W9-CGV-484

Life-Span Developmental Psychology

NORMATIVE LIFE CRISES

CONTRIBUTORS

GARY L. ALBRECHT
ROBERT C. ATCHLEY
JAMES F. CARRUTH
JANICE W. CONE
NANCY DATAN
HELEN C. GIFT
LEON H. GINSBERG
DAVID GUTMANN
DWIGHT HARSHBARGER
ROBERT KASTENBAUM
MORTON A. LIEBERMAN

MARTIN B. LOEB
HELENA ZNANIECKI LOPATA
JOHN LOZIER
WILLIAM H. MIERNYK
LEONARD I. PEARLIN
PATRICIA B. PORTERFIELD
KLAUS F. RIEGEL
ALICE SCHLEGEL
PATRICIA A. SELF
LELAND D. VAN DEN DAELE

LIFE-SPAN DEVELOPMENTAL PSYCHOLOGY

NORMATIVE LIFE CRISES

Edited by

NANCY DATAN and   LEON H. GINSBERG

Department of Psychology
West Virginia University
Morgantown, West Virginia

School of Social Work
West Virginia University
Morgantown, West Virginia

1975

ACADEMIC PRESS   New York   San Francisco   London
A Subsidiary of Harcourt Brace Jovanovich, Publishers

ACADEMIC PRESS, INC.
111 Fifth Avenue, New York, New York 10003

United Kingdom Edition published by
ACADEMIC PRESS, INC. (LONDON) LTD.
24/28 Oval Road, London NW1

Library of Congress Cataloging in Publication Data

Life-Span Developmental Psychology Conference, 4th
    West Virginia University, 1974.
    Life-span developmental psychology, normative life
crises.

    Includes bibliographies and indexes.
    1.   Developmental psychology—Congresses.
I.   Datan, Nancy.   II.   Ginsberg, Leon, (date)
III.   Title.
BF712.L537   1974   155.6   75-3964
ISBN 0-12-203550-X

Contents

NORMATIVE LIFE CRISES:
ACADEMIC AND APPLIED PERSPECTIVES

NORMATIVE LIFE CRISES
IN INDIVIDUAL DEVELOPMENT

NORMATIVE LIFE CRISIS
IN THE FAMILY LIFE CYCLE

NORMATIVE LIFE CRISES
AND THE SOCIAL SYSTEM

List of Contributors

Numbers in parentheses indicate the pages on which the authors' contributions begin.

GARY L. ALBRECHT (227), Department of Sociology, Northwestern University, Evanston, Illinois

ROBERT C. ATCHLEY (247), Scripps Foundation Gerontology Center, Miami University, Oxford, Ohio

JAMES F. CARRUTH (125), Student Counseling Service, West Virginia University, Morgantown, West Virginia

JANICE W. CONE (87), Department of Behavioral Medicine and Psychiatry, West Virginia University, Morgantown, West Virginia

NANCY DATAN (3), Department of Psychology, West Virginia University, Morgantown, West Virginia

HELEN C. GIFT (227), American Dental Association, Chicago, Illinois

LEON H. GINSBERG (11), School of Social Work, West Virginia University, Morgantown, West Virginia

DAVID GUTMANN (161), Department of Psychology, University of Michigan, Ann Arbor, Michigan

DWIGHT HARSHBARGER (285), Department of Psychology, West Virginia University, Morgantown, West Virginia

ROBERT KASTENBAUM (19), Department of Psychology, University of Massachusetts, Boston, Massachusetts

MORTON A. LIEBERMAN (131), Departments of Behavioral Science (Human Development) and Psychiatry, University of Chicago, Chicago, Illinois

MARTIN B. LOEB (155), Faye McBeath Institute on Aging and Adult Life, University of Wisconsin—Madison, Madison, Wisconsin

HELENA ZNANIECKI LOPATA (207), Department of Sociology, Loyola University, Chicago, Illinois

JOHN LOZIER (273), Department of Sociology and Anthropology, West Virginia University, Morgantown, West Virginia

WILLIAM H. MIERNYK (265), Regional Research Institute, West Virginia University, Morgantown, West Virginia

LEONARD I. PEARLIN (183), Laboratory of Socio-Environmental Studies, National Institute of Mental Health, Bethesda, Maryland

PATRICIA B. PORTERFIELD (241), Department of Behavioral Medicine and Psychiatry, West Virginia University, Morgantown, West Virginia

KLAUS F. RIEGEL (97), Department of Psychology, University of Michigan, Ann Arbor, Michigan

ALICE SCHLEGEL (199), Department of Anthropology, University of Pittsburgh, Pittsburgh, Pennsylvania

PATRICIA A. SELF (177), Department of Psychology, West Virgina University, Morgantown, West Virginia

LELAND D. VAN DEN DAELE (51), Teachers College, Columbia University, New York, New York

Preface

Each of the three preceding West Virginia University Conferences on Life-Span Developmental Psychology has been built upon a unifying theme, a unity strengthened by contributors whose principal academic affiliation was in psychology. Contributors did not come exclusively from the area of developmental psychology; for example, Nesselroade and Reese (1973), exploring methodological issues in life-span developmental psychology, brought together participants whose primary commitments were in the areas of theory, measurement, design, and data analysis, inviting them to explore the implications of their work for developmental psychology. Moreover, even within developmental psychology there was substantial variation among major schools of thought, ranging, for example, from the search for formal paradigms in life-span developmental research (Baltes & Schaie, 1973; Goulet & Baltes, 1970; Schaie, 1970) to the relatively more exploratory search for intrapsychic and social changes over the life cycle which has characterized the Chicago school (Charles, 1970; Havighurst, 1973; Neugarten & Datan, 1973). Despite a variety of orientations, however, past participants to the West Virginia University Life-Span Developmental Conferences have shared a common knowledge of the discipline, and their task has been to contribute a particular view to a common theme.

The task of the Fourth Life-Span Developmental Psychology Conference has been quite different. The conference grew out of an effort to create an interface between academic and applied perspectives on the life cycle, the former expressed in the studies of developmental psychology and the latter expressed in the practical efforts of social workers to mobilize the resources of existing social institutions in the service of individual clients.

We soon found that, unlike the underlying unity of preceding conferences, ours rested upon an uneasy dialogue between researcher and practitioner. Moreover, we found that an adequate academic view of the life cycle, for the practitioner, required the incorporation of additional disciplines; and the final form taken by the conference—though it represents no more than a first step toward a successful dialogue between academic and applied perspectives—involved participants from developmental psychology, clinical psychology, community psychology, sociology, anthropology, economics, and social work. Clearly, this group of participants could not claim a common level of familiarity with the literature of life-span developmental psychology; indeed, some participants acknowledged that they discovered the field in the process of contributing to the conference. As the contents of the book indicate, some chapters were presentations of papers, while others came to life as discussions in response to these papers, deliberately chosen to represent alternate and sometimes conflicting points of view.

As we see it, conflict was sharpest not among competing theories in developmental psychology, or across disciplines, but between theorist and practitioner. Stated simply, a model of development, often a model with obvious heuristic value for research, would sometimes be met by a discussant's implied query: So what? That is, how can a formal model of development be translated into the service of the goals of the practitioner, whose purpose is the understanding and assistance of individuals? This translation was attempted by all our discussants, and was often attempted in theoretical statements as well. Nevertheless, practitioners sometimes conveyed a sense of discomfort and skepticism underlying their efforts at translating formal models of development into practical, applicable language.

As editors, we made no attempt to resolve this discomfort. On the contrary, it seems to us that this discomfort is our most valid indicator that our participants were making efforts to cross academic boundaries and to share perspectives that were unfamiliar and uncomfortable. We view this confrontation as a necessary first step toward closer ties between research and application.

Baltes, P.B., & Schaie, K.W. (Eds.) *Life-span developmental psychology: Personality and socialization.* New York: Academic Press, 1973.

Charles, D.C. Historical antecedants of life-span developmental psychology. In L.R. Goulet & P.B. Baltes (Eds.), *Life-span developmental psychology: Research and theory.* New York: Academic Press, 1970.

Goulet, L.R., & Baltes, P.B. (Eds.) *Life-span developmental psychology: Research and theory.* New York: Academic Press, 1970.

Havighurst, R.J. History of developmental psychology: Socialization and personality development. In P.B. Baltes & K.W. Schaie (Eds.), *Life-span developmental psychology: Personality and socialization.* New York: Academic Press, 1973.

Nesselroade, J.R., & Reese, H.W. (Eds.) *Life-span developmental psychology: Methodological issues.* New York: Academic Press, 1973.

Neugarten, B.L., & Datan, N. Sociological perspectives on the life cycle. In P.B. Baltes & K.W. Schaie (Eds.), *Life-span developmental psychology: Personality and socialization.* New York: Academic Press, 1973.

Schaie, K.W. A reinterpretation of age-related changes in cognitive structure and functioning. In L.R. Goulet & P.B. Baltes (Eds.), *Life-span developmental psychology: Research and theory.* New York: Academic Press, 1970.

Acknowledgments

The Fourth West Virginia University Life-Span Developmental Psychology Conference is the outcome of many efforts. Hayne W. Reese, Director of the Developmental Training Committee in the Department of Psychology, gave his support and assistance to the conference at every phase of initiation and planning. The conference obtained its financial support from four university sources: We owe thanks to Ray Koppleman, Provost for Research and Graduate Studies, for his warm response to our proposal for a multidisciplinary conference; to Roger Maley, Chairman of the Department of Psychology, who supported our initial planning and guided its development; to the School of Social Work, which joined the Department of Psychology in its first multidisciplinary co-chairmanship; and to Arnold J. Levine and the Department of Sociology, for co-sponsoring the conference and sharing the tasks of planning.

The preceding Life-Span Conferences have created a tradition of smooth coordination of a multitude of activities. We are grateful to Ford Pearse of the West Virginia University Conference Office and Stan Cohen of the Department of Psychology for helping us maintain this tradition. In addition, the Life-Span Conferences have always owed a large measure of their success to the generous hospitality of the graduate students in the Department of Psychology: Our thanks go to Nancy Treat, Richard Stone, John Haynes, Elle Newton, George Franks, Debbie De Meis, Nedra Reed, Jerrie Ann Will, Sandra Byers, Anne-Marie Deutsch, Gary and Donna Colwell, and Joseph Hannah.

NORMATIVE LIFE CRISES: ACADEMIC AND APPLIED PERSPECTIVES

CHAPTER 1

Normative Life Crises:
Academic Perspectives

NANCY DATAN

WEST VIRGINIA UNIVERSITY
MORGANTOWN, WEST VIRGINIA

ABSTRACT

Philosophers of science suggest that the scientist must be of a higher order of complexity than his object of study. The social sciences, in which men study men, may obey this principle through reductionist study, or violate it by acknowledging through such approaches as participant observation that the object of study is fully as complex as the scientist. The Fourth Life-Span Developmental Psychology Conference brought together academic and applied perspectives, and, in the course of dialogue across disciplinary boundaries, exposed some of the constraints that affect the study of the life span. The time-limited setting in which practitioners work served as a reminder of the temporal constraints that bind the theoretician as well: In the long run we are all short-term. Perspectives from other disciplines which address the social and historical context of development led to a broader sensitivity to the contextual constraints that limit any life-span model of development: These models sometimes seem to emerge by subtraction, as though after removing social, economic, political, and historical influences, what remains is the life-span developmental process, when in fact life-span development does not occur outside a specific context, and thus cannot be studied without it. For the very reasons that the field of life-span developmental psychology is fertile, then, it is bound to fall short of its goal.

I. Introduction

It has been observed by philosophers of science that for effective scientific study, the object of study must be of a lesser order of complexity than the scientist who studies it. I have been troubled by this maxim ever since I first encountered it, for it has seemed to me that the social scientist must violate it, or, in his efforts to obey, must attempt to reduce his object of study to something less complex than himself—or, finally, must generate a new philosophy for the study of human beings.

Many disciplines within the social sciences succeed in abstracting aspects of human life, and this reductionism yields a body of scientific knowledge that is acceptably rigorous as well as a contribution to the study of man: Among these are demography, experimental psychology, sociometry. Other disciplines appear to violate this mandate in various ways: social anthropologists who obtain their data as participant observers; historians, whose uncertain status in the social sciences is expressed by the fact that, as often as not, their department is housed within the faculty of the humanities; clinical psychologists, whose diagnostic skills might reasonably be compared to the art of clinical diagnosis in medicine.

Life-span developmental psychology, viewed from the perspective of "effective" scientific study as it has been defined here, is doomed to failure for a number of reasons that bear examination, since they reflect the implicit and explicit goals of this area, as well as its methods and its findings. The Fourth Life-Span Developmental Psychology Conference, the purpose of which was to explore the interface between theoretical models of development and the application of these models by practitioners, exposed—though it did not resolve—some of the temporal and contextual constraints on the life-span model.

We would be fortunate if we were able to claim that our efforts had brought us to the formulation of a new philosophy for the scientific study of human beings. Instead, practitioners' responses to models of development often expressed a distrust of formal models which was based only in part upon difficulty in application of these models to the clinical setting: The translation from theory to practice was no easier at our conference than it has been anywhere else. Practitioners' responses, however, forced me to reexamine the uneasy interface between academic and applied perspectives.

The conference led me toward a new perspective on theory and research in life-span developmental psychology. Listening to statements of constraints led me to some views on the temporal and contextual limits on life-span models, which will be discussed here. Briefly, I would say that we are bound, by the nature of our subject matter, to fall short of our goal; if Leon Ginsberg can characterize the goals of social work as "modestly majestic," perhaps it is reasonable to say that he and his colleagues have tried to teach us to accept failure with grace.

II.   Academic and Applied Perspectives: The Uneasy Interface

The Fourth Life-Span Developmental Psychology Conference was an effort to address an issue that has received increasing attention over the past decade: the relationship of theory to practice, of "basic" to "applied" research. Theory generates research: A criterion often applied to establish whether a theory is "good" is the amount of research that it generates. By this criterion, disengagement theory, used by Cumming and Henry (1961) to describe the decline in social interaction in the later part of the life cycle, has been regarded as very fruitful, although research generated by the theory has failed to support its central argument, that of a gradual, mutual, and mutually welcome withdrawal by and from society of the aging individual. That is to say: A theory whose fundamental thesis has been disproven may be regarded as successful because of the quantity of research stimulated by the initial theoretical statement, research that serves to clarify the issue raised by the theory, although it does not support the theory.

The goal of applied research, like the goal of the practitioner, is quite different. Both are problem-orientated, and the criterion of fruitfulness that is applied to basic research or to theory is reversed in the evaluation of applied research. Alfred Steinschneider observed that the task of the applied researcher was to publish as little as possible and to put himself out of business as quickly as possible, by finding a solution to his problem by the most parsimonious path.

Though the distinction will quickly become blurred in describing our contributors, it is useful to consider the contrast between, on the one hand, the psychologist, affiliated with a university, with a primary commitment to basic research, and, on the other, a prototypical practitioner in a large clinic, whose training included a review of major developmental theories. Regardless of the practitioner's orientation, his clients seek him out in order to solve a problem. Whatever the nature of the therapy, its goal is a resolution of the client's problem. It is often true that this resolution is promoted by a consideration of developmental change, but the model is employed in the service of the client, and the applicability of any model to a single individual is subject to all the constraints that limit the usefulness of group data as a guide to the understanding of an individual. Models of development are generated from studies of groups of individuals, and represent measures of central tendencies. Such a model cannot predict an individual response, just as a mean score cannot predict an individual score. The model serves the clinician not as predictor but as a context for exploring the client's unique situation. If the clinician is pressured by the clinical context or his client toward a quick solution, a model may tempt with the promise of an answer, mislead, and perhaps disappoint.

The second major difficulty at the interface between theory and practice is also bound up with the factors shaping the clinical interaction—the client in search of help, the helping clinician. As Cone observes in Chapter 5, "All too often, when the symptoms disappear, so does the patient," and the opportunity to study development and change is lost. Members of the helping professions, whether clinical psychologists, social workers, physicians, or nurses, share a task-oriented perspective, and their goal is a solution. If this seems to be a narrow, pragmatic perspective, it must be recalled that the goal is determined by the needs of the client and not those of the clinician. By contrast, the researcher shapes his own goals without reference to his subject's needs: The researcher's goals, which seem to have a broader perspective, may be pursued through investigations that can be insufficiently sensitive to individual subjects. The clinician's responsiveness to his individual clients and the researcher's efforts to obtain parameters of human behavior are complementary and mutually enriching; and without this synthesis, each is incomplete.

III.   Temporal Constraints: A Lesson from Practitioners

The foregoing comparison of the goals of research and the goals of application has incorporated an implicit message that requires explication. The cooperation between the Department of Psychology and the School of Social Work began with some misunderstandings. As Leon Ginsberg points out in his introductory remarks, he and his colleagues found our fascination with "applied" perspectives something of a novelty, since application is the heart of social work; I found a comparable novelty in their fascination with theory and basic research, since these are the foundations of psychology and have been the focus of each of the preceding Life-Span Conferences (Goulet & Baltes, 1970; Nesselroade & Reese, 1973; Baltes & Schaie, 1973). The Fourth Life-Span Conference began with the discovery of difficulties in translation: Novelty for one co-chairman was the daily routine of the other.

In the course of the conference, as I listened to practitioners' responses to current issues in developmental psychology, I heard problems of translation raised again and again. How can this model of ego development be used for today's client? If we accept a theoretical suggestion that death can be viewed as a variable, what are the implications for public policy? Researchers and practitioners seemed to agree that the practitioner's task was to cope with an immediate, pressing problem, while the goal of research was the delivery of laws of human behavior—laws that grew out of a model that in turn was, if not eternal, at least more durable and less transitory than today's client's problem, or today's policy decision. The practitioner by necessity operated under constraints, and the most salient of these were the constraints consequent upon the shortage of time. The practitioner's energies were employed in the service of a short-term goal; the researcher seemed to enjoy the luxury of relatively unlimited time.

In the long run, however, we are all short-term. Nowhere is this limitation more poignantly apparent than in the disciplines that encompass human lives: among them, life-span developmental psychology. We have been seeking, and shall continue to seek, a model of human development that expresses the universal components of the life cycle, from birth to death; but no one of us can hope to live long enough to verify our own models by observing a group of subjects from birth to death. Our own discoveries too are shaped by the constraints of time.

IV. Contextual Constraints: Perspectives from Other Disciplines

In addition to the limitations on the observers, students of life-span developmental psychology have long been sensitive to limitations due to the changing effects of the context of development: the changing social and historical context into which the individual is born, comes to maturity, and dies. It is appropriate that West Virginia University was the setting in which major steps were taken, by Schaie, Nesselroade, and Baltes, among others, toward a methodology that would permit the researcher to distinguish two types of change over time, those due to age changes and those due to cohort effects. This and other advances in life-span developmental methodology became the theme of the Second West Virginia Life-Span Developmental Psychology Conference (Nesselroade & Reese, 1973).

The Fourth Life-Span Developmental Psychology Conference explores some of the "causes" of "cohort effects," observed changes not due to ontogenetic change but to the effect of membership in a particular cohort, born in a particular time and therefore exposed to a specific succession of social and historical changes at certain ages. Developmental models sometimes seem to emerge by subtraction: That is, if an observed change over time in individuals can be shown to be linked to concomitant historical or social change, it is eliminated from the developmental model. Riegel's contribution to this volume takes a broader view of development: He argues that the individual's relationship to his social and historical context is dialectical, and that the developmental process is an outcome of synthetic growth.

Some of our contributors explore sociological, cultural, and economic aspects of the context of development: factors that, in shaping the setting in which the individual develops, also seem to impose constraints on the study of development. But as I listened to the interchanges among psychologists, sociologists, economists, and social workers at our conference, I came to consider that these constraints are essential elements in the study of development. It is obvious, of course, that human development does not occur outside a social and historical context; however, we do not readily recognize the diversity of effects that the social context has on individual development. The social effects of social causes are easily seen: For example, economic change may affect the age of marriage. However, social change may also affect maturational change, as when a raised standard of living leads to a general improvement in nutrition and to earlier menarche in girls. If we also remember that the same forces that lead to a rise in the standard of living tend to prolong the period of education—that is, earlier sexual maturity and later social maturity—we can see in this single example not only the complex interactions among social and biological changes, but also the importance of the social context for the study of human development. As I suggested in discussing the constraints of time, I think that the constraints of the social and historical context are not obstacles to the study of development but components of it.

Baltes and Schaie, in summing up the Third Life-Span Developmental Psychology Conference, acknowledged that, like their predecessors, they too were bound to concede that life-span developmental psychology had not yet come to its maturity, and so efforts at a conceptual synthesis remained a task for the future (Baltes & Schaie, 1973). While I share their faith in the fruitfulness of the life-span perspective, I want to propose some important qualifications on their optimistic view of the future of life-span developmental theory. For the very reasons that the field is fertile—among them, as Baltes and Schaie noted, its dynamic model of the interaction of man and environment—its students, who have taken as their object of study themselves in their own world, must fall short of their goal.

V. From Conference to Proceedings

The central purpose of the Fourth Life-Span Developmental Psychology Conference was to stimulate dialogue across disciplinary boundaries. We directed our efforts toward the exploration of topics from more than one perspective, inviting contributors from the field of life-span developmental psychology, and asking contributors from related fields, including sociology, anthropology, community and counseling psychology, economics, and social work, to address themselves to these issues. The conference generated lively debate across disciplines, which is often reflected in the papers in this volume.

Our contributors have dealt with normative life crises that fall into three categories: normative life crises in individual development, normative life crises in the family life cycle, and normative life crises and the social system. Within these categories there is a tendency to find psychologists dealing with issues of individual development, sociologist and anthropologists dealing with the social system; contributions to the study of the family life cycle represent the broadest range of disciplines, including clinical psychology, developmental psychology, anthropology, and sociology—reflecting the variety of perspectives that have been brought to the study of the family.

Although not all discussants prepared papers for this volume, the diversity of their contributions to the conference enriched not only the conference itself but also the papers in this volume. We should like to express our thanks to those conference speakers who, although their names do not appear in the table of contents, helped us toward our goal of interdisciplinary dialogue at the conference and in its proceedings: Elizabeth Lewis, John J. Miller, and Victor L. Schneider of the School of Social Work, West Virginia University; Ronald Althouse and Arnold J. Levine of the Department of Sociology and Anthropology, West Virginia University; and Joel Shanan of the Hebrew University of Jerusalem.

As these conference proceedings were prepared for publication, I was conscious of two goals. The first was the goal of any editor: concern that each contribution was a satisfactory expression of the approach of its writer to the theme of this book. The second goal was more elusive: to share as much as possible of the conference experience. I have conveyed something of the sense of dialogue and of discord, as well as my own tentative conclusions, in these introductory remarks. This leaves the task of introducing this volume.

We begin with a chapter on death as a normative life crisis. The thought experiment with which that chapter opens was conducted on a bright May morning in West Virginia, with a group of social scientists who were surprised to find death the first topic for our conference. Some years ago, I formulated a definition of human development as the process that occurs between conception and death, reflecting the efforts of the individual to reconcile himself to the two poles of his existence. More recently I found, as one often does, that I was not the first to consider this issue: Kierkegaard wrote, "What is reflection? Simply to reflect on these two questions: How

did I get into this and how do I get out of it again, how does it end?" I
opened the conference with those remarks, and I should like to open this
volume by inviting the reader to reflect with us.

REFERENCES

Baltes, P.B., & Schaie, K.W. (Eds.) *Life-span developmental psychology: Personality and sociali-
zation.* New York: Academic Press, 1973
Cumming, E., & Henry, W. H. *Growing old: The process of disengagement.* New York: Basic
Books, 1961
Goulet, L.R., & Baltes, P.B. (Eds.) *Life-span developmental psychology: Research and theory.*
New York: Academic Press, 1970
Nesselroade, J.R., & Reese, H.W. (Eds.) *Life-span developmental psychology: Methodological
issues.* New York: Academic Press, 1973

CHAPTER 2

Normative Life Crises: Applied Perspectives

LEON H. GINSBERG

WEST VIRGINIA UNIVERSITY
MORGANTOWN, WEST VIRGINIA

ABSTRACT

The application of life-span developmental psychology theory to the education and practice of professional social workers is one of the objectives of the volume. This article discusses ways in which life-span developmental psychology may be useful for social work educators, students, and practitioners. "Human behavior and the social environment" theory in social work education is discussed, as are recent changes in the teaching of that theory in social work education programs. Modifications in the definitions of social problems, the dichotomy between social theory and social work practice, as well as the various sources of social work "Human behavior and the social environment" theory are noted. Life-span developmental psychology theory's potential role and its significance in social work are described. The utility of some of the articles in the volume for social work educators and practitioners is emphasized as is the significance of a theory and a body of knowledge which focus on the total life span from an interdisciplinary perspective. It is concluded that this volume may introduce for some social work educators a new and pertinent theoretical emphasis that is comparable to, but an extension of, more traditional social work approaches to the study of human behavior.

From the point of view of the social work co-editor, this volume and the Fourth West Virginia University Life-Span Developmental Psychology Conference from which its contents are drawn had two major objectives.

The first was to assist in the development and dissemination of applied life-span developmental psychology concepts, particularly those dealing with normal life crises. That process of concept crystallization is a part of the Psychology Department's efforts that long ago earned the School of Social Work's interest, respect, and support. It was rewarding to be involved in their efforts. The second objective was to make a contribution to human behavior theory useful in the education of professional social workers. The development of such materials has lacked recent attention in social work for a variety of reasons, to the disadvantage of the field. Therefore, it seemed to be a worthwhile objective for the West Virginia University social work education program.

The first objective was more easily attained than the second. Over the years, the West Virginia University Life-Span Developmental Psychology conferences have created a tradition to which many of the best thinkers, teachers, and writers in the social and behavioral sciences were willing to contribute their time and effort. The School of Social Work contributed an applied perspective through invitations to social work discussants. In addition, the school drew scholars from related fields who could enrich the development of life-span theory by adding new and complementary, though different, perspectives. The results of those efforts are found in several of the articles and were in evidence, as well, during the course of the conference.

The second objective was more complicated and its achievement was only begun. Readers of this volume may conclude that the conference and its resulting literature took some preliminary steps in the direction of building human behavior theory for social work education.

I. Human Behavior Theory in Social Work Education

The preliminary nature of our contributions to human behavior theory results, as much as anything, from some historical facts and recent changes in the transmission of human behavior theory. What should be taught social workers about human behavior is the source of more than minor controversy and turmoil in the field. That is the result of many factors, not the least of which is that social work is and always has been an applied discipline. That is, it has always been primarily conceived as something that one *does* and only secondarily as something that one knows or believes. No one speaks of "applied perspectives" on social work. Application is understood as the essence of the profession. Of course in attitudinal and knowledge objectives, social work has consistently worked toward the development of a coherent, widely accepted code of ethics and a precise knowledge base for all its practitioners. The transmission of ethical precepts and a formal code of ethics, such as that which has been adopted by the National Association of Social Workers, is always part of social work education programs. Perhaps social work ethics can be accurately characterized as modestly majestic. And the profession takes pride in the social workers' widespread adherence to the code's precepts. But teaching a coherent body of knowledge is less easily achieved.

A. The Growth of Diversity

Difficulties in the transmission of knowledge are due to a variety of reasons, perhaps the most significant of which is the diversity and scope of the profession itself. Social work is historically a conglomerate. It emerged from a variety of eighteenth- and nineteenth-century social reform and social treatment efforts. Although all of them were designed to improve the society in which they were applied, the range of methods for doing so were and remain remarkably different and require a diversity of knowledge. Social workers practice their profession, for example, in mental health programs of all kinds, in medical hospitals, prisons, juvenile courts, public schools, churches, public assistance programs, and child protection agencies. They also work as specialists in community development, social planning, neighborhood recreation and informal education, volunteer youth work, and social action. Over the years, the range of programs using the skills of social workers has grown to the point that social work is one of and perhaps the most diverse of the human service professions. That is advantageous and disadvantageous. While it extends the influence of social work's approach to human problems, it makes interpretation of the profession difficult and leaves educators confused about objectives and content. That second problem was one of the concerns on the agenda for this book.

As social work has grown in the number and range of functions it performs, reaching conclusions about an appropriate theoretical base for practitioners has become more and more difficult for educators. Through most of the profession's recent history, social work's theoretical base was organized into a sequence of courses on human behavior or human growth and behavior or, as it came to be most commonly called in the 1960s, "human behavior and the social environment." But selecting organizing schemes for that instruction and determining the content that would be included became an increasingly complex problem, because the profession became more complex and because practitioners became more dispersed in their activities.

B. Defining Social Problems

A second reason for the difficulties encountered in social work theory building has been the changing nature of the profession's understanding of social problems. There were remarkable modifications in that understanding during the 1960s. During that decade, notions of social causation of human problems became popular in the United States, much as they had in the 1930s. Social workers, as practitioners in all of the social problem areas, became leaders in examining and attempting to apply such theories to their clientele, along with their colleagues in the social and behavioral sciences who were equally interested in such theories. Studying means for working with individuals and helping them overcome their personal and social problems was no longer enough. Individuals were products, perhaps victims, of a social environment that required poverty and ill health to continue, such theories asserted. Some people were advantaged because others were disadvantaged. Delinquency, disease, poor housing, unemployment, and emotional upset resulted from the workings of the social system. Treating people on an individual basis was unproductive and doomed to defeat, many social workers and social scientists believed. And worse, individual treatment diverted attention from efforts that could make a difference. Real solutions required massive changes. Larger systems and the society itself should be the focus of social work's efforts, it was argued.

C. Theory–Practice Dichotomy

Third, it has been the nature of social work and of U.S. human services generally that most of the published theorizing comes from nonpracticing academics. Conversely, most of the application is done by nontheorizing practitioners. Thus there has been a consistent and growing division between theory and practice in the human services. The leading theorists rarely practice and the practitioners cannot or do not, in print at least, theorize. Over the years, the tension between social work's corps of academics and the profession's practitioners has increased. One will find examples of it in the creation of several national commissions, coordinating committees, and other institutionalized attempts to bridge the gap between those who theorize (or, more accurately, those who write and teach) and those who practice.

D. Sources of Social Work Theory

The peculiar nature of theory building in social work is a fourth problem. Useful theories for social work are those that have emerged from practice or those that have been developed in other settings but proven effective in the field through application and rigorous evaluation. But that has seldom been the process. More typically, social work academicians and practitioners have taken popular theories and applied them either through written materials or through practice in the field. Rather than social work theory emerging from practice, theory has tended to be imposed onto practice. That has been the case for most of the profession's history, from the application of psychoanalytic theory, long the most popular and still the most commonly taught and used approach, to the current effort to try a variety of new formulas for human services—behavior modification, transactional analysis, reality therapy, conjoint family therapy, confrontation tactics taken from Saul Alinsky's experiences, and social planning strategies. Because most of these approaches are particular to their developers or their disciples and to the setting in which they were applied, few have been translatable into practice without modification. Those modifications make them something different—different enough, perhaps, to be undefined but identifiable theories or models of social work. But such modifications and applications have been only rarely recorded, which has left social work in the curious position of intervening broadly without a comparable amount of theoretical support.

For all of these reasons, it should surprise no one that the teaching of human behavior and the social environment theory is probably the most difficult of all social work's curriculum areas. Curriculum developers find it difficult to select and define, instructors find it difficult to teach, and, in many social work programs, it is the least popular area of study for students. When it is taught narrowly, as in most schools that adhere to Erikson's stages of psychosexual development, its relevance is questioned. But when the courses try for relevance, the content is often so scattered and diluted that it lacks applicability and coherence.

Life-span psychology theory, as this volume demonstrates, has significant applicability for those who teach and practice social work. For example, it builds upon and is related to the stages of development models of behavior that have been the mode for social work teaching in the past. The contributions by Klaus Riegel and Leland van den Daele, as well as the discussions that follow them, update, extend, and provide perspective on such theories in a manner that ought to be useful to teachers and students of developmental approaches to the life cycle.

II. Life-Span Theory and the Social Work Tradition

Life-span theory is also in the tradition of social work because of its interdisciplinary nature. This volume includes the writings of developmental, social, and clinical psychologists, social workers, sociologists, and an economist. As a field that must draw upon a variety of social and behavioral science disciplines for its knowledge base, an interdisciplinary approach is essential.

Readers will note that most of the papers and discussions deal with crises at various times during the life cycle. These are the normative crises, those that any individual is likely to encounter in a lifetime. Parenting, widowhood, aging, death, depression—the typical, normative crises one may encounter among social work clients—are discussed in depth by the contributors. A profession that has increasingly come to understand the crisis-oriented nature of its service will do well to examine these contributions to the understanding of critical human events.

Of course, the volume is geared to better understandings of individuals and therefore is more useful for social workers involved in clinical or direct practice settings than it is for those who are engaged in social planning and community organization. However, it becomes consistently clearer that social workers engaged in all forms of practice need a sophisticated understanding of the range of human organizations, from the individual to society, if their work is to be informed and effective. The social change agent who does not understand the behavior of the individuals with whom he deals is likely to fail. So is the planner who lacks knowledge of the character of the crises faced by the individuals who seek a satisfactory life in his jurisdiction.

For those reasons, this volume is likely to be of significant utility for social work educators and practitioners. Its concentration on the total life span rather than one period within it has a special significance for a profession that has long been committed to such an approach. Its special emphasis on the normal crises throughout that life span also has merit for social work as a profession.

Perhaps this volume will be the beginning of a new and pertinent theoretical emphasis in social work. It marks the introduction of two disciplines to one another—two disciplines that have needed each other and whose interactions have been postponed for too long.

NORMATIVE LIFE CRISES
IN INDIVIDUAL DEVELOPMENT

CHAPTER 3

Is Death a Life Crisis?
On the Confrontation with Death
in Theory and Practice

ROBERT KASTENBAUM
UNIVERSITY OF MASSACHUSETTS
BOSTON, MASSACHUSETTS

ABSTRACT

Life and death are not strangers to each other. However, life-span developmental theory as such has taken little notice of death and dying. This exploration of possible relationships between the two realms offers a discussion of death as variable, event, state, analogy, and mystery. Detailed consideration is given to a well-known stage theory of dying, and selected problems in theory and practice are then identified. Caution is advised against the premature enshrinement of death as one more "normative life crisis."

I. Purpose and Scope

Participants in the Fourth Life-Span Developmental Psychology Conference were asked by this writer to conduct a little thought experiment. Perhaps the reader would also be willing to try this exercise in self-exploration.

Relax for a moment. When your mind is quiet and without pressure, let a neutral visual field form itself in your mind's eye. When this background field has established itself, visualize the face of somebody you care about, a person who is important to you. See this person's face as though it were a suddenly illuminated light bulb glowing against the nondescript background. Keep this face in view. But now think of somebody else you care about. Watch how this face appears and lights up in your mind's eye as well. You now have the inner presence of two people who are important to you. Now visualize a third person you care about, in the same way as you have visualized the others, who are still present. Now a fourth person. A fifth person. A sixth person. A seventh person. All right, that will do. Your mind now contains visually, explicitly the symbols of seven important people.

One of these people will die before the others. You do not know for sure who this will be, but you do have a guess or feeling about it. Extinguish that person's face. The light goes out where that face had been; the other lights are still on. Time goes by. Another person dies. Watch this person's light go out. The other lights are on, but now there are two dark spots. More time elapses. Another person dies; another light goes out. Three people gone; four remaining. Which light will be the next to be extinguished? Time goes by, and a fourth light goes out. Only three of your important people remain illuminated in your mind's eye. Now another dies. Which of the remaining two will be the next to die, which the survivor? More time elapses. And another light goes out. Your mind's eye, only a few moments ago populated by some of the people closest and most significant to you, now is dark except for a single face.

Halt the thought experiment here and reflect, if you will, upon the following questions:

The survivor in your mind's eye—is this perhaps the youngest of the important people you visualized at the outset?

The first person to die—was this perhaps the oldest of the important people you visualized at the outset?

As individuals continued to die, did you continue to respond implicitly to each death in its full particularity—or, at a certain point, did the mass of accumulated loss take precedence over specific bereavement?

In what ways did your thoughts and feelings fluctuate between concern for those who were gone and those who were remaining? Did you find your mind and your heart divided between the living and the dead?

One final question, if you will: Where does your own face, your own life and fate, belong in this sequence? Would you have been the first to perish? The last? Who of these people do you implicitly expect to survive? Who will survive you?

We cannot do justice to these questions here, but they are useful for hinting at states of being, phenomenological dynamics, and intergenerational relationships that merit our interest both as individuals and as students of life-span development. This little thought experiment, by the way, has been used by this writer in written format for the past 7 years as a research tool to explore the "pecking order of death" (Kastenbaum, 1969). During the Fourth Life-Span Developmental Psychology Conference, a showing of hands revealed that most of the participants had seen their oldest important person die first in the mind's eye, and the youngest survive the longest. Obvious as this result might appear—and it is the typical result—there are some ponderables here. Each person created his own inner representation of those people who were closest to him. It is doubtful that any two minds created inner populations that even approximated the same important people. Nevertheless, deep within personal experience, most people had at least a few outcomes in common. Acknowledge the limitations of this little thought experiment, and of the treatment we can give it here. But think of the implicit dialectics between our own worlds of life and death and having experiences, concerns, and orientations that are common, if not universal.

We contain each other's lives and deaths in our own minds. A multigenerational family has a rich phenomenological tapestry woven of each person's expectations of the other—in which expectations of death and survival are not of small significance. Even if in a tightly affiliated group each member includes all other members (and no outsiders) among his "most important people," the expectations and perspectives are likely to differ appreciably. Think of yourself as the youngest and most "survivable" face within the mind's eye of a very aged relative, and also as the oldest and most "perishable" face within the mind's eye of a very young person. Some of us may actually be represented at both extremes. The core point here, however, is that we have, most of us, deep interconnections with the lives and deaths of others. We may "bury the living" or keep the dead alive. We can be rocked to our foundations when a person dies in the wrong sequence, upsetting our implicit pecking order: "Why isn't Death following the game plan? Isn't He rational?"

Intergenerational dynamics in life-span developmental theory cannot be fully comprehended without careful attention to the ways in which we mind each other's deaths. And, if a personal response is acceptable here, there can be value in the simple act of permitting thoughts and feelings to rise up within ourselves as in the little thought experiment sketched earlier. Appreciation for the people who are important in our lives, while they are still alive, is one of the ways in which focus upon death can enrich their lives and ours.

Yet much theory has been promulgated in the social and behavioral sciences that assumes the nonexistence or nonrelevance of death. Theories that guide or rationalize clinical practice and administrative policy also, in general, take little account of death. Developmental psychology is no exception. As this subject area is usually conceived, taught, researched, and packaged, death is thrown a footnote here and a dated reference there. It is not part of the basic structure of the field. One can move from student to expert without thinking about (let alone thinking through) the mutual implications of life and death. Perhaps, however, there is some point in exploring the interface between life and death within the emerging realm of life-span development. It is a realm in which we might expect both range and perspective, and in which theoretical positions have not yet become fixed and "official."

In this presentation I propose to resist the first temptation and then give in to most others. It would be fashionable to propose death as one more "normative life crisis" among others already acknowledged by the field. But this would be premature. Further, it would deprive us of the opportunity to explore new modes of understanding. Let us neither enshrine nor reject death as a normative life crisis, at least for a while. Instead, let us first examine some of the most relevant meanings of death as a term of discourse. Next, we shall select one major test case of possible relationships between death and life-span developmental theory. The paper will then conclude with a broader sampling of observations concerning death in theory and practice.

II.   Death: Some Definitions and Interpretations

There is little chance of thinking and communicating clearly about death unless we share some definitions in common. What follows here is simply one person's way of differentiating and organizing the multitudinous ways in which death has taken shape in our minds. The treatment is brief, not exhaustive, and intended to be especially germane to life-span issues.

A. Death as a Variable

Begin with the familiar. We all know something about variables. Consider some of the ways in which death presents itself to us as a variable.

1. Death: The Stimulus

A corpse is a stimulus. So is a cemetery. And so is the word "death" itself, as well as such related terms as "fatal," "lethal," "dying," "passed away," and so on. Death words spring out at us from both expected and unexpected sources, from print and from tongue. Certain visual configurations serve as death stimuli through the meanings they have accumulated in our society (e.g., the black border around a card).

Some stimuli convey aspects of "deathness" to almost anybody; other stimuli take on death meanings only to certain individuals or groups who have been sensitized by their experiences. An X-ray plate or laboratory report might register as death stimulus to a physician. From morning through night, from infancy through advanced old age, we are all exposed to a variety of death-pertinent stimuli. It would be interesting to learn what developmental sequence, if any, obtains in the perception of death stimuli.

Death can be a most subtle stimulus. We tend to recoil from the person who we believe, correctly or incorrectly, to be touched by death. It is not necessary that he "look different." We are told: He is a funeral director . . . has fatal illness . . . is a survivor of the H-bomb, and we sense ourselves to be in death's presence although there is nothing deathly to see and hear. Silence when we expect sound, emptiness when we expect content, absence when we expect presence, coldness when we expect warmth, immobility when we expect response—these are among the ways in which a sense of "deathness" may be conveyed to us. Under some circumstances, the very fact that there is "no stimulus" represents death to us. "Nothing" can be the most terrifying and convincing of death stimuli (Kastenbaum, in preparation). Perception of our own inner states can yield death stimuli, as in the psychophysiological state we have characterized elsewhere as "deathly fear" (Kastenbaum & Aisenberg, 1972).

As a stimulus, then, or more properly, as a set of stimuli, death comes to us on occasion in palpable physical dimensions, but also in culturally shaped verbal and nonverbal representations, and in subtle personal encounters. Clearly, in discussing death as stimulus we are not in the realm of rare phenomena.

2. Death: The Response

Death can be response as well as stimulus. A trauma or toxic substance may be the stimulus that elicits the response of death. The stimulus to which death is response can be evident ("Nobody could have walked away from that accident") or problematic ("We just found him like that in his room"). Death may be salient on both the stimulus and response sides, as when a person suffers a fatal heart attack upon hearing of a loved one's sudden demise (Engel, 1971). Death is a possible response to a large number of stimuli and a probable response to others. One cannot be completely certain either as to when a death stimulus might be encountered or when death might prove to be the response to even the most familiar and innocuous-seeming of stimuli.

Organismic death is not the only form of death response. A person may respond to stimulation with death-tinged words and thoughts. Deprivation and stress may lead to "lifeless" behavior, and the individual himself may feel that "something inside me has died." Many of the specific senses in which deathness is conveyed can be expressed either as stimulus or as response. And it often depends upon our own timing and perspective as observers whether we perceive the deathness in a situation as stimulus or response.

3. Death: The Statistical Abstraction

As a psychologist I am accustomed to thinking about real people in real situations. Yet we must acknowledge a more abstracted level in which death figures as a prominent variable. The statistical behavior of death, or death translated into statistical behavior, is of concern to every insurance broker in the nation, as well as morticians, economists, ecologists, demographers, and their varied kith and kin. How many people of what age, sex and socioeconomic echelon will die of what causes, when? Our knowledge of the statistical behavior of death, in answer to such questions, has become more precise and sophisticated over the years (Preston, Keyfitz, & Schoen, 1972). And the answers help the manufacturer decide whether to emphasize diapers or shrouds, the political adviser whether to advocate or oppose birth control, the employer whether to offer the union concessions on holidays and work breaks rather than health insurance, etc.

Every human detail of death has been lost at this level of abstraction; nevertheless, the uses to which this information is put might have profound effect upon both quality and duration of life. An influential book such as *World Dynamics* (Forrester, 1971) exemplifies the seriousness with which some planners take death as social statistic. The "population loop" (birth in/death out) is one of the major sets of variables in conceptualizing, projecting, and perhaps influencing the future of societies. Fraction-of-mineral-resources-remaining-in-the-earth, a pollution quotient, and a crowding index can be juggled in the same formula with projected mortality rate. Decontextualized and abstracted death is a major variable in the description, prediction, and control of congregate human existence.

B. Death as an Event

Death functions as stimulus or response, as independent or dependent variable. But death can also be regarded as an event. It is a happening. We may conceive of it as an active and externally engendered event ("Death strikes!") or as a more passive and internal event ("He has slipped away to his final rest"). In either case, something has happened, and it has happened in a particular place at a particular time. All death certificates are intended to specify the temporal–spatial markings of the event, and at least go through the motions of indicating "cause." Death, when defined as "the act of cessation," can be further understood in terms of two major perspectives that will be briefly delineated in the next section.

1. As a Social-Symbolic Event

Each death takes on a set of significations as a social-symbolic event. These significations vary from culture to culture, but also vary within a culture depending upon who it is that has died under what circumstances. The noninvolved observer might insist that death is death, no matter who, how, and when. In practice, however, the sudden and violent death of a person who is eminent in his culture elicits a response quite different from the expected and "natural" demise of a relatively "inconsequential" person. How important the actual or presumed circumstances of death are in shaping the social-symbolic significations also varies. Some detail of the death event can dominate the signification. In other instances, the death becomes of general interest only because of a function it serves, not because a particular human life has come to an end.

Consider, for example, the last episode of any television gun-play melodrama you might care to name. Typically, one person "gets it" early in the episode and, not uncommonly, several more are laid low before the final commercial is aired. Seldom does the action pause long enough to reflect upon the death of a person as such. The viewer is not expected to care a great deal about the victim, or to draw philosophical or psychological insights from what he has witnessed. Instead, the death event serves chiefly to motivate and advance the plot. For centuries, death has been a stock in trade of authors and playwrights, a dependable way of sustaining interest, moving things along, and scratching out a character no longer needed.

The death event can have significations that are much more consequential. A "big death" may close one epoch of history and open another. The deaths of Jesus and Charlemagne in the past, and of Charles de Gaulle and John F. Kennedy in our own time, have had the effect of marking a change in how-things-were and how-things-will-be-now. When a major wielder of power or representative of cultural tradition dies, the human circumstances of that death event may be secondary in impact to the social disequilibrium that results. Who will succeed to power? Which group will get the upper hand? Will tradition continue or be altered radically?

Within the confines of the family, the death event often poses similar problems. One has thoughts and feelings about the particular individual who has died. But the implications and significations of the death event for the survivors' own lives is also part of the total picture. Why did he die? What are we to do now? Can life ever be the same again? The death event can fall like an iron gate, trapping some of the survivors in the past and liberating others to go forth to a new life style.

As a social-symbolic event, death often challenges our assumptions and beliefs about life in general. The death of a young child may precipitate a religious crisis in the parents: "Are you there, God? I hate you!" The death of a powerful and seemingly invulnerable individual may leave others feeling helpless and exposed: "If death can take even him, what chance do I have?" The death event often is associated with punishment or failure in our culture. It may also be taken to signify the futility of life, or the prelude to eternal bliss. The physician, nurse, hospital administrator and funeral director all have their own significations to bestow upon the death event, involving a configuration of personal, cultural, and occupational responses. The death event sets many little processes into motion in our society. The florist, the clerk in the office of vital statistics, the linotype operator who prepares the death notice, the home office that will demand an explanation of what has happened to holder of charge card #32674–8814–007 are part of this complex configuration.

2. As an Immediate Event

It is only when we have become well aware of the social-symbolic responses to and uses of death that we can focus clearly upon the actual particulars of the death event itself. Even so, it is not safe to assume that we ever witness or analyze death except through the filters of our own preconceptions. What we notice about the death event and when we judge that the event itself has occurred depends much upon our own background, needs, and relationship with the deceased.

Our usual expectations regarding the death event include the establishment of one or more "causes" for an occurrence that can be fixed precisely into our system of temporal–spatial coordinates. We may also be concerned with what the person is experiencing up to and at the "moment of death." Recently there has also been an upsurge of concern for what everybody else should be doing as the death event approaches.

It is worth keeping in mind that these are expectations rather than facts. Each of the expectations deserves to be challenged. Arguments might center around issues such as the following:

(a) Some, perhaps all, deaths do not have "causes" in a simplistic or classical sense of the term. What we choose to call death is itself part of an extraordinarily complex multilevel process that requires an alternative mode of conceptualization to the usual cause–effect model. Sophisticated coroners and pathologists, as well as practitioners of the "psychological autopsy" method, regularly deplore the inadequacy of conventional cause-of-death categories, and some question the basic adequacy of our causal thinking with respect to death.

(b) The death event seldom if ever occurs at a precisely specifiable moment. Similar pressures to specify "time" and "cause" do result in statements being made. But there are both methodological and judgmental problems involved in determining the time (and therefore, also, the place) of death which maintain a large potential error range. A more radical challenge comes from the view that, method aside, the death event has an extended temporal trajectory both before and after any arbitrarily selected "moment."

(c) There is a market for transcendental "last words" and for a general romanticization of death that goes far beyond the actual experiences and utterances of most people who are at point of exitus. It may be that people do not experience anything at the moment of death, or that what they experience must remain forever beyond the knowledge of the survivors. Further, as more people receive heavy medication and are maintained in a marginal zone between life and death, we might expect even fewer significant experiential states on the death bed. Most unfortunately perhaps, attention too often is devoted to the awaited last words or last breath, when the attention would have been more valuable for everybody concerned if it had been given consistently during the total course of the dying process.

(d) Those who habituate the hospital environment know that the death event often arouses the need to be doing something or, failing that, to watch somebody else doing something. "Going away," physically or mentally, is a kind of doing something about the death event for those who can devise no other activity. The *need* to do something in the face of the death event should not coerce us into assuming that there really are many things that should be done at the hypothetical moment of death, or that these activities can be governed by a standard administrative ritual.

The emerging conception of the death event in our own society emphasizes technical description and control. Most people who find themselves in frequent contact with the death event would feel more comfortable if death could be classified, predicted, and explained in a simple and systematic manner. An authoritative scientific model of death, bolstered by new legislation to cover most contingencies, would relieve anxiety. But this preference for the technical and the systematic does not of itself demonstrate that the death event is best regarded in such terms. It just implies that there will be continuing pressure to arrive at consensus, to agree upon what should be done in the death situation—and probably diminished tolerance for those who view the death event differently.

C. Death as a State

The death event can be regarded as an act of separation or rite of passage. Whether or not death in fact has its special moment, it suits many of us to think of a sudden and decisive event that evicts one from the world of the living. But how are we then to understand what follows the death event? We court confusion by using the same term to refer to both an event and a state. Does death (the event) make us dead (the state)? In practice as well as theory we can create difficulties for each other by failing to distinguish between these two uses of the term. Of two people who are equally afraid of death, for example, one might have his apprehensions focused upon a possible specific mode of dying, while the other is fixed in terror upon the prospect of eternal damnation. To remind ourselves that death as a state can be conceptualized in more than one way, we shall briefly characterize some of the approaches that have been taken by individual thinkers or cultural traditions.

1. More of the Same

After the death event, "life" might continue much the same as before. The deceased passes from one realm to another. However, personality, motives and challenges remain little affected by the transition. This view, held by a number of tribal societies (Hertz, 1960), makes it clear that *continuation* after the death event is not identical with immortality. Life after the death event is imagined to follow the same general outlines as the life that is familiar to the community, with allowances made for encounters with menacing or kindly gods. Death as a state can have its vicissitudes and crises, just as life before the death event. It is even possible for the dead person to be destroyed again. As outsiders to this concept of the death state as continuation of previous existence, we might wonder about the logical consistency of such double death, or the status of the twice deceased; this would be our problem, though, and not one that troubles those who see death in the terms sketched above.

2. Perpetual Development

Today's life-span developmental theorist has yet to match the broad conceptualizations offered by some philosophers and scientists of previous generations. Inspired by various inputs, such as the excitement of evolution theory, the crumbling of the block universe, a whiff of oriental cosmology, imaginative thinkers described a universe in which the primary principle is development. A bare temporal–spatial manifold is in process of "flowering into deity," in Samuel Alexander's poetic phrase (Alexander,1920), and human growth is part of this process. Both Gustav Fechner (known to the history books for an achievement that was only secondary in his own mind; the establishment of psychophysical methods in experimental psychology) and the American philosopher William Ernest Hocking specified individual and conditional trajectories of development. At any particular point in the life span, an individual might be more or less advanced in his own progress toward fulfillment. The same holds true at the point of the death event. Accordingly, death as a state varies from person to person, contingent upon the kind of development that has already been achieved (Fechner, 1906; Hocking, 1957). "Awareness," "enlightenment," "higher consciousness" —any of these terms would be suggestive of the basic dimensions of development. The opportunity for perpetual development both before and after the death event exists for all of us. But there are no guarantees. One can flunk developmental tasks on both sides of the grave. Death, then, is not a fixed state. The death state can vary from a complete depletion of awareness to an experiential heightening beyond our powers of imagination. The death state is linked both with the individual's previous developmental career and with the general status of our in-process universe.

3. Less of the Same

More common than either the continuity or perpetual development models of the death state is the decremental model. The death event is not simply a transition to either a postmortem replica of previous life or a new realm for conditional development. Instead, we are plunged into a dark pit from which there is no escape, only a gradual submergence. This is the "underworld" of miserable shades whose individual characteristics erode with time until all differentiation has disappeared. In ancient Mesopotamia, for example, the deceased became an *edim* or *etimmu*, a "grisly being" condemned to *kur-nu-gi-a*, "the land of no return" (Brandon, 1967). The death event is catastrophic in this view. Even the mightiest ruler and the fairest maiden lose all power and beauty. The dead are equal and undifferentiated in their low estate. So dreadful was this prospect that it formed the core challenge to human courage and creativity in the earliest major work of literature to reach us over the centuries, the *Epic of Gilgamesh*.

Hebrews of the Old Testament period faced the gloomy prospect of *Sheol*, the final common meeting place where the dead subsist without joy or hope, mere wretched shadows and remnants of what they once had been. The death state was especially terrifying to the living because it signaled isolation from the power and glory of Yahweh. As Bultmann observes:

> It is really here that the actual sting, which death had for OT religion through the centuries, resides. Yahweh is the god of life in a quite exclusive sense. Death and its realm stand outside the stream of power which has subdued all areas of life, and the absence of a theological point of orientation for the concepts of the state of death resulted in the fact that, within the Yahwistic faith, these have been preserved in an undecided and unreconciled state not otherwise found in the OT [Bultmann, 1965, pp. 10-11].

Perhaps, then, the death state is to life as aging is to development. Both involve decrement that cannot be escaped. Yet our ancestors revered many of their aged and attempted to bring comfort to them. A person might still have significant psychosocial value, though very old or very sick. The death event, however, tended to repel those who had cared faithfully for the aged and the sick. Who would want to touch a body that was now beyond the pale of life and, by so doing, dip one's own hand into the dark and dismal stream of *Sheol?*

4. Waiting

Many people today and in centuries past have conceived of the death state as an exercise in waiting. It would be more precise, perhaps, to speak of it as a state of restful waiting. After the death event, the deceased (or some component thereof) reposes until the Day of Judgement. One then moves to the final destination or state. This is a triphasic conception. The first phase of the death state resembles sleep or suspended animation. The middle phase is that dramatic moment when disposition is made of the soul. Finally, the deceased takes his or her "place" for "eternity" or for "all time" (fundamentally different concepts but, for most people, functionally equivalent).

A particular individual or society may emphasize one of these phases more than the others. Among Christians, for example, some associate chiefly to the "taking-a-good-long-rest" phase. Others rivet their attention upon the critical moment of judgment, and still others concentrate upon the penultimate phase when sorrows have passed, justice has been done, and one exists at last in undisturbed radiance and peace.

I have characterized this conception of the death state as *waiting* to emphasize its temporal characteristics. A certain tension is established between the death event itself (usually regarded here as a sudden and decisive happening) and the end state. The death event does not tell the entire story; there is more to come. The idea that the dead are in some sense waiting deserves consideration within the broader context of our culture's relationship to time. Many observers have seen us as time-obsessed, achievement-oriented, gratification-delaying creatures who are much too busy doing to be. The concept of development itself strongly implies a directional change that is incessantly moving us from one way station of life to the next. We are always in motion, and hopeful that we are getting somewhere. This concept of time as a medium through which development and achievement occurs seems to extend beyond the death event. Not only is there the basic triphasic structure of the death state just sketched, but individuals sometimes conceive of further "doings" when the dead shall awaken. In fact, the notion of a "do-nothing eternity" seems repugnant to many who retain belief in an afterlife death state. Perhaps we have become so accustomed to change and striving that the idea of any final state (before or after the death event) is alien to us.

It is not only the dead who wait. Aged men and women who see themselves as abandoned and rootless here on earth often wait for the death
event, as do some terminally ill people of any age. For some who are ready
to resign from life, it is a wait for release to be taken away. For others, it is
a wait for the new life, the transfiguration, the reunion with loved ones
under perfect conditions. This distinction can be important from the standpoint of both the individual himself and those who would be of help to him.
But in either case, the waiting signifies a phenomenological state that is
somewhere between life and death: "I am here, but not really; I am only
here because I am not yet there."

Time is important in this view of the death state in other ways as well.
The time lag between the death event and judgment/transfiguration may be
conceived as both instantaneous and extremely protracted. The deceased
may have to wait in Phase I until all mortal souls are available for judgment. This would represent a very long period of time as measured by
conventional human standards (if not all time). but, subjectively, might be
experienced as instantaneous. Or one might believe that judgment comes
very soon after the death event for every individual. Should one be foolhar-
dy enough to ask, "How long does death [the state] last?"; a host of logical
and semantic as well as theological problems arise. It is enough for our
purposes here to note that the traditional triphasic conception of the death
state in our culture does imply temporal duration in some sense of the term.
More than one believer finds himself thinking that time ends with the death
event, but continues to anticipate a further sequence of events that lend
themselves to conceptualization in familiar temporal terms.

5. Recycling

One of the most radical conceptions of the death state is also one of the
most traditional and popular. In our own as well as in ancient times there
have been many who regard the death state as but a temporary and alternating condition. The individual seems to pass from life to death. But, in
some essential sense, the dead return to the world in one form or another.
This general view has many variants, but its common theme is the conserva-
tion of identity and/or energy. The core of one's being (however this may
be conceived) cannot be destroyed (or only under very special circumstances). Each of us is obliged, priveleged, fated, or doomed to put up with
ourselves through round after round of recycling. There are abundant
anthropological observations on beliefs and practices associated with the
recycling of identity through birth–death–rebirth loops (e.g., Ellis, 1968;
Frazer, 1966; Henderson & Oakes, 1971).

The death state can be seen as one position on the constantly revolving
great wheel of life and death (e.g., Kapleau, 1970). It can be conceptualized

in cosmological and theological terms, or as an extension of scientific principles (e.g., matter–energy interchange and indestructibility). But recycling also can be regarded as a transposition of the child's view of reality. Cyclical experiences are much in evidence in infancy and early childhood, and probably exercise considerable influence upon the development of cognitive structures (Kastenbaum & Aisenberg, 1972). It is not difficult for our bodies to believe that every ending has its new beginning, and every sleep its awakening. Cultures that live close to the seasons, to the rhythms of earth and tide, are also likely to be impressed with the predictable return as well as with the predictable departure of natural phenomena. With or without the trappings of elaborate conceptualizations, the basic notion of the death state as part of a fluctuating relationship with life continues to have its hold on many of us.

6. End Point of Biological Process

In recent years the medical, legal, and scientific communities have taken renewed interest in another traditional interpretation of the death state: as the end point of a biological process. Under precisely what conditions can we act with the secure knowledge that the death event is no longer in progress, but that the death state itself has been reached? This question is of concern to people involved with organ transplants, cryonic suspension, and the euthanasia–death-with-dignity issues. Others are finding the problem fascinating for basic research purposes apart from practical implications, and still others believe that a more accurate and "modern" view of the death state should be established and then incorporated into our legal, educational, legislative, and social institutions. *Updating Life and Death* (Cutler, 1969) is the title of one book, but represents the task that many have set for themselves.

The borderlands between death as event and as state are the site of exploration and controversy. The distinction between "clinical death" and "biological death" has become well established in principle, if still unsettled in detail. Cessation of vital signs is accepted by some physicians and medical researchers as indicating "clinical death." In our terminology, this is both an event and a state. It is not, however, the final death state, because ordinarily it will be followed by irreversible damage to biological structures, after which the body can no longer support life even if heroic measures are instituted. If and when qualified observers agree upon specific criteria for biological death, then the two-phase process of death in progress can be said to have given way to a final state of lifelessness.

There are methodological, philosophical, and even political problems to contend with in establishing either the general or specific case of biological death. The definition of "irreversible damage," for example, has been changing for at least 200 years. There is no reason to believe it has achieved a fixed form today. Social, political, and economic values influence decisions reflecting our judgments on who is dead and who worth keeping alive. In short, there is both scientific and humanistic hazard in the rigid and premature establishment of a final death state. The aura of objective medical science might persuade the easily persuaded that we now really do know what, when and how death is. A more appropriate interpretation would be that we are merely continuing exercises in the "pragmatics of death" (Kastenbaum & Aisenberg, 1972) that were begun for us long ago by thoughtful and attentive observers that history has chosen to neglect.

What we have, in effect, is increased social need for sharp definitions of death, along with more sophisticated methods to monitor the condition of the organism. Physicians and researchers still have many options before them in making such determinations, and the more informed they are, the more options. And everybody involved in the process is subject to many pressures and influences that are external to the death phenomena. Furthermore, it is doubtful that anything new has been learned about the death state as such. The layman can say, "Death is the nothing that begins when everything else has ended." The physician cannot say even this much when he stays within his proper role. He is trained in observing and influencing life-related processes. If he limited himself to his own expertise, he would say only: "There is nothing here that responds to me. There is nothing more for me to do. This stimulus–response vacuum is what I mean by the state of death, and that is all I can say."

7. The Nonstate

But *is* death a state—of any kind? Perhaps we begin in confusion and can end only in confusion when we think of death as a state. Whatever is attributed to the death state refies an abstraction, or makes a "something" out of "nothing."

Taking this approach, we would be wary of those habits of thought and language that lead to positive conceptualizations of death. By assuming death to be a state among other states, we blink its crowning distinction: "nothing, nothing . . . nothing at all." This, however, is easier to propose than to follow through consistently. It is very difficult to unthink and unspeak death as a state. Our needs for logical development and sheer cognitive–affective comfort will find little nourishment in the barren, alien vision of a nonstate. We know little about nothing, and much prefer to convert nothing into anything (Kastenbaum, in preparation). Whether or not we can relate ourselves effectively to death as the nonstate, however, this does comprise one of our options.

8. The Nonliving

"Being dead" and "not being alive" are not necessarily identical states. The nonliving is a category that can include the dead (depending upon one's definition of the death state), but has other members as well. Inorganic nature is not dead in the usual senses of this term, but shares certain characteristics in common with the once alive (lack of development, more restricted modes of exchange with the environment, etc.). How much of nature properly belongs in the category of nonliving? What is not alive but not dead depends upon one's knowledge and perspective. The people who seem most expert in observing and analyzing phenomena bordering "organic" and "inorganic" also seem most willing to entertain open and flexible conceptions (e.g., Hoffman, 1957). Theoretically, it is helpful to distinguish the dead from the unalive, but, in practice, definitive language is as elusive here as elsewhere.

D. Death as Analogy

So powerful a term as death recommends itself to us in many contexts. We may speak of the death of a railroad, an empire, or a dream. Others understand what we mean, even if the statements do not bear critical scrutiny. Loss, emptiness, lack of response, and termination of a process are among the many meanings of death. However, there is no fixed set of phenomena to which death can serve as analogy. We use the term death as we do many other terms, to meet the expressive needs of particular circumstances. "Ow-wow! That killed my knee-bone!" The child who has just tumbled from his bicycle ensured that the experience will be communicated with the deserved vigor and significance by using a death verb as intensifier. The "dead" battery in our car or the letter we fear has ended up in the "dead letter office" are just two more routine examples that could be cited.

Of more interest here are some of the ways in which the use of death as analogy pertains to our relationships with other people and, at times, with ourselves. Three types of usage will be briefly described (Kastenbaum & Aisenberg, 1972).

1. Social Death

A person may be "cut dead" by family, friends, or the entire community. In the emergency room some accident victims are treated as though they were "as good as dead." The process of regarding another human being as socially dead can be as formal and ritualistic as a bone-pointing ceremony, or as casual and unexamined as the total snubbing of a "unimportant" person.

The concept of social death centers upon words, attitudes, and actions of other people rather than the characteristics of the "dead" person himself. To determine whether or not a person is socially dead. we observe how he is treated by others. A complete absence of life-relating behaviors (speaking to him, making a place for him at the table, etc.) would suggest that the social-death condition is in effect. In special circumstances we may also observe patterns of behavior that positively treat the person as though dead, as distinguished from the suspension of normal life-acknowledging interactions.

Social death has two characteristics not usually associated with "real" death: It can vary from partial to complete, and it can be temporary or reversible. Current concepts such as the clinical/biological death distinction do give "real" and "social" death more kinship than what might appear to be the case on the surface. In any event, social death is a concept implicit in some of our interactions with others, lends itself to observation and analysis, and seems to have a kind of socioemotional validity in its own terms, no matter how we view its relationship with other forms of death.

2. Thanatomimesis

An organism, human or subhuman, may give the appearance of being dead. The opposum's knack for "playing dead" is justly famous, but is by no means the only example to be found in the animal kingdom. In our own species, thanatomimetic behavior has frequently been observed. A few generations ago, for example, many people here and in Europe were aghast at the prospect of perhaps being buried alive. Learned journals as well as the popular press discussed alleged instances of a living person being mistaken for one from whom all life had fled. Perhaps it was more than coincidental that public anxiety about premature burial and the incidence of hysterical forms of behavior disturbance—including swoons, catalepsies, and "ecstasies"—peaked at about the same time. Temporary loss (or apparent loss) of consciousness could yield the impression of death, even, at times, to physicians.

Thanatomimetic behavior can be purposeful (e.g., feigning death to avoid a truly fatal blow in combat), unintentional (e.g., the diabetic coma or post-seizure state), or somewhere in between. It can also be an artistic form: the yogi or other master of bodily process who displays his philosophy and skills by suppressing respiration and other vital signs. It can be a form of learning and anxiety control through play, as in children's death games through the centuries (Opie & Opie. 1969). Perception of another as dead obviously involves the sensitivities and expectations of the observer as well as the objective appearance of the observed. A nonresponsive aged patient, for example, may be taken for dead (thanatomimesis) by one staff member and treated as though nonalive (social death), while a colleague with more experience or a different orientation sits by the bedside, touching and speaking to the "deceased."

There is much to be learned about thanatomimetic phenomena. The essential point for us here is that a deathlike appearance does not invariably represent the actual condition of the organism.

3. Phenomenological Death

A person may also be "dead to himself." Phenomenological death can take either of two general pathways. A role or part function of the individual may die. The surviving self observes and mourns. One of the most predictable trajectories of this type is the fate of the professional athlete who, as Roger Kahn (1971) notes, "has two deaths to face." Although still relatively young and in good health, the individual may be "washed up" as a competitive and celebrated athlete. The locus of death can be even more specific, as when a "dead arm" ends the career of a pitcher who otherwise has his reflexes and youth intact. In this general form of phenomenological death, a surviving observer self experiences the loss of a partial self or role function. The process of grief–mourning–working through can be compared with the reaction to the death of another person, although not identical.

But phenomenological life may flicker and fade in toto. The person no longer experiences as freshly, perceives as clearly, feels as deeply. The light of awareness that has illuminated all else for the individual itself is subject to failure. Phenomenological death is a term most aptly applied to those who no longer appear to have any experiential capacities remaining, even though the body continues to support life. Nevertheless, it is also possible to conceive of phenomenological deadness–aliveness as a dimension of everybody's functional status at all times. The vibrant child may be more "alive" than the routinized adult, and each of us may vary within our own range of deadness–aliveness throughout the day and from one day to the next. Soft-drink advertisements urge us to "Come alive!" and we speak of being "turned on" by certain people or experiences. These usages hint the viability of a deadness–aliveness dimension on the phenomenological level. Difficulties in conceptualizing and studying phenomenological states need not be deterrents to acknowledgment of the fact that we are sometimes more alive than at other times, and perhaps owe this phenomenon more attention than it has yet received.

E. Death as Mystery

Our inclination to think of death in rationalistic, logical, control-oriented terms does not prove that death is, in fact, rational, logical, and controllable. Indeed, in most of us, as in our culture in general, there are countertendencies. "Irrational" thoughts and feelings about death exist side by side with our most polished and respectable conceptualizations. Even the intolerant distinction between rational and irrational reflects some of the bias of our times. Others have lived with a rich mixture of the rational and the irrational, never feeling compelled to root out all implicit contradictions.

Perhaps death is truly a mystery. We cannot "know" death in the way that we can hope to know other subjects. It is at once too close and too alien to us. This view does not require us to abandon our efforts to comprehend death in modes familiar to us (e.g., as subject of empirical research or logical analysis). But it does raise the possibility that death is, in principle, a mystery. Among other implications, this would mean that we respect the limits of our knowledge and not overly assimilate death to concepts and observations with which we have greater knowledge and affinity.

F. Death Concepts and Developmental Theory and Research

Presumably death concepts will appear with increasing frequency in developmental theory and research: These concepts could hardly appear with less frequency than they have in the past. We will be performing a service to ourselves and to each other if we exercise care in matching word to concept, and communicating precisely what type of death we have in mind in a given context. There is little point in generating elaborate theory and research if we are confused about the central terms involved.

Awareness that death has multiple meanings and usages should also make us more useful to individuals whose lives intersect with our own. We should be less likely to assume that somebody else thinks of death as we do (or as we think we think we do). And quick generalizations about the development of death thoughts and orientations throughout the life span might give way to alert and patient observation.

There are more potential points of contact between death and developmental theory than can be sketched here. What we can do, however, is to examine one problem area that is of substantial interest for both human well-being and systematic understanding—the process of dying. Even more specifically, attention will focus upon the proposition that we die in stages.

III. Do We Die in Stages?

The concept of stages is abundantly familiar in developmental theory and research. Freud, Erikson, and Piaget are perhaps the most influential of the theorists who have offered stage-progression approaches, but there are many others also available to choose from. Stage theories are characterized by emphasis upon qualitative differences that are thought to appear in a relatively fixed sequence. Change along a simple quantitative dimension is usually not regarded as the stuff of stage theory. The 12-year-old is taller than the 6-year-old, but it is the contention that he *thinks differently* that constitutes the grounds for locating him in a different stage.

Popular as a technique for organizing observations and for teaching, stage theory might also be expected to surface in the area of dying and death, which until recent years has attracted few researchers, theoreticians, and clinical specialists. With the publication in 1969 of Elizabeth Kubler-Ross's *On Death and Dying,* such a theory did become available and widely disseminated. It is this approach that will be described and examined in the next section.

A. A Stage Theory of the Dying Process

1. The Five Stages

Kubler-Ross proposes that the dying person passes through five stages. These begin with the impact of mortal tidings, and terminate as life itself terminates. Individuals may differ in the rapidity through which they move from stage to stage. Further, some people do not reach the final stage at all. One can be caught or arrested at a particular stage of dying, as in any stage in life-span development. The stages are normal modes of responding to the harsh reality of death. Further, there can be some slipping back and forth between stages, and the coexistence of two stages.

Denial is the first stage. The person is, in effect, saying "No!" to death. This stage takes place whether terminal status is communicated by medical authorities or surmised by the individual himself. Denial can be displayed in straightforward fashion or obliquely. By words and actions the person resists acknowledging the reality of impending death.

Anger comes next. The lid blows off. Angry feelings may be vented upon family, medical staff, the environment. Even God is not exempt. It is as though somebody must be blamed for the overwhelming disaster, which is no longer denied. The typical question the person is struggling with at this time is "Why me?" Frustration builds and anger overflows as the question resists satisfactory answer.

Bargaining is the middle stage. The person attempts to make a deal with fate. He changes his strategy and asks for a favor. Kubler-Ross compares this maneuver with the child whose request for an overnight visit with a friend has been turned down. After stamping his foot, "No!" and expressing anger, the child eventually comes around to ask, "If I am very good all week and wash the dishes every evening, then will you let me go? [Kubler-Ross, 1969, p. 72]." The terminally ill patient attempts to bargain for an extension of life, a postponement of the death event. Much of the bargaining is likely to proceed covertly between the dying person and God, but the process sometimes can be seen as well in interactions with others.

Depression sets in "when the terminally ill patient can no longer deny his illness, when he is forced to undergo more surgery or hospitalization, when he begins to have more symptoms or becomes weaker and thinner, he cannot smile it off anymore. His numbness or stoicism, his anger and rage will soon be replaced with a sense of great loss [Kubler-Ross, 1969, p. 75]." The depressive state may involve feelings of guilt and unworthiness, fear of dying, and attenuation of communication with family and others.

Acceptance is the final stage. The struggle is over. Tired and weak physically, the patient nevertheless is no longer sunk in the anguish of depression. "Acceptance should not be mistaken for a happy stage. It is almost void of feelings. It is as if the pain had gone, the struggle is over, and there comes a time for 'the final rest before the long journey' as one patient phrased it [Kubler-Ross, 1969, p. 100]."

2. Context of the Stage Theory

Kubler-Ross illuminates her presentation of each stage with brief synopses of terminally ill people she has interviewed, and transcribed dialogue between the patient and herself. This sharing of clinical material helps the reader to grasp the essence of the various stages. Moreover, it provides a person with "something to go on" or "something to look for" when entering into a relationship with a dying person oneself. She also comments upon some of the ways in which family or staff might respond helpfully to the dying person in each stage. The difficult problem of relating to the dying person when anger is the dominant affect, for example, receives her attention. A separate chapter is devoted to examples from her therapeutic efforts with the dying.

Interwoven through all five stages is the phenomenon of *hope*, which also is discussed in a separate chapter. Perhaps her key point here is that

> In listening to our terminally ill patients we were always impressed that even the most accepting, the most realistic patients left the possibility open for some cure, for the discovery of a new drug, of the last minute success in a research project. . . . It is this glimpse of hope which maintains them through days, weeks, or months of suffering. It is the feeling that all this must have some meaning, will pay off eventually if they can only endure it for a little while longer. It is the hope that occasionally sneaks in, that all this is just like a nightmare and not true . . . [Kubler-Ross, 1969, p. 123].

B. Stage Theory of Dying as a General Contribution

The stage theory of dying has made a number of contributions to our culture's general orientation toward dying and death. Not the least of these is the awakening or legitimation of interest in a topic that has been taboo to many Americans, whether laymen or professionals (Feifel, 1959). Kubler-Ross has reached the feelings of people who previously did not know where to begin in relating themselves toward their terminally ill friends, family or patients. *On Death and Dying* became for many their first exposure to systematic description of the dying process, and their first guide for their own explorations. Although books on death have been published before and after, it is this contribution by Kubler-Ross that established the topic as one of general concern.

Thoughts and feeling stirred by this book have added to the impetus of a nationwide death education movement. The existence of stage theory also has provided a coin of communication: The social worker from Utah meeting the nurse from New York can both talk about Stage 3, and the student of death education has his or her five stages to copy down and memorize.

The book, then, has opened the subject of death and dying to many people and provided a basis for communication. This stepping-over-the-threshold is significant action, when we reflect that even experienced health professionals often place physical and emotional distance between themselves and the palpabilities of dying and death. The humanism and the case material account for part of this effect. What about the stage theory itself? It is my impression that the stage theory gained rapid acceptance because it is a clear, understandable schema that provides structure and reduces anxiety for the reader. Death becomes subsumed under dying, and dying transformed from a vague, overpowering, and terrifying mass to a delimited, coherent, orderly sequence. There are rules now to govern this part of the universe that has for so long been considered out of bounds. The reader, researcher, or health professional thus can approach the topic with less anxiety and foreboding.

It is not surprising that many people have felt remarkably better after becoming acquainted with the stage theory of dying. Anxiety and lack of cognitive structure are replaced by the security of knowledge. The reader now knows what happens during the process of dying, has greater feeling for the patient's situation, and has some idea about what might be done to be of value to the patient or his family. There is no doubt that stage theory has increased the dialogue, both oral and written, about care of the dying person. And there is little doubt that more people have taken heart to draw closer to the dying person. Not all the consequences have been favorable, however, and some of the problems involved will be examined in what follows.

C. Stage Theory of Dying as a Contribution to Knowledge

We raise now a sampling of those questions that come to mind in evaluating any model of human behavior. Particular attention will be given to issues that link the stage theory of dying with other developmental approaches.

1. Overview

The stage theory of dying draws primarily upon the clinical experiences of psychiatrist–author Elizabeth Kubler-Ross. In her words, this theory is intended "to summarize what we have learned from our dying patients in terms of coping mechanisms at the time of a terminal illness [Kubler-Ross, 1969, p. 33]." The theory is intended to encompass feelings and behaviors of the dying person from awareness of terminality to the death event itself. In company with other stage theories, the stage theory of dying specifies a strongly directional set of transitions with each way station characterized by fairly distinct phenomena. The source, intention, and general nature of Kubler-Ross's theory do not present any difficulties. Personal experience with dying patients is obviously a sensible basis for deriving the principles of a theory or general formulation. The stage theory of dying comes into being as a means of summarizing and sharing those experiences. And the idea that the process of dying can be usefully viewed in terms of some orderly progression of adaptive states does not tax credibility. In broad outline, then, the theory deserves consideration as a plausible approach toward understanding the dying process. Does it also deserve acceptance as the "true account" or the "most useful" theory? This is quite another question.

2. The Data Base

Experiences with approximately 200 terminally ill people provided the basis for the stage theory of dying; since that time Kubler-Ross has interviewed approximately another 200 terminally ill in her own setting, and has seen many others as consultant–lecturer. It is clear that her theory is grounded in relevant information.

However, virtually every operation that might be performed on clinical information for conversion into research data has been neglected. The sample itself has not been described. Terms have not been defined. Transcripts have not been subjected to analysis and no interrater reliability procedures that might demonstrate the existence of the five stages have been performed. The interaction between the method of data gathering and the results has not been discussed. The most basic types of statistical information have not been provided. (How many patients, for example, were seen for what periods of time? How many, in fact, did die while the interview series was in process? How many were interviewed only on a single occasion?, etc.).

There are sensitive issues here that could easily be distorted. Systematic research and finesse may be unreasonable to expect when a person is helping to pioneer and emotion-laden growing edge of knowledge and concern. One-to-one with a dying person, a psychiatrist or other interested person has more pressing concerns than the abstract demands of science. Kubler-Ross had to discover her own pathway to understanding the terminally ill, and then had the generosity of spirit to share it with others.

But all of this does not permit us to relax standards of evidence. Perhaps a theory has emerged whose ties with its original data base are personal and difficult to share or open for objective evaluation. This circumstance in itself neither supports nor undercuts the specifics of Kubler-Ross's theory. However, the rapid acceptance of the stage theory of dying has quite outdistanced any attempt to examine the theory empirically or logically. It is taken typically as proven fact. But the fact is that the theory was not offered with a close and coherently developed data base at the start, and no effort has been made to test out the theory as it continues to become more widely disseminated and applied. Few who center their approach to dying and death around the stage theory of dying see it as in need of analysis, examination, evaluation. It is useful in some way, therefore it is self-perpetuating. Moreover, as will be seen later, those who find this theory less than useful tend to drop it without necessarily subjecting either the theory or their own uses of it to searching analysis. In short, there is conviction that the stage theory of dying is an empirically valid formulation of human experience during the dying process, when little effort has been expended to study the relationship between theory and fact. The present criticism is not directed at the paucity of information brought forth to support or test the stage theory of dying, but the attitude that research is superfluous.

As a person who has some experience with the terminally ill, I appreciate the fact that companionship, caring, and intervention cannot wait until scientific formulations have been purified and validated. Sounding the caution about a particular theory is not equivalent to discouraging people from bringing their best selves to interactions with the dying, or to using whatever insights the theory provides. But I must reject the contention that the stage theory of dying is so important and useful that research can wait. It is precisely because the experiences of the dying person and all those around him are so important that we ought not to base our work indefinitely upon an untested theory. If the theory is substantially correct, then we should use it for all that it is worth; if it has decided limitations or inaccuracies, then we should move without delay to find alternatives.

3. Factors Insufficiently Considered by the Stage Theory of Dying

It is here suggested that Kubler-Ross's theory suffers from what could be described either as overreliance upon one component of the total situation or underappreciation of the total context. In this regard, the theory perhaps is suffering a flaw common to most stage theories. Mentioned in the following paragraphs are several other sources of variance that are neglected by the emphasis upon the five hypothesized stages of individual adaptation to terminal illness.

Nature of the disease.   There have always been physicians who maintain that a person "dies the death of his disease." In other words, the patterning of the pathology dominates all else. This contention, like those of the stage theory of dying, has yet to be tested critically. But it is evident that the nature-of-the-disease process can greatly affect pain, mobility, trajectory of dying, and the social stimulus value of the dying person, to mention just some of the dimensions involved. Within the realm of cancer alone, for example, the person with head or neck cancer looks and feels different from the person with leukemia. The person with emphysema, subject to terrifying attacks in which each breath of air requires a struggle, experiences his situation differently from the person with advanced renal failure, or with a cardiovascular trajectory. Although Kubler-Ross's theory directs welcome attention to the universal psychosocial aspects of terminal illness, we also lose much sensitivity if the disease process itself is not fully respected.

Sex differences. Do men and women experience terminal illness identically, even if both are afflicted by the same condition? Clinical experience suggests that the sexes differ with respect to the type of discomfort, impairment, and limitations of function that are of greatest concern. Some of our research in progress further suggests that pain, dependency, and loss of occupational role rank very high for men, while women are more distressed by the impact of their illness and death upon others. It is possible, then, that sex-role attitudes may be a significant source of variance in adaptation to terminal illness.

Ethnicity. Is it legitimate to die in a hospital or other public institution? How is pain to be experienced and expressed? Is it most important to keep up the strong front or the family name? Does the death event signify triumph and release or dismal failure? For some people, the answers to these questions may be found most clearly in their ethnic identity. The total interpersonal situation that surrounds a terminally ill person as well as his own responses can differ radically depending upon the ethnic patterns involved—as thousands of nurses can testify.

Personality or cognitive style. Whatever makes a person the particular person he is has much to do with the nature of his terminal phase of life. No single personality or cognitive style is invariably adaptive; in fact, any of a number of cognitive style variables might be equally adequate. The point is that we approach our death to some extent as the type of person we have always been—reflective or impulsive, warm or aloof, whatever. A view of the dying process that excludes personality as such must also exclude much of reality.

Developmental level. The meaning of dying and death differs for the infant who has known little of life and for the aged man or woman who has known much. Additionally, whatever merit there is in classifying people according to developmental level applies as well to appreciating their experiences in the terminal phase of life. People come to death as more or less mature organisms, and with very different positions along their own potential life cycles. In other words, the person's general developmental situation must be taken into account as well as any modes of development that are specific to the dying process itself.

Sociophysical milieu.   What is the nature of the environment in which the person is dying? Is it an efficient, professionalized world of strangers? A slow-paced nursing home? A room in the house where the person was born many years before? Is the environment over or underprotective? Does it value expression or suppression of feelings? Is this an environment in which there are clear, conflicting, or no expectations of the dying person himself? However we may choose to analyze the sociophysical milieu, it is obviously a major source of variance in influencing what the dying person says and does, and perhaps also what he feels.

Formulations of the dying process could be derived from each of the areas sketched earlier. Some appear as promising or more promising than a stage theory, some less promising. Useful theories of dying could be grounded, for example, in the sociophysical milieu. The work of Glaser and Strauss (1965) moves in this direction. The milieu also has the advantage of being somewhat amenable to change. A formulation that incorporates two or more sources of variation could be even more powerful (e.g., the developmental and the sociophysical). There is no compelling reason to limit our thinking to any single realm.

Even if Kubler-Ross's theory could be supported as an accurate representation of adaptive strategies on the part of the dying person, it would still tell us little that we need to know about the interaction with disease process, ethnicity, personality style, and so on. Were less claimed for her theory, more could be granted to it. Hastily accepted as *the* account of the dying process, Kubler-Ross's theory emphasizes one possible set of dynamics to the virtual exclusion of all others.

One of the consequences is establishment of the image of *the* dying person moving through the universal five stages. Yet it is always a specific person dying in a specific environment that has its own social and physical dynamics, and the person approaches death through one or more specific disease modalities, responding in terms of the idiosyncratic integration of personality, ethnic, sex-role, and developmental resources. Viewed in this light, each death is individual. The five stages, if they do exist, are found within the context of the situation but do not necessarily dominate it.

4. Other Problems with the Stage Theory of Dying

In keeping with most developmental theories, the stage theory of dying assumes a single primary path of movement. We grow up one way. We die one way. Variations are acknowledged, but are seen as deviations from a central mode of progression. This approach is objectionable in the stage theory of dying as well as other forms of developmental theory—objectionable because the uncritical perpetuation of the one-path conception (a) impedes the appreciation and discovery of alternate approaches and (b) has the effect of stereotyping uncommon or idiosycratic patterns as deviant.

Both the stage theory of dying and developmental theories in general sometimes fail to distinguish adequately between what usually happens and what *should* happen. The problem may, however, be more severe in the present use of the stage theory of dying, where conception and application are closely linked, and both under intense emotional pressure. Kubler-Ross herself has cautioned that people should not be rushed through the stages. Yet the theory implies that there is a valued destination to be reached, and that one should keep moving toward acceptance, if at his or her own pace. Less a problem of the theory itself than of some of its applications, there is nevertheless a disturbing tendency for description to be converted imperceptibly into prescription. In general, the relationships between fact and surmise, surmise and theory, and theory and value orientation remain obscure and vulnerable in the stage theory of dying.

Clinical research concerning the dying process by other investigators does not clearly support the existence of the five stages or of any universal form of staging. A recent review of the literature, scant as it is, finds no evidence for five predictable stages of psychological adaptation. Other investigators' data "show the process of dying to be less rigid and even stageless. There is some consensus among all researchers that terminal patients are depressed shortly before they die, but there is no consistent evidence that other affect dimensions characterize the dying patient [Schulz & Alderman, 1974]." We must add that this negative conclusion is based upon studies conducted by various clinical investigators with equally various populations, techniques, and objectives, none of which were to make critical tests of stage theory. Nevertheless, the fact that available data do not make a strong case for the stage theory of dying obviously must be kept in mind.

D. Concluding Note on the Stage Theory of Dying

Although this has been perhaps the most systematic exploration yet made of the stage theory of dying, much remains to be learned and discussed. It is possible that the theory, either in its present or a revised form, might eventually become established as a faithful representation of central facts in the dying process and a dependable guide to education and action. For the moment, however, what we have is the early social history of a simple formulation about some vital aspects of human existence. This theory fills various individual and social needs; it is illuminated by the experience and insight of its author; and it can be appealing to those who are avid collectors of stage theories. We hope to have suggested that the application of stage theory to significant—literally life-and-death—experience should be accompanied by the critical and self-correcting perspective of science, no matter how we might want to believe that the truth is at hand. Those who have taken up the theory only to abandon it after clinical trials might also find it useful to examine their own reasons for both acceptance and rejection. What was expected or demanded of the theory? Were these expectations appropriate? What can we require realistically of any formulation of the dying process, and what must we require directly of ourselves? No matter what base of external knowledge or what theoretical perspective we bring to the dying situation, there is no substitute for confronting and in some manner accommodating ourselves to the prospect of our own deaths—a central theme in the work of Kubler-Ross and most other pioneers in this field.

IV. Death in Theory and Practice: Selected Problems

A. Steady State or Change?

Developmental theorists find their various ways of coming to terms with two sets of dynamics that might appear to be independent or oppositional. One can emphasize the forces that hold the individual together, enable him to retain "homeostasis," "steady state," or "equilibration" (these terms being used uncritically in the present discussion). But one might emphasize instead the dynamics of "change," "maturation," or "development." Major theories usually incorporate both dynamics, but seldom achieve "equilibration" of the steady state versus change components.

In this very limited discussion, I intend only to suggest some of the considerations that become more salient when aging and death are recognized as well within the compass of developmental theory. Emphasis in developmental theory traditionally is placed on the early years. This means, of course, that we are concerned with growth, expansion, and energy expenditure, all at a relatively brisk pace. Some type of change or directional model recommends itself to accommodate the empirical facts. The more subtle observer and thinker, such as Piaget, does give attention to homeostatic mechanisms as well. Because so much of developmental psychology has come under the influence of facts and theory deriving from the early years, we may inherit unexamined assumptions and stereotypes that are applied naively to phenomena of midlife and beyond.

The relationship between steady state and change dynamics, for example, is not necessarily the same when we are concerned with the (seemingly) slower tempo of affairs in midlife. The constricting, slowing, entroping, energy-conserving phenomena of later life comprise a different context for steady state/change dynamics than the growth spurts of the early years.

Perhaps an even more challenging problem involves the nature of who or what changes (or remains constant). Is there a core of personal identity that persists throughout the adult years, although behavioral and somatic parameters change? Should we, in fact, regard identity preservation as the goal of the various changes and adaptations observable in the later years of life? There are formidable semantic and methodologic problems here. We should want to know, for example, precisely what it is about the individual's identity that might serve as the goal of equilibration through change. When in doubt, it is sometimes permissible to ask the individual himself. How has he been experiencing his own life? What are his own inner constancies, and where his growing edges? The phenomenological approach to life-span developmental psychology has not yet had the input that might be expected from it; eventually, our understanding should be much enriched from this source.

The prospect of death may set into motion other dynamics, or hasten some of the changes already in process. One may organize himself around the family name, his bank account, or a very personal, idiosyncratic identity core known only to himself. It is this symbol of himself that he most wishes to protect against the onslaught of aging and/or terminal illness. The sensitive friend, the professional care-giver, and the life-span researcher all have reason to be concerned about the individual's priorities of self-constants as stress increases, threat mounts, and resources fail. We need, in other words, a life-span developmental approach that can bear the full length and weight of human experience.

B. Death as Life Crisis

Let us finally touch upon the title question: *Is* death a life crisis? If magnitude of consequence is the criterion, then death would come highly recommended as a life crisis. But we have already seen that death is a term with many meanings, and rare is the person who is consistently clear about his own meanings, let alone those of others. The fact that perspectives on death differ within as well as among individuals suggests that a simple answer to our question is unlikely.

Consider first that death is not a crisis from the statistical standpoint. A death for every birth is a certainty. The "death system" (Kastenbaum & Aisenberg, 1972) of our culture and most others has built-in provisions for death. The suspension of death, as imagined in several works of fiction, might constitute more of a social crisis than the orderly, predictable demise of thee and me. A particular death may shock, confound, or disorganize. This cannot be said of all deaths. Note how many deaths daily pass through us with scarcely a blink. A crisis atmosphere may develop when we are confronted with the wrong death, death in the wrong way, or too many deaths at once. Viewed in this light, death is just one of many phenomena that have variable social consequences, ranging from piddling to profound, from immediate to delayed, from debilitating to strengthening the social order—for instance, the fine state funeral that reinforces national unity and pride when the death itself is of a long-used-up public figure.

Death is not invariable a crisis from the individual standpoint, either. There are people among us who seldom give thought to death. Some of these people come to death before death has come to mind—accidents, foul play, sudden traumata of various kinds. A crisis was neither anticipated nor experienced in such instances.

Others among us do think of death, but minus the doomsday visions. There are people who seem to view personal annihilation with equanimity, and other who are serene because, for them, death does not represent annihilation. Still others feel sorely troubled with the life they are experiencing, and death is seen as the solution rather than the problem. Concepts of death are closely linked to our ideas of time, both structurally (e.g., how extended our projections and retrospections, how many events anticipated, etc.) and through the affective–thematic coloration (e.g., a future for ambitions to be achieved, or deserved pleasures to be relished). As one future prospect among others, the phenomenological status of death is influenced by our total relationship to time. Some temporal orientations may lend themselves more readily to crisis perception than others.

The dying process itself can be a time of crisis—but this, too, is contingent upon many factors. Our clinical and research experience accords with an underlying if unstated premise of Kubler-Ross's theory: Most people do not just fall apart as death approaches. A chaotic state that persists through terminal illness strongly suggests that treatment has been mismanaged, badly. Something important has been done wrong, or left undone. The dying person is also a living person. General laws of personality and behavior and those specific rules that have developed for a particular individual are not suddenly suspended because death is in prospect. Although in my judgment it is premature to declare that people die according to certain stages, it is also incorrect to suppose that we are entirely defenseless or random in our response. We are not obliged to accept the premise that it is normal for dying to be a crisis. We are, however, well advised to hone our own sensitivities to the situation of the dying person and those who stand by him, without imposing a ready-made theoretical orientation.

C. In Conclusion

A peculiar paper, this one. Perhaps it is because I am a kind of developmentalist who is frequently involved in dying, death, and lethal behavior, but also a kind of "deathnik" who is involved with developmental phenomena. One of me wants to tell the other that developmental principles and methods can help to illuminate what takes place in and around the death situation. The other me wants to reply that life-span developmental theory is incomplete until it opens up decisively to death phenomena—and that, in so doing, it should not assume that existing concepts and methods will do justice to these phenomena.

Both of me want to avoid the premature acceptance of theoretical frameworks in either field, and to invite the company of others in exploring the life–death interface. It is with amity aforethought that we have refrained from handling death over as a neatly packaged normative life crisis. The topic is too significant to receive anything less than the most alert and thoughtful attention we can bring to it.

REFERENCES

Alexander, S. *Time, space, and deity.* London: Macmillian, 1920
Anon. The epic of gilgamesh. Edition consulted: Alexander Heidel, *The gilgamesh epic and old testament parallels.* Chicago: Univ. of Chicago Press, 1963.
Brandon, S. G. F. *The judgment of the dead.* New York: Charles Scribners, 1967.
Bultmann, R. *Life and death.* London: Adam & Charles Black, 1965.
Cutler, D. R. (Ed.). *Updating life and death.* Boston, Massachusetts: Beacon Press, 1969.
Ellis, H.R. *The road to Hel.* Westport, Connecticut: Greenwood Press, 1968.
Engel, G. L. Sudden and rapid death during psychological stress. *Annals of internal medicine* 1971, **74**, 771–782.
Fechner, G. *The little book of life after death.* Chicago, 1960.
Feifel, H. (Ed.), *The meaning of death.* New York: McGraw-Hill, 1959.
Forrester, J.W. *World dynamics.* Cambridge, Massachusetts: Wright-Allen Press, 1971.
Frazer, J. G. *The fear of the dead in primitive religion.* (1933). Edition consulted: New York: Biblo & Tannen, 1966.
Glaser, B.G., & Strauss, A. *Awareness of dying.* Chicago: Aldine Publishing, 1965.
Henderson, J. L., & Oakes, M. *The wisdom of the serpent.* New York: Colliers Books, 1971.
Hertz, R. *Death and the right hand* (1907). Edition consulted: Glencoe, Illinois: Free Press, 1960.
Hocking, W.E. *The meaning of immortality in human experience.* New York: Harper, 1957.
Hoffman, J. G. *The life and death of cells.* New York: Dobleday, 1957.
Kahn, R. *The boys of summer.* New York: Signet, 1971.
Kapleau, P. *The wheel of death.* New York: Harper, 1970.
Kastenbaum, R. Death and bereavement in later life. In A. H. Kutscher (Ed.), *Death and bereavement.* Springfield, Illinois: Charles C. Thomas, 1969. pp. 27–54.
Kastenbaum, R. On the future of death: Some images and options. *Omega* 1972, **3**, 319–330.
Kastenbaum, R. *Nothing.* In preparation.

Kastenbaum, R., & Aisenberg, R. B. *The psychology of death.* New York: Springer, 1972.
Kubler-Ross, E. *On death and dying.* Toronto: Macmillan, 1969.
Opie, I., & Opie, P. *Children's games in street and playground.* London: Oxford Univ. Press, 1969.
Preston, S. H., Keyfitz, N., & Schoen, R. *Causes of death.* New York: Seminar Press, 1972.
Schulz, R., & Alderman, D. Clinical research and the "stages of dying." *Omega,* 1974, **5,** 137–144.

CHAPTER 4

Ego Development and Preferential Judgment in Life-Span Perspective

LELAND D. VAN DEN DAELE

TEACHERS COLLEGE, COLUMBIA UNIVERSITY
NEW YORK, NEW YORK

ABSTRACT

Contemporary unitary, terminal models of ego development often confound value-laden description with formal characteristics of cognitive development. Virtue is associated with cognitive maturity, and the converse with cognitive immaturity; but within broad limits, cognitive maturity is neither necessary nor sufficient for virtue. An alternative model, derived from an axiomatic theory of ego organization, provides for the nonevaluative classification of preferential judgment. The development of preferential judgment involves the successive reorganization of subjective, objective, and normative content at successive levels of cognitive complexity. The stages of preferential judgment are exemplified through classification of observations and interview material selected from more than 1000 subjects between the ages of birth and 41 years. Empirical evidence consistent with developmental divergence and developmental order of stages is presented, and the conditions of developmental transformation discussed.

I. Introduction

The problem of the ego and the self is variously the problem of identity (de Levita, 1965), continuity (Tracy, 1907), meaning (Symonds, 1951), responsibility (Cooley, 1922), and, from certain perspectives, the core problem of philosophy (Frankenstein, 1966) and psychology (Allport, 1943). The myriad roles of the ego arise, in part, from the mulitple orientations that have governed its definition and description (Kuc & van den Daele, 1974). The ego is sometimes a mentalistic and sometimes an empiricist construct and sometimes both. Whether, however, mentalistic or empiricist, idealistic or reductionistic, the ego is attributed a central role in the organization of personality and conduct.

The ego represents a general executive function that organizes self-image, interpersonal style, and the general conduct of behavior:

> Subject is ego, object is self,
> whether man, elephant, or elf.
> Ego directs, self obeys,
> complementary in innumerable ways.

The ego is a central control device that monitors, interprets, and evaluates need disposition, need restriction, and their coordination.

II.   A Critical Evaluation of Life-Span Ego Theories

Current life-span theories of the ego selectively characterize the development of ideal self, relatability, conscious preoccupation, interpersonal maturity, and character. With few exceptions (Ausubel, 1952; Erikson, 1963), current theories adopt a simple, unitary, terminal model of development (van den Daele, 1969). With such a model the only meaning that may be imputed to individual differences is difference in rate of progression through stages.

A naive examination of these stages reveals a general typological similarity: Early stages are amoral (Peck & Havighurst, 1960), exploitative (Fromm, 1947), hedonistic (Kohlberg, 1963), impulse-ridden (Loevinger & Wessler, 1970), and capricious (van den Daele, 1968). Later stages are rational–altruistic (Peck & Havighurst, 1960), productive (Fromm, 1947), principled (Kohlberg, 1968), and spontaneous (Loevinger & Wessler, 1970).

Kohlberg (1969), Loevinger (1966), van den Daele (1968), and others (Edwards, 1973; Sullivan, McCullough, & Stager, 1970) have suggested that the similarity of stages described for different populations with different methods affirms the generality of ego stages. An alternative though nonexclusive explanation resides in the common ancestry of ego theorists. The parental and filial connections of theorists are illustrated in Figure 1. With few exceptions, current theories arise from an amalgamation of the psychologies of early Piaget (1926, 1932), George Herbert Mead (1934), and the psychoanalytic psychosexual stages (Fenichel, 1945).

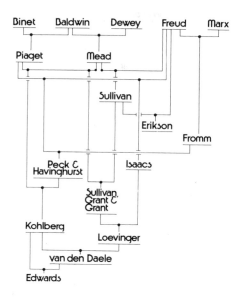

Fig. 1. Genealogy of life-span ego theory. Parent–offspring relations were induced from author's acknowledgments, concourse in a common nest, i.e., the University of Chicago, or theoretical similarity. Primary sources for the genealogy not cited in the text include Costa and Kessler (1972), Isaacs (1956), Sullivan, Grant, and Grant (1957), and Warren (1966). The orthodox analytic theorists, Spitz, Hartmann *et al.*, are adequately reviewed in Décarie (1965). The orthodox theorists, along with Ausubel (1952), are primarily concerned with ego and behavior in infancy and early childhood, and hence are omitted from the genealogy and review of life-span ego theory.

The common ancestry illuminates a common anti-Rousseauian bias. From the orthodox psychoanalytic perspective, the child's innate dispositions to sex and aggression are only gradually socialized. The immature ego is buffeted by strong urges from the id, and only through the development of various stratagems, repressions, compensations, and sublimations does the ego obtain a certain independence.

If the neo-Freudians, Adler (1927), Sullivan (1953), Fromm (1947), and others (Horney, 1950), rejected the extreme biologism of orthodox psychoanalysis, they did not reject the model of man as impulse and demand successively socialized to some ideal of conduct. In the psychoanalytic tradition, immaturity is characterized by personal–social irrectitude, and maturity by personal–social propriety.

Peck and Havighurst's early stages are characterized by "whims and impulses," "lack of control," "amorality," and "selfishness" (1960, pp. 5–6). Loevinger's early stages are described in terms of "blatant opportunism," "deception," "coercion," and "sexual and aggressive impulsivity" (Loevinger & Wessler, 1970, pp. 56–58). In these examples, and in other representative typologies, value-laden descriptions are mixed with selected preoperational cognitive characteristics.

The adultocentric characterization of children's motivation and behavior is amusingly parodied by Lewis Carroll (1964, p. 105):

> Speak roughly to your little boy
> and beat him when he sneezes.
> He only does it to annoy
> because he knows it teases.

Kornei Chukovsky, the Russian children's poet, provides a large number of observations inconsistent with the immaturity-is-vice paradigm. He characterizes the child as "a linguistic genius," "a tireless explorer," and "a poet." One of his subjects, Lialia, a 5-year-old, expresses her concern for humanity in the following discourse:

> Look. All these grown-up men and women—what are they busy with—with funerals. Of course, I am not afraid. No. But it's a pity—they bury and they bury and it's human beings they bury. Let's go and inform the militia—I feel sorry for these dead people [Chukovsky, 1968, p. 50]

Elizabeth Davoren, in a discussion of the battered child, describes the behavior of a toddler:

> I remember watching an 18-month-old soothe her mother, who was in a high state of anxiety and tears. First, she put down her bottle she was sucking. Then she moved about in such a way that she could approach, then touch, and eventually calm her mother down (something I had not been able to begin to do). When she sensed her mother was comfortable again, she walked across the floor, lay down, picked up her bottle, and started sucking it again [1968, p. 155; cited in Demause, 1974].

A well-known moral philosopher provides the following anecdote: His 4-year-old son knew that it was wrong to kill people, and one day, in conversation, his son found that people were animals. His son concluded that, therefore, it was wrong to kill animals, let alone to eat them after killing them. For almost 6 months after this conclusion, he refused to eat meat. He had become a committed vegetarian in spite of the reiterated appeals of his parents to eat meat (Kohlberg, 1968, p. 24). Of course, in some sense, the child's mode of reason was immature, but was his vegetarianism an outcome of "blatant opportunism," "sexual and aggressive impulsivity," "hedonism," or even "fear of punishment"?

The corollary to immaturity-is-vice is maturity-is-virtue, and this too is represented in contemporary ego theories. In these formulations, rectitude is joined to formal thought to yield a characterization that implies more formal persons are more virtuous persons, or less strongly, formal thought is prerequisite to more humane forms of ego expression. More formal persons are more virtuous persons because more formal persons can better compute the multiple aspects of a situation and better derive an appropriate virtuous solution. In Peck and Havighurst's view, later stage subjects are "dependably honest, responsible, and loyal [1960, pp. 7–9]," and in Loevinger's scheme, mature subjects are "realistic," "objective," and "unprejudiced" (Loevinger & Wessler, 1970, p. 100).

Whether more formal persons employ more virtuous justifications or behave in more virtuous ways is surely problematic. As Lewis states to the the protagonist in Colin Wilson's *Glass Cage:*

> Does it follow that I'm totally incapable of murder . . . ? What you mean is that you hope I'm never driven to the point where I commit one. I'm more capable of murder than most people in this town because I'm more intelligent, and consequently more inclined to nervous strain. More frustrated, if you like [1967, p. 31].

In conflict with the "formal thought is prerequisite to higher virtue" postulate, even a naive examination of literature and experience implies that higher computational ability is ubiquitous with reference to conduct, value, and belief.

Formal reason can rationalize a variety of orientations, from elitism to egalitarianism, from idealism to cynicism. Western history and culture embody myriad perspectives formulated and justified by formal reason. Even the apparently innocuous terms "realistic," "objective," and "unprejudiced" presume some standard for their evaluation, so one man's realism is another man's prejudice.

What then promotes the fiction that immaturity-is-vice and maturity-is-virtue, and how is it that personal–social rectitude became wedded to maturity at all? I believe the prima facie acceptability of contemporary ego theories rests on at least three supports: First, a general cultural belief in progress extends to progress-in-virtue. Second, the child is a convenient object for adult projection (Demause, 1974). And third, bourgeois ideals of proper conduct and belief are legitimized. With virtue associated with maturity, psychology proves virtue better.

III. Metatheory for a Theory of Ego Development

Any theory or scheme of ego development makes certain presuppositions about the organization of the psychological universe. Often these presuppositions are latent, but when latent, they nevertheless operate to shape conclusions and explanations.[1] It is better at the onset to formulate the latent theory so the interplay of metatheory and theory is consistently presented. The latent theory indentifies and describes certain natural systems or structures that are presumed to determine behavior and decision. Any theory of ego development that aims at completeness must be formulated in a sufficiently general way to include the universe of potential decision rationales. Accordingly, the theory of ego development is introduced in axiomatic terms. The axiomatic treatment yields a set of primary systems and a secondary system that maps aspects of the primary systems. The interaction of these systems determine the pragmatic–semantic and syntactic features of behavior and rationale.

A. The Primary Systems

The ego interprets, with a directed and finitistic computational capacity, a subordinate set of multidimensional, interactive systems. Let there be a system A, and a distinct system B, and an intersection or interface between systems A and B, and call it system C. The systems A, B, and C may be represented as interrelated functional or propositional statements, directed graphs, or in any consistent calculus. Let the systems A and B intersect or interface in various ways. Only from A are the elements in system A known, only from B are the elements in system B known (and only from C, or A and B coordinated, are the elements in system C known) where A, B, and C are perspectives on systems A, B, and C. Call the systems A, B, and C the primary systems.

Coincident with the primary systems A, B, and C, three interdependent natural systems operate to influence or determine behavior. These are the *need-directive system*, the *need-restrictive system*, and the *coordination system*. The systems are presumed to possess both an objective and phenomenological status. These systems may be represented in various ways and given various meanings, but any empirical representation reflects a provisional characterization.

1. Need-Directive System

The need-directive system describes the organization of dispositions that subserve biological integrity (Figure 2). The dispositions are hierarchized

---

[1] The proposed scheme of ego development arises from a number of influences: These include developmental structuralism (Piaget, 1970; van den Daele, 1969, 1974b, 1974c, 1974d, 1975b), formal logic (DeLong, 1970; Reichenbach, 1947), psychocybernetic models (Miller, Galanter, & Pribram, 1960), and cognitive developmental theory (Kohlberg, 1969; Inhelder & Piaget, 1958).

$$A \cdot f(x_1 \ldots x_n) \cdot Vq(y_1 \ldots y_n) \cdot V(\exists h) D(h) \cdot B \cdot h(z_1 \ldots z_n)$$
... or any consistent calculus.

Fig. 2. Need-directive system. The need system summarizes a set of biologically based dispositions and reactions. The operation of this system may be described in the language of any consistent formalism, i.e., Nowakowaska's motivational calculus (1973).

and interdependent, and engaged under specified system conditions. Need directives are either specific or general. Specific need directives implicate specialized tropisms and action patterns associated with particular physiological and social dispositions (Eibl–Eibesfeldt, 1970). General need directives implicate action patterns that operate to maintain general biophysical equilibrium (van den Daele, 1970a, 1971, 1974a).

The operation of the need-directive system is relatively unambiguous in early infancy. Infant action patterns are largely stereotyped and subserve need directives in a direct manner, but with maturation these action patterns are displaced or combined to yield complex and sometimes disguised patterns of need gratification. The particular action patterns subordinated to need directives change, but need directives with some exceptions may be presumed to remain relatively invariant. The ego, as a control device, copes with a relatively common set of specific and general need dispositions throughout development.

2. Need-Restrictive System

The need-restrictive system describes the organization of physical and social regularities that operate to condition or constrain behavior (Figure 3). Like need dispositions, need restrictions are either specific or general. The combination of physical and sociocultural aspects and specific and general aspects yields four classes of need restriction: Specific physical restrictions denote seasonal, geographic, and economic constraints, and general physical restrictions, universal physical–causal invariances. Specific sociocultural restrictions implicate roles, procedures, and ceremonies, and general sociocultural restrictions, invariant features of the human condition.

In contrast to the need-directive system, the need-restrictive system within Western society is presumed variable. Specific physical restrictions shift with season and location; specific sociocultural restrictions vary with age,

Fig. 3. Need-restrictive system. The physical–social structures that inflect or modify the expression of need directives, transcribed into any consistent calculus.

status, and family; and general sociocultural restrictions alter with secular and generational change. Nevertheless, the restrictive system is not completely mutable. Seasonal–geographic constraints are often cyclic, while the forms of sociocultural restriction reflect the forms of human interpretation (Levi-Strauss, 1949), and possess linkages to the imperatives that arise from human need dispositions (Gutmann, Chapter 10, this volume).

3. Coordination System.

The coordination system describes the organization of action–event stratagems conditioned by disposition and restriction (Figure 4). Like need dispositions and restrictions, coordinations are either specific or general: Specific coordinations describe action patterns that are associated with particular physiological or social dispositions and particular physical or sociocultural restrictions. General coordinations embody action patterns linked to general biophysical equilibrium and general physical or sociocultural restrictions. The utility of specific coordinations is restricted to particular organism–environment states, while the utility of general coordinations is relatively unrestricted. The coordination system is a primary adaptive organization.

Specific coordinations are complexly determined and inherently variable. The progress of specific coordinations is surveyed in maturational schedules of social and adaptive behavior (Gesell & Ilg, 1943). Age-independent regularities of the coordination system are broadly specified in classical learning theories (Hilgard, 1956). Learning theories describe the sufficient conditions for coordinations between need dispositions and environmental contingencies as evidenced in behavioral change.

B. The Secondary System

Impose a metasystem of the primary systems and call it the secondary system. Allow the secondary system to map the systems A, B, and C, but

$$A \cdot m \mid f \cdot q(x_i \cdot a_i \ldots x_n \cdot a_n) \mid V$$
$$D \cdot N \mid g \cdot r(y_i \cdot b_i \ldots y_n b_n) \mid$$
... or any consistent calculus.

Fig. 4. Coordination system. The coordination system represents the organization of behavior codetermined by need and restriction, and its formal representation, in some consistent calculus, reflects this intersection of systems.

allow it only one perspective A, B, or C at a time. Restrict its capacity to map to the forms it possesses. The forms of the secondary system may be represented in any consistent calculus, but represent the forms of the secondary system in the same calculus as the primary systems. The dimensionality and complexity of forms are ordered and, as they are ordered, the dimensionality and complexity of mappings are ordered.

Coincident with the secondary system is the interpretive system. The interpretive system reflects and transforms information that arises from the need–directive, need-restrictive, and coordination systems. Information from these systems provides a natural object to the interpretive system. Like the primary systems, the interpretive system possesses a postulated structure. Its structure undergoes successive reorganizations with development.

1. The Interpretive System.

The interpretive system may be characterized from a number of theoretical perspectives. These perspectives include informal and formal characterizations of cognition and development. In the former category are Baldwin (1895), early Piaget (1926), Werner (1948), and others (Sully, 1896); in the latter category, later Piaget (Inhelder & Piaget, 1958), Pascual-Leone (1970), Witz (1971), and others (Cunningham, 1972; Klahr, 1974). Formal perspectives engender relatively idealized models of cognition that provide more or less rigorous characterizations of stages of cognition.

Cognitive development may be conceptualized as a successive evolution of interpretive forms represented as directed graphs or various models within category theory (van den Daele, 1975c). The salient developmental features of cognition in the theory of forms are the *dimensionality* and *complexity* or *depth* and *breadth* of rationale. The depth of an argument identifies its functional order or abstractness, and the breadth of an argument its complexity or scope.

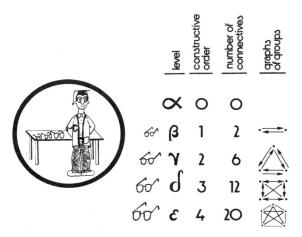

Fig. 5. Interpretive system. The larger the glasses, the larger the computational space. Constructive depth and connective breadth covary with computation space and define levels of interpretation. Levels of interpretation constrain permissible cognitive transformations, represented in the illustration as the graphs of groups of successive orders of complexity.

The depth of an argument is equivalent to the orders of its construction or decomposition (van den Daele, 1974b, c). Higher order rationales coordinate lower order functions. In a zeroeth-order construction, no components are specified; in a first-order construction, object referents are identified; in a second-order construction, classes of referents are established; in a third-order construction, classes are subordinated and organized; and in a fourth-order construction, systems of coordination are defined and morphisms designated.

The breadth of an argument describes the number and relationship of coordinated connectives and nodes. It specifies the form of relationship among assertions. The form of relationship is the form of justification. If connectives are represented as the edges of directed graphs, the number of connectives approximates $L_n (L_n - 1)$ where L_n is designated the level of interpretation. A zeroeth-order construction corresponds to a first-level or alpha interpretation with $1 (1 - 1)$ or zero connectives; and an nth order construction, to a nth + 1 level or omega interpretation with $L_n (L_n - 1)$ connectives (Figure 5). The breadth of argument covaries with the depth of justification.

The theory of forms is a syntactic theory of permissible arguments associated with interpretive levels. Within the theory of forms, the truth functional evaluation of justification is restricted to the evaluation of the relation of argument phrases. Truth is interpreted as syntactic consistency. The scope of syntactic consistency varies with interpretive breadth: Primitive rationales are consistent within a narrow scope, and advanced rationales within a broad scope. The development of justification is not a development from irrational to rational, but a development from a restricted to a more general consistency.

2. The Aptmat

The interpretive system operates under a general constraint that corresponds to the notion of "common sense." *Common sense is not sense in the sense of intelligence as everyone with common sense senses.* Rather, common sense describes the way in which intelligence is applied to the data of experience. Common sense identifies the degree of pragmatic, semantic, or syntactic aptness of an argument, rationale, or action. To the extent form and designata are morphic to the structure and content of a primary system under interpretation, an argument, rationale, or action is apt.

The relation of interpretive form to primary structure is mediated by the *aptmat* (Figure 6). The aptmat is an adjunct to the interpretive system that monitors and evaluates the morphism between representation and content. Among the universe of interpretations available for some representation, a large number are filtered and only a few are considered. Among the set considered, an inapt interpretation is sensed as inappropriate; a partially apt interpretation as incomplete; and an apt interpretation as appropriate

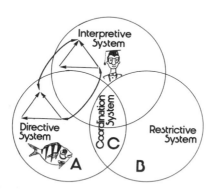

Fig. 6. An interpretive map. The interpretive system intersects the primary systems, and maps a form onto a form. The form of form covaries with interpretive level, and the fit of form with *aptmat* capacity.

and complete. The aptmat provides the intuitive foundation of judgments of conceptual fit, representational adequacy, and paradigmatic utility.

As syntactic consistency is independent of semantic reference, so interpretive sophistication is independent of aptness. An interpretively primitive rationale may be apt or inapt. The association of cognitive level with aptness within ego theories reflects a confusion of the syntactic and semantic bases of truth functional evaluation. Lower level arguments are not necessarily "worse," and higher level arguments "better": The adequacy of a rationale is a joint function of interpretive level and interpretive aptness. The interpretive forms and the aptmat are the minimum apparatus of the control device called the ego.

IV. Stages of Ego Development

The description of stages of ego development arises from the metatheory: The need-directive, need-restrictive, and coordination systems are identified by the letters of the Roman alphabet, A, B, and C respectively, and coincide with domains of criterial discourse. The domains restrict the semantic–pragmatic content of rationales. The domain of discourse associated with the need system arises from assertions of affect, feeling, desire, and intent. Subjective dispositional criteria organize rationales. The domain of discourse associated with restriction system arises from assertions of consequence and order. Objective criteria determine justifications. The domain of discourse associated with the coordination system arises from assertions of compromise, agreement, and contract. Relational criteria organize judgment.

The levels of form are identified by the letters of the Greek alphabet, α, β, γ, δ, ϵ respectively, and coincide with *levels of interpretation*. The levels restrict the syntax of rationales. The levels of interpretation are termed preconstructive, uniconstructive, biconstructive, triconstructive, and quadconstructive to designate the order of functional abstraction. The successive levels correspond to the Piagetian periods, sensory–motor, preoperational, concrete operational, and formal operational, with the exception of the quadconstructive level, which implicates methods associated with the examination of the metatheoretical properties of systems.

The union of a domain of discourse, A, B, or C, with a level of interpretation, α, β, γ, δ, and ϵ yields a mode of rationale. The intersection of three domains of discourse with five levels of interpretation generates 15 modes. The modes are assimilable to a variety of developmental models. Under a unitary interpretation, the modes correspond to successive stages αA, αB, αC, βA . . . ϵC. The stages determine the pragmatic–semantic and syntactic criteria for the classification of empirical response (Table 1).

Table 1

A Periodic Table of Ego Development[a]

Levels of interpretation	Domains of discourse		
	A Subjective – directive	B Objective – restrictive	C Relational – coordinative
α	$\alpha - A$: homeostatic – tropistic	$\alpha - B$: action – efficacious	$\alpha - C$: objectal – interactional
β	$\beta - A$: voluntaristic	$\beta - B$: functional – attributive	$\beta - C$: categorical – regulatory
γ	$\gamma - A$: preferential – hierarchical	$\gamma - B$: pragmatic – utilitarian	$\gamma - C$: instrumental – normative
δ	$\delta - A$: individual – relativistic	$\delta - B$: definitional – deductive	$\delta - C$: consensual – valuative
ϵ	$\epsilon - A$: existential – reflective	$\epsilon - B$: systematic – constructive	$\epsilon - C$: ontotelic – paradigmatic

[a]Note: The designation of stages derives from the classification of empirical response described later in the text.

A. Empirical Exemplification of Stages: Preferential Justification

The stage of the ego is revealed in rationale, argument, justification, and behavior. While the scheme is both general and complete for the domains of discourse and levels of interpretation specified, empirical response embodies specific historical–cultural content. Empirical response semanticizes need, restriction, and coordination in terms of cultural formulas, definitions, and labels. In the present analysis, the empirical exemplification of stages arises from preferential justifications about the worth of personal goals, values, and ideals, and with preconstructive subjects, the display of directed behavior (Table 2). The corpus of observations includes data from three general sources: first, infant records obtained from home observation; second, depth interviews with subjects about physical, material, occupational, and social preferences (van den Daele, 1968, p. 247); and third, biographical reports derived from the general literature (Cantril & Bumstead, 1960; Lynd, 1958; Olney, 1973; Rosenthal, 1971).

Table 2

*Observations for Empirical Exemplification
of Stages of Ego Development*

Group	N	Age	Source	Reference
Indiana:				
Preschool	18	5	interview	
Grade school	72	7 – 14	interview	
High school	36	14 – 18	interview	van den Daele (1968)
Illinois:				
Preschool	66	3 – 6	interview	
Grade school	62	6 – 15	interview	van den Daele (1970b)
High School	32	14 – 19	interview	
Mississippi:				
Headstart	134	3 – 6	interview	
Pennsylvania:				
Infants	12	0 – 3	behavior	
Adults	21	18 – 41	interview	
National sample:				
Follow-through	480	8 – 10	interview	Roberts (1974)

Preferential inquiry, or observation of directed behavior, imposes no a priori constraints on the pragmatic–semantic or syntactic features of a rationale, or action pattern. Alternative judgmental tasks such as the identification of factors in physical causality (Inhelder & Piaget, 1958) and decision about the morality of acts (Kohlberg, 1969) restrict the range of permissible constructions. In the first case, purely objective demands constrain solution; and in the second case, social mandates constrain evaluation. This is not to argue that preferential judgment is independent of cognitive or moral features (it is not), or that valuable information about the status of ego development may not be derived from these sources. Rather, preferential inquiry evokes a relatively unrestricted set of rationales and behaviors that include formulations associated with more specialized judgments. Preferential inquiry, or analysis of directed behavior, constitutes a general strategy for assessment of cognitive–affective organization.

B. Preconstructive Period: Alpha Level Stages

Alpha level stages are prejustificatory. The interpretive system is zeroeth constructive and zeroeth connective. The dynamics of behavior are under the control of the primary systems. The forms of behavior are the forms associated with the uninterpreted operation of the primary systems. System dominance is inferred from behavioral orientation. The preconstructive period is a period of rapid evolution of primary behavioral competence.

The alpha level parallels Piaget's sensory–motor period (Flavell, 1963). The sensory–motor period is divided into a set of stages that commence with the use of reflexes and conclude with the internal representation and manipulation of sensory–motor schemes. The final stages of the sensory–motor period are transitional to the preoperational period, as the alpha C stage is transitional from preconstructive to uniconstructive representation. In general, the C phase of any level is transitional and shares some of the characteristics of the successive level of interpretation.

In Piaget's theory, changes in the complexity of behavior are associated with shifts in control from internal to external to interactive dominance. In the theory of ego development, behavioral complexity and behavioral orientation are conceptually independent, but, in the alpha period, empirically interdependent. Behavioral complexity and behavioral orientation are associated with a progressive neuromaturational organization. The need, restriction, and coordination systems represent an ontogenetic hierarchy.

1. Alpha A: Homeostatic–Tropistic Stage

The primary preferential directive of the homeostatic–tropistic stage is the maintenance of physiological equilibrium. Specific and general need directives act in concert to determine action patterns. The regulation of behavior derives from endogenous control mechanisms. These control mechanisms subserve relatively universal, species-specific, biologically based dispositions. A disposition represents a characteristic state in the subject manifest in behavior which is maintained until the conditions that aroused the disposition are altered.

The need directive that signals hunger probably derives from a hypothalamic monitoring device that samples blood glucose, among other constituents. At some threshold value, the behavior pattern cry-for-food is initiated, along with appropriate thrashing and periodic mouthing behaviors. Introduction of nipple or nipple substitute in the mouth cavity suppresses the crying behavior and initiates the sucking reflex. At satiation, sucking is terminated and a sleeplike state ensues. Complications of the action pattern may occur: If the infant is unable to breathe owing to some obstruction, the sucking pattern is interrupted with an arching movement of the body. In this sense, directives are interdependent and control a system of contingent action patterns.

2. Alpha B: Action–Efficacious Stage

The primary preferential directive of the action-efficacious stage is the manipulation and control of immediate sensory experience. The subject strives to repeat or engender fortuitous occurrences. He is oriented to the external environment and consequences of behavior or action within that environment. Exteroceptive stimuli dominate enteroceptive stimuli.

Piaget provides a large number of observations that illustrate behavior at this stage. A representative example is the behavior of his 5-month-old daughter:

> Lucienne tries to grasp the rattle . . . when it is attached to the bassinet hood and hangs in front of her face. During an unlucky attempt, she strikes it violently: fright, then a vague smile. She brings her hand back with a doubtless intentional suddenness: a new blow. The phenomenon then becomes systematic: Lucienne hits the rattle with regularity a very great number of times [1952, p. 167].

Behavior is instigated and maintained by extrinsic events. With changes in these events or event contingencies, behavior changes.

3. Alpha C: Objectal–Interactional Stage

The primary preferential directive of the objectal–interactional stage is the attainment of goals or goal stages associated with self-social interaction. These expectancies coordinate need or intent with action–event contingencies. Affect and behavior are coordinated to imagistic scenarios of physical–social interaction. The self obtains the status of an identity element that coordinates discrete experiences to a common referent.

At 1 year, 9 months of age,

> B.B. has just finished a shower. His mother indicates his hair must be dried. He runs off with his mother in pursuit. When he comes to the end of a hall, he anticipates being caught and looks around for an escape with a devilish look. When his mother approaches him with a towel, B.B. falls to his knees and puts his head down to make the operation more difficult. He laughs uproariously while he moves his head from side to side and peeks out from under the towel to look at his mother with glee.

B.B. engages his mother in a game of catch-me-if-you-can. The game coordinates his intent and action with the reciprocal intent and action of another. In another eipisode, at 1 year, 11 months of age,

> A.G. has a toothbrush his father wants to retrieve. A.G. says "No!" and scoots from the bathroom. His father follows him and grasps the toothbrush. A.G. holds it tightly and drops to the floor, protesting, "No, no." He looks intently at the father with very sad, very large eyes, ready to cry. The father relinquishes the toothbrush, and A.G. appears content: He carries the toothbrush about the house, places it in his mouth from time to time, and eventually returns it to the bathroom sink.

The father's attempt to interrupt a program of action evoked a verbal appeal with expressive gestures, and the father relented. In the interaction of child and father, one is tempted to see the precursor of adjudication of interpersonal conflict, but it is only later, in the interpretive periods, that the issue of self and social demand is rendered explicit.

C. Uniconstructive Period: Beta Level Stages

The beta level of interpretation commences with the onset of a symbolic or semantic code that maps elements in the primary systems. Beta cognition is largely referential: Interpretation concerns elements within the primary systems as experienced. The forms of reason correspond to trivial inverses, simple implications, binary "and" and binary "or" statements respectively. Essentially, the full range of basic logical connectives is available in the beta period, but within a restricted range of propositional complexity.

The beta level of interpretation parallels Piaget's preoperational period. Verbalization at this stage is action-ridden, imagistic, and from a truth-functional perspective, often inconsistent. In Flavell's (1963) apt characterization, rather than organize, reorder, and transform events, subjects regurgitate reality sequences. Justification proceeds from one particular to another. Since thought is not organized in terms of a hierarchical classificatory system, questions that require explanations or justifications usually are assimilated to statements of desire, function, attribute, or demand.

1. Beta A: Voluntaristic Stage

The primary preferential criterion is consistency with one's wish or desire. The voluntarism of the beta A stage is a generalization of affective disposition that arises from the need system. Two features predominate at this stage of preferential rationale: First, intention subordinates choice; and second, justification is trivially circular.

When T.L. is asked where he would like to live and why, he responds, "I want to live in a trailer . . . I like trailers." S.M. states, "I would like to see a doggie [out the window] . . . because I love dogs." R.A. would like "to see a fire" because he just "wants to." In these examples, the terms "want," "like," and "love" are affective expressions of pragmatic significance: The terms serve as operators that bind the self in some function–argument relationship.

Like R.A., Q.L. is oriented to the unusual: "I would just like to see planes fly by . . . I just like it." Choice of the spectacular and flamboyant, objects with speed and motion, or persons with physical prowess or agility identifies an orientation to excitation (van den Daele, 1968, 1970b). This orientation is presumed to arise from a general dispositional tendency to stimulus variation. While the orientation is undisguised at the voluntaristic stage, the orientation to excitation identifies a content that may be assimilated to a variety of forms.

2. Beta B: Functional–Attributive Stage

The primary preferential criterion is the attainment of a consequence or attribute associated with choice. The subject apprehends that choices imply functions, uses, and outcomes. The form of justification includes trivial circularities and simple implications. Choice is subordinate to phenomenal consequence or attribute.

Attributive justifications are syntactically identical to the redundant affirmations or tautologies of volitional intent. When asked what he would like his parents to think of him when he grown up, S.M. responds, "Be a big boy . . . cause I'm big." B.T. wants her friends to think, "I'm a nice lady . . . because I think she's a nice lady." Functional justifications are more common. The reason for choice is identified with its function or immediate consequence. Frequently, such responses appear to implicate some kind of gain, payoff, or concrete advantage. Q.R. wants "a big house . . . so we can play in it." C.F. states, "I love [my mother] . . . because she wakes me up in the morning." Successive "why" questions from the interviewer elicit functional chains: H.T. responds she would like "thirteen dollars . . . to spend on food . . . to buy sugar and bread." R.S. would like to see "a car out the window . . . so I could have my own car . . . so you could go anyplace you want." Functional strings usually terminate after two and rarely three connected statements.

The content of consequences is strongly influenced by subpopulation at this and other stages. The formulation of consequences depend upon immediate experience. C.S., a rural black child, asserts he would like "a wife . . . to feed the chickens and the rabbit." J.T., another rural black child, states he would like to be "a father . . . to beat his children." Early associations and definitions may ramify in the formation of later values (van den Daele, 1970b).

3. Beta C: Categorical–Regulatory Stage

The primary preferential criterion is an orientation to a set of concrete regulations associated with physical–social interaction. The regulations are behavior-specific and symmetrical. Volition and consequence are subordinated to categorical assertions that possess an unqualified truth value. The subject strives to conform to generic rules of conduct.

The categorical–regulatory orientation segregates disposition and consequence into generic categories of acceptable and unacceptable. The symmetry of regulations often arises with implication followed by negation, or less frequently, with the negation of an implication. The implication, however, is not systematically explored, but posited without qualification. T.R. argues, "Boys don't suppose to have aprons . . . because they not a girl." V.T. wants "five dollars . . . because I didn't want to take the whole world, the whole world's money . . . [because] the people wouldn't have any money." Sometimes regulations are associated with simple implication: L.O. surmises, "Boys can't go to the girl's bathroom . . . cause it's the law." J.M. asserts, "To be bad is mean and nice is laughing . . . I don't like fights . . . cause that's not nice." In spontaneous justifications, a symmetrical implication is sometimes unexpressed: When B.W. was asked to stop throwing a knife, he replied, "Fred was throwing the knife." If Fred, who is the same age, could throw the knife, the implication follows that B.V. could throw the knife, and if he should not, Fred should not. The beta C subject coordinates restriction and intent through successive contrast relations that eventuate in generic regulations.

D. Biconstructive Period: Gamma Level Stages

Rationales of the gamma level introduce higher order operators and new relationships among assertions. General categories organize referential language, but since the categories are only one step removed from the tokens that map phenomenal experience, thought remains relatively concrete. The forms of reason permit the solution of nontrivial detourers and compositions, the application of simple syllogisms, and the union of conjunctive and disjunctive arguments in the specification of reasons and consequences associated with choice. Logical connectives are coordinated within a restricted range suitable for the solution of practical problems in nonformal contexts.

The gamma level parallels Piaget's concrete operational period. In problems of logic and judgments of physical causality, the subject possesses the competence to pose and unpose classes, to hierarchize, and pool classes in various ways. The subject can render judgments of equivalence and order and combine these to obtain various inferences. With reference to preferential judgment, typical applications of concrete operational thought are judgments of correspondence (whenever x is true, y is true), asymmetry (if x, then y, then z, but not if x, then z), limitation (too much or too little), and covariation (the more, the more).

1. Gamma A: Preferential–Hierarchical Stage

The primary preferential criterion is conformity to a relatively consistent hierarchy of wants and satisfactions. The subject possesses the competence to compare the self's pleasure–pain in one situation or another, but in a practical, situation-specific way. He may mentally reverse a preferred choice and specify consequences of a nonpreferred choice. Enumeration of these consequences is typically item symmetric: For example, "I don't like noise; I like quiet. . . . I don't like crowds, I like trees," etc. Subjects at this stage may readily shift orientation from a preferred to a nonpreferred alternative and generate empirically consistent statements.

B.C. reports he would like to "stop getting homework . . . because I want to go out and play. I don't want to do the homework . . . it takes me till late to do my homework and then I don't have time to play." A.H. prefers to see "trees and flowers" out the window because "it's better than seeing all those smokestacks and everything." T.M. states, "I like the afternoon better than the morning, like you do everything in the morning, then in the afternoon, you sometimes stay with friends and talk." Frequently choice is justified by reference to outcomes with strong affective significance: C.D. expostulates, "If I don't count, than I don't speak, and then I'm dumb . . . and if I can't add or subtract, I *dumb* [sic] too because if you can't add, you can't add money, and money is the same as numbers." H.L. wants to paint the school's wall, "because the owner of the school come and see the wall dirty, they would *blame* me, and the teachers would *blame* me." In C.D.'s and H.L.'s protocols, "dumb" and "blame" are terms with a negative valence in the hierarchy of wants and satisfaction which appear prepotent in the determination of choice.

2. Gamma B: Pragmatic–Utilitarian Stage

The primary preferential criterion is the instrumentality of action associated with performance. Choices are ordered along objective dimensions that include considerations of economy, "It's cheaper"; durability, "It lasts longer"; utility, "It does more things"; efficiency, "It works better"; and expediency, "It's easier to use." Justifications are construed in relation to function, task, job, or external demands and requirements. Rules of correspondence describe a concrete order of benefits and exchanges.

D.O. asserts he would like to "make more houses . . . because maybe for that you can get paid because that's hard work . . . [and] you can't just do hard work for nothing." E.K. wants to see "nature" out of his window "because if you had hills and mountains, then maybe you could think about writing a story about them. It gives you ideas. It lets you think about things." The subordination of preference to task yields explicit statements of competence, effectance, and curiosity: G.A. states, "I just like to learn about God . . . I wonder what happened years and years ago . . . because it doesn't happen now . . . and was there a boss like God or, um, a big cheese. . . ?" F.N. desires to be an artist, since "you can draw what you think and people can see it. . . . I like to see how well I can draw, how well I can picture my thoughts."

3. Gamma C: Instrumental–Normative Stage

The primary preferential criterion is conformity to a set of norms derived and justified by experience. In contrast to the more particularistic regulations of the beta C stage, the norms of the gamma C stage are inductive generalizations with a qualified scope. The subject conceptualizes a set of rules of correspondence between certain modes of behavior and the reactions of others. Conformity to social expectation is utilitarian to self-interest: Self and social interest coincide.

"You should be yourself," M.S. explains, "cause people are nicer if you never tell people something that you didn't do. They'll like believe if you tell people a lot of stuff, and after awhile, they don't believe you or anything 'cause you keep saying that you have so much good stuff, and then all of sudden, at a certain point, they're gonna want to see it all, and you just can't show it to them." M.S.'s justification is reminiscent of an appeal to Mead's generalized other (1934). Compare I.G.'s explanation why "troublemakers" should be expelled from school: "Because they are causing trouble . . . and little kids . . . are getting beat up, and are getting hurt, and that's not a good reputation for this school, and why should a few kids spoil the whole reputation of the school?" Often gamma C rationales make an appeal to role-taking: J.B. argues people should have manners, "cause it's rude and disgusting and if I was chewing, let's say a potato with my mouth open, it looks disgusting, the mouth when it's full of food, not gum."

E. Triconstructive Period: Delta Level Stages

Delta level justifications organize and coordinate categories and operations in a systematic way. Categories are imposed upon categories, and operations upon operations. Categories are twice removed from experience, so there is no necessary appeal to a phenomenalistic language. The forms of reason include permutations of assertions of affirmation and negation with existential and universal quantification, the coordination of discrete perspectives to obtain equivalent results, and the application of extended syllogistic strings in justification. Logical operations are objectified and organized to render a set of conceptual programs for the analysis of operative relations.

The delta level of interpretation is analogous to Piaget's formal operational period. The subject is not merely concerned with the simple justification of choice by rules of concrete cooorespondence, but with the role various factors play in the determination of choice: He spontaneously separates out relevant variables and attempts to organize them in a coherent way. He possesses a general scheme for the determination of preference which takes account of the possible as well as the actual. Justification is rendered a priori rather than a posteriori.

1. Delta A: Individual–Relativistic Stage

The primary preferential criterion is consistency with the rational feelings, needs, and dispositions of the self. A set of affective priorities organizes judgment and determines categories of preferential choice. Dominant affective priorities include an orientation to personal autonomy and independence. Persons are characterized by different abilities and aptitudes: The self possesses distinct personal and role attributes. Each person should be "true to himself." Self-interest and social expectation are delineated.

"If I were a criminal lawyer," L.M. states, "I would be miserable. I couldn't handle the responsibility for another person's future, even if I got good money for it. If one of my clients were sentenced and I knew he was innocent, I would blame myself for my inadequacy." M.W. asserts, "I enjoy the city. I'm exhilarated by the people in the subways and on the streets . . . My mind requires action and my body demands adrenal stimulation." A.B. explains, "Whatever anybody else might say, I admire my father. I admire his capacity to understand people. I like the way he thinks and speaks . . . not that I would like his job, I just like him, and would like to be like him."

The importance of independence is expressed by S.J.: "I don't marry just because somebody is special . . . I don't give myself away in exchange for a marriage certificate. . . . Rich or poor, handsome or ugly, young or old, I have no intention of becoming Mrs. So-and-so." A general disposition to autonomous experience subordinates and integrates previous normative and instrumental criteria: T.G. digresses, "A lot of people can say that it's right, but that doesn't mean that it's right. And even if they think it's right and even if it is right, it's nice to find out yourself. It's fun to do it and find out things you didn't know before."

2. Delta B: Definitional–Deductive Stage

The primary preferential criterion is conformity to the requirements mandated by a rational, objective order. An objective order represents a coherent set of assumptions associated with certain necessary corollaries and conclusions. The postulated order is "objective" in the sense that other rational persons would identify the same salient features, given the same assumptions and experience. The self's preferences are subordinated to the requirements implicated by that order. An objective order may embrace different contents, but among the majority of subjects, it is usually restricted to occupational and social requirements.

"As a father," V.O. explains, "I would mold my children to be responsible citizens, so they could keep a job and take care of their families, when they have families. It's important to do this for society, not just for myself or my pride or something. . . ." M.C. Comments, "I would prefer to live in a community that provides essential services in an effective way. This is a first priority . . . I mean schools, health care, and sanitation service. . . . Otherwise the task of family management is more complicated."

Subjects are concerned with personal competence or the adequacy of the self's attributes in relation to task or occupation. Purely affective considerations usually are minimized. "I work with my hands well and have a good sense of visualization," H.B. states, "so I opted to be an architect." The objective characteristics of the occupation are enumerated: "Architecture provides an opportunity for creative expression. Each client presents a certain problem and with compass and straight edge, you form a solution."

3. Delta C: Consensual–Evaluative Stage

The primary preferential criterion is consistency with a set of values that balance individual needs with social demands. These values arise from the rational consideration of personal interest as conditioned by social experience. Any choice is presumed to possess both personal and social consequences that ramify in the interaction of self and environment. The delta C stage is the holistic embodiment of the concerns of earlier delta stages. Affective and restrictive concerns are coordinated.

L.D. states, "My parents would be happy, and I would be happy, if I met my obligations to myself and my family. Children reflect on their parents, and with their choices they affirm or negate the intents and values of their parents. In this sense, I'm fortunate because my parents communicated to me the value of individuality and respect for the individuality of others." A similar statement is provided by T.B.: "You can't just deal with clients, you have to respect them. . . . Although a lawyer provides a professional expertise, we are all people, and although people come in different shapes, sizes, and colors, we share a common humanity."

While the above justifications embody generalizations of normative social values, some statements of coordination provide alternative formulations. Y.C. argues, "Man don't really care about man. Everybody's worried about his own lawnmower. . . . We grin and nod to oil the social machine." O.T. states, "Those cats gotta have a share of pie too. . . . Jus' 'cause you black or fat, or a mean crocodile, don't mean you gotta eat up what's in the way of you mouth. You give a little to your brother and he give a little to you, and the little you give, and the little he give is twice as much. Ain't no man ain't my brother."

F. Quadconstructive Period: Epsilon Level Stages

Rationales of the epsilon level of interpretation coordinate relations and transformations of systems of organization. Constructions are thrice removed from experience to subordinate structures that organize operations. The forms of reason are augmented to include the derivation of triple compensations and the generation of connected syllogisms with collateral formulations. Systems are systematized to reveal the general features by which the world is organized and defined.

The epsilon level possesses no direct counterpart in Piaget's theory of cognition unless Piaget's works *Structuralism* (1970), *Biology and Knowledge* (1971a), and *Insights and Illusions of Philosophy* (1971b) are interpreted as exemplifications of a metatheoretical perspective. While the formal level coordinates factors within a structured whole, the "postformal" level coordinates structured wholes. The operative emphasis shifts from computation of truth values within some predicated formalism to a consideration of the formalism itself as an object among objects. The postformal perspective engages the examination of formal consistency, completeness, economy, and universality, and ramifies in the pursuit of general philosophic, esthetic, and pragmatic formulations.

1. Epsilon A: Existential–Reflective Stage

The primary preferential criterion is congruence with coordinated subjective intuitions. The ontological foundations of identity, purpose, and freedom are examined. Significance and intent are organized within a matrix of generalized disposition and phenomenal imperative. The subjective is systematized to define the boundaries and conditions of personal realization. The antinomies of estrangement and engagement, anomie and integrity, illusion and reality provide polarities of discourse with various resolutions.

The systematized expression of subjectivistically contingent rationales is embodied in a variety of sources from romanticism to existentialism (Ford, 1957; Kaufmann, 1956). In literature and poetry, romantic and existential constructions universalize the subjective. The self metaphorizes experience to structure and organizes its being-in-the-world.[2] Nonetheless, the world of the epsilon A rationale reflects a bounded cultural–historical perspective. The subjective is in counterposition to the nostrums of an enlightened conventionality. In a digression about his relation to his wife, D.V. states:

---

[2] Consider, for example, Rilke's First Elegy, "Who, if I cried, would hear me among the angelic orders? [1939, p. 25]" and Ginsberg's America, "America, I've given you all and now I'm nothing [1956, p. 31]."

I would possess her—every vein and tendon of her being; I would partake of her fluid and substance; I would capture her consciousness and interpenetrate it. But she resists and I cannot command and no matter, we are locked in the prisons of our minds, and only occasionally is there a little light which we glimpse, or think we glimpse, in a world which might exist, or ought to exist. It is our damnable role to be rendered with the will of angels and with the finesse of gorillas.[3]

2. Epsilon B: Systematic–Constructive Stage

The primary preferential criterion is consistency with the requirements of a general formal orientation. An explicit appeal is made to an objective or necessary order that organizes and subordinates various preferential perspectives. The themes of this period concern formal adequacy, examination of the objective foundations of conduct, and the implications of a constructed order for human action.

Well-formulated, objectivistically contingent justifications are exemplified in a large set of traditional philosophical systems. The philosophies range from medieval scholasticism to modern positivism (Bochenski, 1956). In all these world views, the primary problem is the nature of the world or the world as known. Given some formulation of the organization of the world, certain modes of behavior, action, and conduct are permissible. Man flaunts the demands of a necessary order only at his peril. K.T. asserts that only within the "good" society may a person find purpose and general harmony with the world and his fellow men. She continues:

> Some societies are viable, and others, nonviable. They are viable to the extent that they satisfy in an equitable manner the demands of various subgroups within the society. These demands arise out of a partition into stratified age, sex, and interest groups. To some extent, any such partition is a "natural" outgrowth of individual differences, but it also comes about through definitions imposed by the society itself . . . . The question resolves itself to the distribution of efforts and rewards.

K.T. fills out her argument by reference to several alternative models and concludes other models are either incomplete or, otherwise, inconsistent.

3. Epsilon C: Ontotelic–Paradigmatic Stage

The primary preferential criterion is congruence with a universal paradigm that arises from generalized subjective intuitions and universalized features of the human condition. Ontotelic paradigms coordinate the metaphors by which the self may mythologize the world with the systems by which the world may be organized. The forms of subjective possibility and objective necessity are rendered interdependent.

---

[3] Any epsilon justification is considerably richer than the exemplifications provided in the text, which are foreshortened.

Ontotelic formulations reside at the intersection of generalized disposition and universalized restriction. In literature, philosophy, and religion, epsilon C rationales embrace cyclic, dialectic, and hierarchical paradigms of man-in-the-world. Within these paradigms, the content and form of disposition and restriction are subordinated to a more general construction. Cyclic formulations imply a cosmic cycle of indefinite repetition (Keyser, 1956); dialectic formulations affirm a bipolarity, opposition, or contradiction as the fundament of dynamic systems (Marx, 1973); and hierarchical formulations presume an internal dynamic or evolutionary imperative that propels man, individually and collectively, to higher stages of consciousness (Brown, 1959; Theilhard de Chardin, 1962). The paradigms of transformation are merely empty if rendered without a symbolism of universal intent.

> the periphery of [justification] has a infinite number of points. Every noble and gifted man has, before reaching the mid-point of his career, come up against some point of the periphery that defied his understanding, quite apart from the fact that we have no way of knowing how the area of the circle is ever to be fully charted. When the inquirer, having pushed to the circumference, realizes how logic in that place curls about itself and bites its own tail, he is struck with a new kind of perception: a tragic perception which requires, to make it tolerable, the remedy of art [Nietzsche, 1954, p. 95; cited in De Long, 1970].

An ontotelic formulation is a construction on an art form.

V. An Illustrative Empirical Evaluation

The protocols of 60 subjects divided into six age groups were selected from the subject pool (Table 2). Protocols were *episoded* into *behavior* or *response units* by a procedure adopted from Barker and Wright (1954): A behavior or response unit is a natural segment of activity or verbalization organized around a common theme (van den Daele, 1973). Each response unit was coded for a stage of preferential justification, and each subject was assigned a modal stage and stage distribution.

Although the composition of groups varied for sex, socioeconomic status, and cohort, the general distribution of modal stage by age group was consistent with a developmental model (Table 3). The modal average of stages increased until age 16 and declined at age 32. An evaluation of intraindividual response distribution for subjects classified by modal level revealed a general compatibility with a cumulative, unitary model, along with *individual singularities* consistent with a cumulative, multiple model (Table 4). Individual singularities reflect *nonstandard* intraindividual response distributions: In Table 4, the response distribution of the epsilon B subject reveals a zero incidence of subjectivistically oriented justifications. Either this subject suppressed or subordinated need-derived rationales that were once

Table 3

Modal Ego Stage by Age Group

Percent distribution of modal stage	Stage	Log age					
		½	2	4	8	16	32
α	A	60	0	0	0	0	0
	B	40	10	0	0	0	0
	C	10	40	0	0	0	0
β	A	0	30	20	0	0	0
	B	0	20	60	10	0	0
	C	0	0	20	20	0	0
γ	A	0	0	0	40	10	10
	B	0	0	0	20	10	20
	C	0	0	0	10	20	20
δ	A	0	0	0	0	20	10
	B	0	0	0	0	30	20
	C	0	0	0	0	10	10
ε	A	0	0	0	0	0	0
	B	0	0	0	0	0	10
	C	0	0	0	0	0	0

in his repertoire, or he progressed through a developmental pathway almost wholly organized around objective demands. Group data tend to mask these singularities that are undisguised in individual protocols.

VI. Discussion of Selected Issues

A large number of problems of general interest arise from the theory of the ego. These include the determinants of developmental individuality, the relative stability and utility of various rationales within various environments, sex differences in development, the range of permissible content within domains of discourse, the empirical realization of postepsilon (quinconstructive) rationales, aptmat strategies, aptmat performance with hyperabstract constructions, interpretive transformation, and the scheme as a model of social–historical evolution. The set of problems may be multiplied, but the set enumerated is sufficient to exemplify the content and form of problems associated with the theory of the ego. In the present section, the issues examined are restricted to the relation of theory of the ego to alternative schemes, and the problem of *crisis* in life-span development.

Table 4

Response Distribution by Modal Ego Stage[a]

Percent distribution of response		Modal stage														
		α			β			γ			δ			ε		
		A	B	C	A	B	C	A	B	C	A	B	C	A	B	C
α	A	65	35	0	0	0	0	0	0	0	0	0	0	0	0	0
	B	30	55	20	0	0	0	0	0	0	0	0	0	0	0	0
	C	5	10	60	20	5	0	0	0	0	0	0	0	0	0	0
β	A	0	0	20	70	20	10	5	0	0	5	0	0	0	0	0
	B	0	0	0	10	55	15	10	5	0	0	0	0	0	0	0
	C	0	0	0	0	20	50	25	10	10	0	0	5	0	0	0
γ	A	0	0	0	0	0	20	40	15	15	15	5	0	0	0	0
	B	0	0	0	0	0	5	15	45	20	10	10	5	0	10	0
	C	0	0	0	0	0	0	5	15	35	10	10	15	0	5	0
δ	A	0	0	0	0	0	0	0	5	15	40	10	10	0	0	0
	B	0	0	0	0	0	0	0	5	5	15	40	20	0	35	0
	C	0	0	0	0	0	0	0	0	0	5	25	45	0	10	0
ε	A	0	0	0	0	0	0	0	0	0	0	0	0	0	0	0
	B	0	0	0	0	0	0	0	0	0	0	0	0	0	40	0
	C	0	0	0	0	0	0	0	0	0	0	0	0	0	0	0

[a]The response distribution for each subject was computed and pooled with his modal group. The group distribution was rounded to the nearest 5%. Read across for modal stage and down for distribution.

A. A General System of Classification

The general formulation of the theory of the ego permits the classification of alternative stage schemes (Table 5). Alternative schemes represent *specializations of content* appropriate for some subset of the population or some restricted judgmental task. While the examples of behavior and verbalization described in Section II are problematic from the perspective of alternative models, the examples may be readily classified with the proposed scheme: The behavior of the 18-month-old toddler described by Davoren (1968, p. 155) is *objectal–interactional;* the verbalization recorded by Chukovsky (1968, p. 50) and the anecdote provided by Kohlberg (1968, p. 24) are *categorical–regulatory;* and Lewis's statement in Wilson's *Glass Cage* (1967, p. 31) is *individual–relativistic.*

Table 5

Classification of Representative Ego Stages within Proposed Scheme[a]

Levels of interpretation	Domains of discourse		
	A Subjective – directive	B Objective – restrictive	C Relational – coordinative
α	Baldwin's preprojective Décarie's "early" Piaget's "reflexive"	Baldwin's projective Décarie's "intermediate" Piaget's "acquired adaptations"	Baldwin's subjective Décarie's "advanced" Piaget's "mental combinations"
β	Baldwin's "ejective" Loevinger's "impulse ridden" Peck & Havighurst's "amoral"		Kohlberg's "punish- ment and obedience orientation"
γ	Hunt's "0" Loevinger's "opportunistic" Peck & Havighurst's "expedient"	Kohlberg's "instrumental hedonism"	Hunt's "1" Kohlberg's "good boy morality" Loevinger's "conformist" Peck & Havighurst's "conforming"
δ	Hunt's "2" Piaget's "adolescent egocentrism"	Kohlberg's "authority maintaining" Loevinger's "consci- entious" Peck & Havighurst's "irrational conscientious"	Hunt's "3" Kohlberg's "contractual" Loevinger's "autonomous" Peck & Havighurst's "rational altrustic"
ε		Kohlberg's "universal principles of conscience"	

[a]Note: The theories classified are Baldwin's (1895), Décarie's (1965), Hunt's (Hunt & Halverson, 1964), Kohlberg's (1963), Loevinger's (Loevinger & Wessler, 1970), Peck and Havighurst's (1960), and Piaget's (1952). The classification is provisional only.

The most complete alternative scheme is Kohlberg's (1968) characterization of the development of moral judgment. The stages span the late beta

period to the middle epsilon period, which conforms, more or less, to the expected stages for subjects within the age range evaluated for construction of his scheme. The Kohlberg stages of moral judgment represent a moral philosophical perspective on justifications constrained by restrictive and coordinative demands, exclusive of subjective dispositional rationales. The latter are inadmissible as moral justifications from Kohlberg's moral philosophical perspective. In the codification of moral response, the set of subjective rationales are assimilated to "premoral" stages, which accounts in part for the reported moral "regression" in late adolescence (Kohlberg & Kramer, 1969).

B. Discrepancy, Stress, and Crisis

In contrast to a simple, unitary progression, inspired by stage conceptions in embryology, the form of ego development is cumulative.[4] Subjects possess a repertoire of rationales for the regulation of behavior and justification of preference. The availability of alternative rationales renders plausible cognitive deliberation, indecision, and conflict, independent of stage, and simultaneously renders a set of alternative adaptive strategies.

The set of rationales available to the subject are organized around needs, restrictions, and coordinations, differentiated and semanticized earlier in development. In the usual decision problem, aptmat and rationale operate in tandem to provide an optimal solution. A transformation in the morphism of structure and rationale for which no map is apt instigates a reconsideration of the forms of rationale and their semanticization: An "apt" aptmat signals the inadequacy of interpretive constructions, and the subject experiences an unease proportional to the formal discrepancy.

Formal discrepancy varies from weak to strong: Weak discrepancy implicates interpretive incompatibility within a restricted scope, and strong discrepancy, interpretive incompatibility within a broad scope, where scope designates the depth and breadth of available rationale. The unease associated with discrepancy is linked with behavior: The stronger the formal discrepancy of structure and rationale, the more probable defensive and withdrawal maneuvers. In part, these maneuvers serve to maintain functional integrity through reduction of interpretive load.

As Nicholas explains in John Fowles' *The Magus*:

> The move, packing things, upset us both . . . the need to get up early, to introduce order into our life, was too much for us. We had two dreadful rows. The first one she

[4] In embryological development, a later structure necessarily replaces an earlier structure: The gastrula replaces the blastula. In psychological development, a later structure may coexist with an earlier structure: An earlier structure may remain in memory.

Table 6

Sources of Stress, Quasi-Crisis, and Crisis in Adult Subjects

Formal discrepancy	System in transformation			
	Need	Restrictive	Coordinative	Interpretive
Weak	menses	school transition	definitional ambiguities	fatigue morning-after effect
Moderate	puberty pregnancy menopause	divorce widowhood	normative incompatibilities double binds	maturational shift
Strong	pituitary dysfunction	sensory deprivation traumatic separation	valuative discontinuities	cerebral decay hallucinogens

started, and stoked, and built up a white-hot outpouring of contempt for men, and me in particular. I was a snob, a prig, a twopenny–halfpenny Don Juan—and so on. The next day—she had been icily mute at breakfast—when I went in the evening to meet her, she was not there. . . [1965, p. 36].

Any weak interpretive incompatibility is tantamount to a "stress" situation, and any strong interpretive incompatibility is tantamount to a "crisis" situation. Selected sources of interpretive incompatibility classified by system and strength are summarized in Table 6. Although these sources may be treated as conceptually independent, a transformation in any one system usually precipitates changes in other systems. The correlative transformation of several systems expands the scope of discrepancy and augments stress. Discrepancy is additive.

1. Normative Transformation

Transformation of structure associated with interpretive discrepancy is linked, in part, to normative biomaturational and social changes, correlated with development. These normative changes arise in the need system, restriction system, coordination system, and interpretive system respectively, and ramify in behavior and rationale.

The *need system* is biophysically based and subserves species survival. Among the set of normative changes in the need system, puberty, pregnancy, the postpartum period, and menopause often effect general reorganizations of dispositional tendencies to yield transformed hierarchies of needs and feelings. A candid 20-year-old male reminisces:

When I was in in sixth grade, all I did was play basketball and trade baseball cards. The most important thing in my life was the Saturday morning serial. . . . Girls were funny things with skirts and panties, and they couldn't play basketball worth a damn. But when I was in the ninth grade, creation played its abominable joke, and girls became relevant. I dropped the baseball cards, and substituted skin. I haven't been the same since.

The *restrictive system* embodies the objective organization of the physical and sociocultural environment. Contemporary Western society imposes various milestones in social development that sometimes abruptly transform the physical and interpersonal milieus. These milestones include maternal separation, primary and secondary school transition, college entrance, marriage, parenthood, career adaptation, military induction, divorce, widowhood, and retirement.

A sufficiently strong transformation of the restrictive system may radically alter earlier behavior. A 31-year-old male, who had graduated *summa cum laude* in literature, reflects on his military experience:

I slept for 3 hours, maybe 4 hours a night. I was harassed, harangued, and humiliated by turns. I was praised for endurance, toughness, leadership, and all the manly virtues. I forgot my Dante and Virgil, and got in line. . . .

The *coordination system* characterizes behavior and response conditioned by subjective disposition and objective demand. Specific coordinative changes are largely interdependent with biophysical and social transformations of the need and restriction systems. The magnitude of specific changes reflects, in part, the magnitude of structural changes in subjective disposition and objective demand.[5] The transformation of coordination sometimes yields a general reorganization of self-definition and interpersonal response. An 18-year-old female explains:

I found out how to do it: I found out how to make people feel at ease and listen to what I had to say. . . . I guess it was the enthusiasm and poise with which I presented my ideas. . . . I'll never be a wallflower again. . . .

The *interpretive system* rationalizes and defines the forms of the need, restrictive, and coordination systems. The forms of the interpretive system, by which the forms of the primary systems are mapped, are constrained by available computation space. Computation space increases with development, and new forms, previously unavailable, are reflected or constructed in the interpretive system.

[5] Nevertheless, the coordination system is conservative in its general features: It operates, in part, to compensate internal and external variations to maintain behavioral equilibrium.

An increase in computation space precipitates a semanticization of the newly acquired morphisms of interpretive form and primary structure. The subject engages question-and-answer to embody his intuitions of reason and reality. The terminus and commencement of interpretive levels define developmental periods of heightened inquiry. The crucial role of semanticization in the identification of morphisms and their retrieval renders periods of interpretive shift, periods of particular individual susceptibility to social–cultural influences and propaganda.[6]

2. Adaptation to Transformation

In adaptation to change, the subject *rerationalizes* the system under transformation at a level of interpretation that may not exceed the operative level at the time of change. The operative level depends upon the state of the neural system, which itself varies with general health, age, and transient factors, such as fatigue. In aged or ill subjects with reduced interpretive capacity, a change in enviornment may precipitate a radical regression to subjectivistically contingent concerns.

In Gide's *The Counterfeiters,* La Perouse, an old man, separated from his wife and home, has taken a position as a tutor in a private school. Although La Perouse is a failure with his classes and scorned by the children, he abjures a friend, "I'm perfectly comfortable, I assure you . . . [but I'm] rather too far from the kitchen. Sometimes during the night, I want something to eat . . . when I can't sleep. . . . I must tell you that I sleep very badly [1955, p. 357]." La Perouse fails to perceive the objective sources of his anxieties and enumerates a set of somatic complaints.

Although the rerationalization of the system under transformation may not exceed the operative level of the subject at the time of change, it may not equal it. An aptmat possesses a finite, real-time capacity for the evaluation of interpretive aptness. A system under transformation is reinterpreted at an apt level, that is, at a level commensurate with aptmat capacity.

The need, restriction, and coordination systems represent an ontogenetic hierarchy of adaptive significance and formal complexity. In benign adaptations to change, the subject reinterprets successive systems to recapitulate the paradigmatic form of development.

---

[6] Normative interpretive transitions occur at 2, 7, and 14 years, and perhaps at 20 and 32 years more or less. If normative shifts are set to equal 2, 6, and 12 years, then by the formula $x_i (x_i - 1)$, the expected values for residual interpretive transitions are 20, 30, 42, and 56 years respectively. Typically, interpretive transitions are accompanied by a dominance or resurgence of subjective rationale. The dominance of subjective justification reflects an "unease" that arises from aptmat evaluation of new intuitions and old definitions that are incomplete or inadequate vis-á-vis the primary structure under interpretation.

VII. Summary Characteristics of the Proposed Scheme of Ego Development

The scheme is *general:* It allows a variety of ways of semanticizing the need system, the restrictive system, and their coordination. It does not bind the developmental investigation of behavior and rationale to a particular sociocultural characterization. The scheme requires only the identification of a form of interpretation and a domain of discourse. Their intersection determines a mode of justification. For this reason, the scheme promotes examination of commonalities and differences within diverse expressive motifs. Subjects are not placed within a procrustean bed of restricted content.

The scheme admits *developmental individuality.* The scheme makes no necessary commitment to a unitary model. The investigation of a developmental convergence and divergence is admissible: Evidence of "atypical" developmental pathways need not be treated as error.

The scheme is *dialectical* (van den Daele, 1975a): The need system and restriction system are in relative opposition and their coordination in some more or less adequate way, the resolution of opposition, is implicit at each level of interpretation. The resolution may occur only through a synthesis that coordinates need and restriction in a more general way.

The scheme is *recursive:* Ego development is characterized in terms of the successive rationalization of needs, restrictions, and their coordination. That is, the need system, the restriction system, and the coordination system are reinterpreted at successive levels of form, so, in this sense, there is no once-and-for-all solution to the problem of the self, the world, or the relation of the self to the world.

The scheme posits *no terminus.* All interpretive constructions are, in some sense, isomorphic to conceptual structures. *The mind is its own mirror: Mind models itself; and itself models "mind," as "mind" models. Mind walks backward with "mind" one step behind in an indefinite regress to an unknown limit.*

ACKNOWLEDGMENTS

I owe this work to a number of colleagues who by their encouragement or support provided an impetus for its conclusion: Lawrence Kohlberg, Walter Emmerich, Irving Sigel, Herman Witkin, Klaus Riegel, Brian Sutton-Smith, Joseph Grannis, and Joseph Roberts. I thank my students at Columbia University who assisted in the third stage of delivery: Marta Kuc, Tom Stevens, M'Lou Caring, Frank Eaddie, David Abrams, and Stephen Gass, who provided the illustrations for this chapter. The proposed scheme of ego development was conceived while the author was a visiting research psychologist at Educational Testing Service in Princeton, New Jersey.

REFERENCES

Adler, A. *The practice and theory of individual psychology.* New York: Harcourt, 1927.

Allport, G. W. The ego in contemporary psychology. *Psychological Review,* 1943, **50,** 451–478.

Ausubel, D. P. *Ego development and the personality disorders.* New York: Grune, 1952.

Baldwin, J. M. *Mental development: Methods and processes.* New York: Macmillan, 1895.

Barker, R. G., & Wright, H. F. *Midwest and its children.* Evanston, Illinois: Row, Peterson, 1954,

Dochenski, I. M. *Contemporary Furopean philosophy.* Berkeley, California: Univ. of California Press, 1956.

Brown, N. D. *Life against death.* Wesleyan, Connecticut: Wesleyan Univ. Press, 1959.

Cantril, H., & Bumstead, C. H. (Eds.) *Reflections on the human venture.* New York: New York Univ. Press, 1960.

Carroll, L. The duchess' lullaby. In W. Cole (Ed.), *Beastly boys and ghastly girls.* New York: World, 1964.

Chukovsky, K. *From two to five.* Derkeley, California: Univ. of California Press, 1968.

Cooley, C. H. *Human nature and the social order.* New York: Scribners, 1922.

Costa, P., & Kessler, R. Ideal-self development. Paper presented at the meeting of the Eastern Psychological Association, Boston, Massachusetts, April, 1972.

Cunningham, M. *Intelligence: Its Organization and development.* New York: Academic Press, 1972.

Davoren, E. L. The role of the social worker. In R. E. Helfer & C. H. Kempe (Eds.), *The battered child.* Chicago: Univ. of Chicago Press, 1968.

Décarie, G. *Intelligence and affectivity in early childhood.* New York: International Universities Press, 1965.

de Levita, D. J. *The concept of identity.* The Hague: Mouton, 1965.

DeLong, H. *A profile of mathematical logic.* Reading, Massachusetts: Addison-Wesley, 1970.

Demause, L. The evolution of childhood. *History of Childhood Quarterly,* 1974, **1,** 503–575.

Edwards, J. B. Chosen ideal person, least ideal person, and judgments about moral wickedness: A developmental study. *Journal of Moral Fducation,* 1973, 379–399.

Eibl-Eibesfeldt, I. *Ethology: The biology of behavior.* New York: Holt, 1970.

Erikson, F. *Childhood and society.* New York: Norton, 1963.

Fenichel, O. *The psychoanalytic theory of the neurosis.* New York: Norton, 1945.

Flavell, J. *The developmental psychology of Jean Piaget.* Princeton, New Jersey: Van Nostrand-Reinhold, 1963.

Ford, D. (Ed.) *The Pelican guide to English literature: From Blake to Byron.* Vol. 5. Middlesex, England: Pelican, 1957.

Fowles, J. *The magus.* New York: Dell, 1973.

Frankenstein, C. *The roots of the ego.* Baltimore, Maryland: Williams and Wilkins, 1966.

Fromm, E. *Man for himself.* New York: Holt, 1947.

Gesell, A., & Ilg, F. L. *Infant and child in the culture of today.* New York: Harper, 1943.

Gide, A. *The counterfeiters.* New York: Modern Library, 1955.

Ginsberg, A. *Howl and other poems.* San Francisco, California: City Lights, 1956.

Hilgard, E. R. *Theories of learning.* (Ref. ed.) New York: Appleton, 1956.

Inhelder, B., & Piaget, J. *The growth of logical thinking.* New York: Basic Books, 1958.

Isaacs, K. S. Relatability: A proposed construct and an approach to its validation. Unpublished doctoral dissertation, Department of Psychology, Univ. of Chicago, Chicago, 1956.

Kaufmann, W. *Existentialism from Dostoyevsky to Sartre.* New York: World, 1956.

Keyser, C. J. The group concept. In J. R. Newman (Ed.), *The world of mathematics.* New York: Simon and Schuster, 1956. Pp. 1538–1557.

Klahr, D. An information-processing approach to the study of cognitive development. In A. D. Pick (Ed.), *Minnesota symposia on child psychology*. Minneapolis, Minnesota: Univ. of Minnesota Press, 1974.

Kohlberg, L. The development of children's orientations toward a moral order. *Vita Humana,* 1963, **6,** 11–33.

Kohlberg, L. Education for justice: A modern statement of the platonic view. Ernest Burton Lecture on Moral Education, Harvard Univ., April 23, 1968.

Kohlberg, L. Stage and sequence: The cognitive developmental approach to socialization. In D. A. Goslin (Fd.), *Handbook of socialization theory and research.* Chicago: Rand McNally, 1969. Pp. 347–380.

Kohlberg, L., & Kramer, R. Continuities and discontinuities in childhood and adult moral development. *Human Development,* 1969, **12,** 93–120.

Kuc, M., & van den Daele, L. D. Ego development in psychological theory. Metatheoretical studies, Columbia Univ., New York, 1974.

Levi-Strauss, C. Les structures élémentaries de la parente. (2nd ed.) The Hague: Mouton, 1968. (First edition published 1949.)

Loevinger, J. The meaning and measurement of ego development. *American Psychologist.* 1966, **21,** 195–206.

Loevinger, J., & Wessler, R. *Measuring ego development.* Vol. 1. San Francisco, California: Jossey-Bass, 1970.

Lorney, K. *Neurosis and human growth.* New York: Norton, 195n.

Lunt, D. E. , & Halverson, C. F. Manual for scoring sentence completion responses for adolescents. Unpublished manuscript, Syracuse Univ., Syracuse, New York, 1964.

Lynd, H. M. *On shame and the search for identity.* New York: Harcourt, 1958.

Marx, K. *Collected works* (3 Vols.). New York: International Publishers, 1973.

Mead, G. H. *Mind, self, and society.* Chicago: Univ. of Chicago Press, 1934.

Miller, G. A., Galanter, E., & Pribram, K. H. *Plans and the structure of behavior.* New York: Holt, 1960.

Nietzsche, F. *The portable Nietzsche* (W. Kaufmann, Ed.). New York: Viking, 1954.

Nowakowska, M. *Language of motivation and language of actions.* The Hague: Mouton, 1973.

Olney, J. *Metaphors of self.* Princeton, New Jersey: Princeton Univ. Press, 1972.

Pascual-Leone, J. A mathematical model for the transition rule in Piaget's developmental stages. *Acta Psychologica,* 1970, **32,** 301–345.

Peck, R. F., & Havighurst, R. J. *The psychology of character development.* New York: Wiley, 1960.

Piaget, J. *The language and thought of the child.* London: Routledge and Kegan Paul, 1926.

Piaget, J. *The moral judgment of the child.* Glencoe, Illinois: Free Press, 1932.

Piaget, J. *The origins of intelligence in children.* New York: International Universities Press, 1952.

Piaget, J. *Structuralism.* New York: Basic Books, 1970.

Piaget, J. *Insights and illusions of philosophy.* New York: World, 1971. (a)

Piaget, J. *Biology and knowledge.* Chicago: Univ. of Chicago Press, 1971. (b)

Reichenbach, H. *Elements of symbolic logic.* New York: Free Press, 1947.

Rilke, R. M. *Duino Elegies.* London: Hogarth, 1939.

Roberts, J. B. A cognitive-developmental study and evaluation of the pupil role as decision-maker. Unpublished doctoral dissertation, Department of Early Childhood Education, Columbia Univ., 1974.

Rosenthal, B. G. *The images of man.* New York: Basic Books, 1971.

Sullivan, C., Grant, M. Q., & Grant, J. D. The development of interpersonal maturity: Applications to delinquency. *Psychiatry,* 1957, **20,** 373–385.

Sullivan, F. V., McCullough, G., & Stager, M. A developmental study of the relationship between conceptual, ego and moral development. *Child Development,* 1970, **41,** 399–411.

Sullivan, H. S. *The interpersonal theory of psychiatry.* New York: Norton, 1953.

Sully, J. *Studies of childhood.* New York: Longmans, Green, 1896.

Symonds, P. M. *The ego and the self.* New York: Appleton, 1951.

Teilhard de Chardin, P. *Phenomena of man.* New York: Harper, 1962.

Tracy, F. *The psychology of childhood.* Boston, Massachusetts: Heath, 1907.

van den Daele, L. D. A developmental study of the ego-ideal. *Genetic Psychology Monographs,* 1968, **78,** 191–265.

van den Daele, L. D. Qualitative models in developmental analysis. *Developmental Psychology,* 1969, **4,** 303–310.

van den Daele, L. D. Modification of infant stage by treatment in a rockerbox. *Journal of Psychology,* 1970, **74,** 161–165.

van den Daele, L. D. Preschool intervention through social learning for disadvantaged children. *Journal of Negro Education,* 1970, **29,** 296–304. (b)

van den Daele, L. D. Infant reactivity to redundant proprioceptive and auditory stimulation: A twin study. *Journal of Psychology,* 1971, **78,** 269–276.

van den Daele, L. D. A manual for evaluation of ego development and preferential judgment. Unpublished manuscript, Fducational Testing Service, Princeton, New Jersey, 1973.

van den Daele, L. D. Natal influences and twin differences. *Journal of Genetic Psychology,* 1974, **124,** 41–60. (a)

van den Daele, L. D. Infrastructure and transition in developmental analysis. *Human Development,* 1974, **16,** 1–23. (b)

van den Daele, L. D. Organization and transformation. In K. Riegel & J. Meacham (Eds.), *The developing individual in a changing world.* Vol. I. The Hague: Mouton, 1974. Pp. 69-78. (c)

van den Daele, L. D. Ego development in dialectical perspective. *Human Development,* 1975, in press. (a)

van den Daele, L. D. A Cook's tour of development. *Journal of Genetic Psychology,* 1975, in press. (b)

van den Daele, L. D. Form and rationale. In L. D. van den Daele, J. Pascual-Leone, & K. Witz (Eds.), *NeoPiagetian perspectives in cognition and development.* New York: Academic Press, 1975, in press. (c)

Warren, M. Q. Interpersonal maturity level classification. California Youth Authority, Sacramento, California, 1966.

Werner, H. *Comparative psychology of mental development.* New York: International Universities Press, 1948.

Wilson, C. *The glass cage.* New York: Random House, 1967.

Witz, K. Models of systems of sensory-motor schemes in infants. Unpublished manuscript, Univ. of Illinois, Urbana, Illinois, 1971.

CHAPTER 5

Formal Models of Ego Development:
A Practitioner's Response

JANICE W. CONE

WEST VIRGINIA UNIVERSITY
MORGANTOWN, WEST VIRGINIA

ABSTRACT

Theories of ego development and the practice of psychotherapy have historically had an intimate, interdependent relationship; most models have evolved from clinical settings. Similarly, van den Daele's model of ego development provides a theoretical basis for many issues important to the practitioner. However, it is no longer possible to assume that the relationship is direct and interdependent. Therefore, my response to van den Daele's discussion requires that the relationship between the two also be examined.

The first three sections of this discussion are directed at some of the issues raised by van den Daele which are pertinent to practitioners. While there are clinicians who continue to conceptualize their work within the constructs of ego psychology, these remarks come from one who is no longer totally identified with that theoretical framework. In this discussion, the terms practitioner and clinician are used interchangeably to describe those whose professional efforts are primarily the application of principles and theories of human behavior. The last section is designed to clarify some of the changes in the relationship between practitioners and ego theory.

I. Overview of Selected Issues

The synthesis of cognitive development and needs is one of van den Daele's most important contributions for the practitioner. Traditional models of ego development have frequently been based upon a triadic organization of need fulfillment, sociocultural constraints on their fulfillment, and a system for coordinating these opposing forces. However, the role of cognition has not been as clearly defined.

Earlier theories restricted growth or change to what van den Daele calls the primary systems. Changes were, for the most part, focused on the interrelationships of the three systems. The conceptualization of the relationship between cognition and need in a 3 x 5 matrix, with changes occurring on the vertical, offers the clinician a theoretical frame of reference that relates to his activities and thinking.

The therapeutic process is no longer limited to an experiential–insight orientation. Many models of therapy regard change as occurring through cognitive, didactic, and educational means; thus, a recognition of the interplay between reason and cognition to human feelings and behaviors. The first orientation is primarily concerned with *why*, with etiology; the assumption is that when an individual understands the origins of his problems, he will be able to change his behavior. The second orientation is more concerned with *what*—what processes are operating in the present; what maintains the problem; and what changes in emotions, behavior, thinking, or perception are necessary in order for growth or improvement to occur.

Although the change or growth process may be conceptualized differently, most therapeutic models are, in the end, addressing similar, basic questions of self, its separateness and relatedness to others and the world, self-esteem, and emotions. Another common issue in evaluating human functioning is the system around which decisions and feelings are organized; for example, the personality constructs of id, ego, and superego, and need directive, need restriction, coordination.

A high percentage of adult clients seem to have been overburdened by need restrictions, whatever their levels of cognition. The needs and values of others in society are viewed as more important and more valid than their own. This orientation has been so consistent through their development that it becomes nearly impossible for them to conceptualize and verbalize their needs. A number of assumptions result, such as: "My needs are less important than those of others"; "It is selfish to overtly assert my needs"; "Others will disapprove, become angry, and/or not love me if I pursue my needs." Society tends to reinforce this orientation, placing negative values on the needs of self and equating a need-directive orientation with immaturity. The social roles of wife and mother, for example, seem to be primarily oriented around need restriction, with self-esteem measured by one's success at pleasing others.

Two final issues raised by van den Daele deserve comment in this over view: the cultural and theoretical bias in most models of development against earlier stages, and the overall emphasis in his scheme on justification. For the most part, earlier stages are described in terms that are socially undesirable. The result is a double bind for the child; if he develops normally, his personality and behavior are perceived negatively. The immature personality is conceived as primarily id or need directive, with progress resulting from the inhibition of those impulses.

Practitioners who work with children have long observed that the "abnormal" behaviors of children frequently serve as a convenient scapegoat for adults. The behavior of the child overshadows the more basic problems experienced by the parents. In addition, it provides adults with a socially acceptable reason for seeking professional help. Family therapy sessions reveal a number of such patterns. Children can be observed over a number of sessions misbehaving at the point of marital conflict. This behavior serves as a decoy, an event around which the parents and therapist will refocus their attention. Adult belief in the lack of sensitivity of children is expressed in a number of ways. For example, children might be asked to leave the session because they do not really understand their family's problems. An adult may consistently answer questions directed at the child, "because he didn't understand or know the answer." However, with encouragement, young children make apt, brave perceptive observations of their family interactions and its so-called secrets, despite their "lower" cognitive abilities.

Van den Daele offers a number of reasons for the bias against earlier stages. Among those suggested was the belief that reason and virtue are the same. Another, which is discussed later in this paper, is the goal-oriented nature of both society and developmental theories.

Discussion of some additional problems between adults and children may serve as a vehicle for demonstrating the importance of justification of the decision-making process to the clinician. Initially, parents appear to be most concerned about the behavior of their child. However, a second issue becomes quickly evident, concern with the child's decision making, his justification for the behavior. And it is this that frequently interferes with the success of behavioral approaches. For example, the presenting problem may be that of a child's breaking family rules, such as arriving late for supper. A more basic problem seems to emerge when the child is asked why he did it. Punishment is often for his justification and not for his behavior. What occurs is a process of "plea bargaining." If the child can state an acceptable reason for his behavior, punishment may be reduced. The most unacceptable reasons seem to be "I don't know" or "Because I wanted to." The legal system in the larger society is in some ways similarly oriented. It is not the offense that determines the degree of guilt, but the strength of the justification.

II. Development: An Open-Ended Process

Adherence to models advocating a single path of normal development leading to a fixed end has largely served to restrict our understanding of human behavior, particularly "abnormal" or "dysfunctional" behavior. Efforts to understand and treat mental illness often focus on searches into the past for earlier dysfunctional development that is interfering with present functioning. In practice, this search for a cause has frequently been transformed into a search for blame. Blame rarely produces growth. Instead, it tends to justify present difficulties, and is used as an excuse for *not* changing. Patients or clients will often be enthusiastic in this search and free in offering their insights, such as: "I'm fat because my mother was uninvolved and didn't love me"; "I can't study or perform because I'm anxious, which is caused by hate for my father, who was always critical of me." Perhaps most frustrating are the assumptions that follow insights—change or growth is deemed impossible since the causes of problems are in one's past, which cannot be changed. These justifications are in no way limited to lower levels of cognition. They are more closely related to the aptmat process described by van den Daele.

The *aptmat,* or aptness of a given rationale or action, receives much attention in the therapeutic process. The numerous steps in thinking are examined: what is perceived and how (through what senses), the validity of the perceptions, how was it interpreted (as to content as well as meaning to the self), what were the response, behavior, and action that resulted?

Studies among clinical populations would appear to validate van den Daele's view of the developmental process as accumulative and recursive. He suggests that earlier, less formal levels of cognition are always available. It frequently appears that individuals who demonstrate ability to function on a higher, more formal level can at other times be observed behaving on a lower level. The determinant appears to be the specific social stimulus.

Therapy with interpersonal relationship problems requires attention to the aptness of the cognitive level in a given situation. What frequently occurs is usefully described as an interaction of mixed levels of cognition. For example, problems will undoubtedly result if one spouse responds to the other's statement of love with a theoretical discussion of the relativity of the concept, questioning its existence except as an abstraction. By contrast, the treatment of sexual disorders may require assisting individuals to operate on an almost preoperational/functional level.

Interpersonal relationships often seem to operate on lower levels of cognition. That is, despite the potential for functioning at more abstract levels when there are problems in interpersonal relationships, an individual usually conceptualizes and perceives them at lower levels. A number of common inapt, dysfunctional rationales emerge. Most people appear to "forget" the relativity of perceptions, that words and ideas are merely abstractions, that most judgments are merely preferences, and the nonexistence of "right" and "wrong" or "truth" in the context of interpersonal relationships. In addition, there appears to be insufficient acceptance of interindividual differences—that two individuals can prefer or like different kinds of music, for example, without one being "wrong." This lack of acceptance is frequently visible in marital interactions: "If you loved me you'd like what I like" or "If you loved me you'd know what I want without my telling you." The practical problems of this kind of thinking are obvious, since it is nearly impossible for any two people to have exactly the same likes, dislikes, or wants at any given time. And while not impossible, it is highly improbable that one can accurately "read another person's mind."

The last decade has seen the incorporation of existential philosophy into therapeutic theory. Van den Daele offers a viable theory of ego development to which this change can be related. He suggests no final terminus, level, stage, or goal of development, no point at which questions of the self and its relationship to the other and the world are finally answered. Rather, development is described as a never ending process of successively "new" or different interpretations and justifications for these central questions.

Prior to the change in orientation toward existentialism, practitioners attempted to pursue final stages or states as the ultimate goals and measures of success of their professional endeavors. Much of the frustration experienced by the practitioner was related to the vague and arbitrary nature of such final stages as "normality," "health," and "maturity." Even if the achievement of those goals were theoretically possible, other factors make them unrealistic. For example, a large portion of the patient or client population seeks help primarily to remove specific feelings or problems for the purpose of restoring a previous state of emotional homeostasis. Theoretical models notwithstanding, all too often, once the symptoms disappear, so does the patient—perhaps eroding, as he departs, a bit of the therapist's belief in the usefulness of models of development. This kind of symptomatic treatment, whether through chemicals or through the therapist's taking the role of an interested and concerned friend, has its place in therapy. However, it is frustrating for the therapist who wants to change the personality substantially. It is equally problematic for the patient, because dependence on therapy easily follows.

may have been a reflection of the goal-oriented nature of society in general, or a reflection of the extent to which theory has successfully influenced society, or both. Despite their emphasis on symptoms, most patients organize their lives around the notion of a final stage in development. Their goal appears to be reaching a point when they will not experience depression and anxiety and will make only rational decisions. They measure present and past functioning against this rather formidable goal. The result has been, of course, that the present always falls short. The individual frequently attempts to rid himself of these "abnormal" feelings, rather than recognizing them as one means of discovering new skills and potentialities.

Existential philosophy has contributed an important perspective on man and therapy, the notions of *being* and *becoming*. Pogers (1971) has perhaps most clearly communicated the view of man as a process, not composed of fixed traits, but of ever changing potentialities. This view is essential in the questions and problems of self-esteem. Ellis (1970) has suggested it is probably better to relate self-esteem or self-worth to the process of being and becoming, rather than measuring it by the external, arbitrary notions and values of a society. Numerous therapeutic schools and techniques have emerged whose focus is on assisting individuals to see themselves as a process and to be more aware and accepting of their being. In a sense, they hope to help the individual like himself and to change in order to make himself better. This merely signifies a difference in the motivation to change, and it is not meant to imply that the focus or direction cannot be determined. Stated differently, once it is recognized that one's present is the future's past, it seems more likely that change and the assumption that one can control it are possible.

Van den Daele's model suggests that much of our bias against early stages of development—against children—is related to the goal orientation of adults and their unawareness of their own process of development. The process seems to be perceived as subordinate to the goal. The behavior and thinking of the young child is measured against that of the final state. The resulting judgments and definitions of the child also appear to be final. But most young children have a *being* orientation. They are spontaneous, curious, open, and aware of their perceptions and feelings of the present, skills that many adults must be taught. It seems reasonable to suggest that we both admire and resent children for their having these qualities.

III. Crisis Theory

There is much in the literature of the past 15 years on theory and models for crisis intervention or therapy. For the most part these models are consistent with the model suggested by van den Daele. Parad (1965) and others discussed and identified those "normal" life events that were potential sources for psychological crisis and which would require new forms of integration, cognition, new definitions of self, and the development of new coping skills for the meeting of needs. The events identified included death of a relative, illness, marriage, birth of a child, and a child's leaving home.

Crisis therapy, as described, had a twofold purpose (Small, 1971). The first purpose was the restoration of previously effective ego functions or states of equilibrium. Second, it was thought that because of his disequilibrium, the individual might be able to move on to the discovery and development of new skills and levels of integration, that is, "reorganization" of the personality.

Although crises were considered normal events, these earlier models of crisis theory appear covertly to assume that an individual's vulnerability to crises, as well as the quality of the experiences, are determined by "abnormalities" in ego development.

When the cumulative, open-ended nature of the van den Daele model is considered along with the earlier discussion of man as a process, it appears that the individual requires reorganization of the self at many points in his life. Practitioners or therapists are most familiar with those individuals who are experiencing a situation for which they (1) have no readily available solution or (2) no solution presently existing in their repertoire.

IV. Whither Theories of Ego Development and the Practitioner?

A number of external and internal pressures and changes have resulted in the assumption by many practitioners that their professional activities and the concepts of therapeutic models have little relationship to ego development, and vice versa. A cursory examination of therapeutic models reveals development by each of a specialized language and concepts, apparently unlike the semantics and concepts of ego psychology. One is more likely to hear a clinician discussing such things as "double bind," "counterrole," "strokes," "life scripts," and "dyads" than the language of traditional models.

The content and focus of therapeutic models have also changed. The models have become increasingly concerned with techniques, with the interactions between people, behavior change (as opposed to structural change), and the changing of larger social systems. Some of the pressures that stimulated these changes included recognition of the inefficiency of traditional insight-oriented, one-to-one long-term therapy in the presence of continually increasing patient populations; the inapplicability of a highly

verbal process to a large segment of the population; the demands for prevention and accountability; and increased awareness of the relationship
between social roles and conditions to individual adjustment or health.

While it should not be concluded that theories of ego development have
nothing relevant to offer the practitioner, the changes described awaken a
number of conflicts with theories that inhibit their examination and assimi-
lation by practitioners. Van den Daele's model offers some potential resolution for aspects of this conflict.

A. Applications of Theory

For the most part, translating the abstractions of theories to specific
behavioral referrants and the specifics of techniques has been seemingly
impossible and frustrating to the practitioner. It appears that two responses
are common: (1) acceptance of the "impossibility" by compartmentalizing
one's interest and study into theory at one extreme, and techniques or
application on the other, and (2) for the practitioner to question whether
any theory will relate to his concerns. Many clinicians have focused much
of their effort around the theoretical and philosophical issues related to
their patients, with less overt attention to the process of intervention. This
imbalance is also visible in the content of training and education efforts.
The theory certainly cannot be made totally responsible for the way it is
used by practitioners. However, traditional models of ego development
have tended to reinforce ideas that adequate insight will lead directly to the
techniques necessary for behavior change.

B. The Medical Model

The medical model basis for dysfunctional behavior and the organization
of services has become unpopular, controversial, and, in the minds of some,
inappropriate. Practitioners have often equated ego psychology with the
disease model. Therefore, in their efforts to disengage themselves from the
medical model, the concepts and language of ego psychology were also
discarded.

C. Changing Definitions of Clients

In the last two decades, the patient or client has been redefined to include
two or more persons, such as married couples, families with children, or
even larger groups. In such cases the understanding of the system and its
change requires more than an understanding of its individual parts. Therefore, theories of individual development appear to overemphasize the role
of personal, internal structures and functions in the change process.

Since the practitioner's role in the therapeutic process is that of an external influence on the individual, research and theoretical needs extend beyond descriptions of internal developmental processes and content. We need to know how normal development is influenced by external factors, the environment, in order that we can more accurately replicate and accelerate the process, clinically.

D. Clinicians and Academicians

One basic difference between clinicians and academicians is the clinician's ambivalence toward science. More specifically, clinicians have internal conflicts over such philosophical issues as objectivity versus subjectivity and determinism versus freedom and individuality. At times we are committed to the pursuit of the causes of human problems, to those events that shape man's development, and the techniques or methods that will conclusively change the course of that development. Much of that commitment is supported by a desire to be a part of the scientific community. However, the methods of scientific inquiry are threatening because they might substantiate our subjective impression that we cannot be sure that what we do helps people.

Concurrent with our respect for scientific efforts is a conflicting belief in the freedom and individuality of man, a desire to see him as having the ability and responsibility for changing himself. Each new discovery of a factor that plays a part in shaping behavior seems to attack the free will of the individual. Determinism runs counter to our efforts to convince clients—and perhaps ourselves—that they can change their behavior and the course of their development.

Determinism also stimulates concern for and fear of the power of science and its potential for manipulating others. Public and professional reactions to the theory and techniques of behavior therapy reflect varying attitudes regarding power and control. What emerges is a fear and rejection of the power for potential manipulation of individuals by a rather select group such as clinicians. It is interesting that most of the criticism is directed toward the theory; indicating a seeming unawareness that clinicians already hold a powerful upper hand in their relationship with clients. Thus, despite the clinicians' conflicts regarding power and control, it seems to me that since this power exists, random, noncontingent, "unknowing" use is much more frightening.

The scientific process must objectify people and the therapeutic process, striking another sensitivity of practitioners, particularly those who were a part of the movement that emphasized experiential learning over didactic, formal learning. Their response to research, then, is that because the researcher is an uninvolved observer, he cannot really know anything about the process or event being studied.

V. Conclusion

This discussion of some of the issues that complicate communication between practitioners and academicians has a secondary purpose. The ideas and concepts of theories combined with these issues offer clinicians the kind of challenge and conflict that ensures their own personal and professional growth and vitality. Such issues can ensure the *being* and *becoming* or clinicians, as well.

REFERENCES

Berne, E.*What do you say after you say hello.* New York: Grove Press, 1972.
Ellis, A. *Reason and emotion in psychotherapy.* New York: Lyle Stuart, 1970.
Parad, H.J. (Ed.), *Crisis intervention: selected readings.* New York: Family Service Association, 1965.
Rogers, C.R. *On becoming a person.* Boston, Massachusetts: Houghton-Mifflin, 1961.
Small, L. *The briefer psychotherapies.* New York: Brunner-Mazel, 1971.

CHAPTER 6

Adult Life Crises:
A Dialectic Interpretation of Development

KLAUS F. RIEGEL

UNIVERSITY OF MICHIGAN
ANN ARBOR, MICHIGAN

ABSTRACT

Crises, conflicts, and contradictions ought to be regarded as constructive confrontations and the basis for development rather than in a negative manner and as causes for disruption. In this chapter the course of general adult development is analyzed, as well as the career development of the normal and exceptional scientist—in particular, of Jean Piaget and Wilhelm Wundt. Individuals through their constructive development create historical changes; the sociocultural conditions, in turn, will change the individual. These double interactions produce conflicts or crises between individuals, between groups, and between individuals and groups. Several cases of conflicts are described and a general model for developmental progression through crises resolution is proposed.

I. Introduction

A. Prologue

Since the time that I was asked to discuss crises in adult life, I have felt uncomfortable about the topic. On one hand, I cannot deny that incisive crises occur during adulthood and old age; on the other hand, I do not like the pathological and often fatalistic implications of this term. Searching through my vocabulary, I thought for a while that terms like "developmental leaps," "critical choice points," or "existential challenges" might somewhat better describe the condition under concern. Failing to convince myself of the preference for these substitutions, I began to realize that it would be necessary to devote large parts of this chapter to an analysis of the concept of crisis and its underlying philosophical model and ideology.

The concept of crisis is antithetically connected with those of equilibrium, stability, consonance, and balance. The notion of equilibrium as a desirable goal has thoroughly penetrated the thinking of behavioral and social scientists and defines crisis in a negative manner. Thus, the concept of crisis attains meaning only as a disequilibrium when viewed as a long-term condition, or as the act of interrupting a state of tranquillity and as the shock of being thrown off balance when viewed as a short-term imposition. But since contrastive states or events are closely interdependent, the concept of equilibrium cannot be understood without the concept of disequilibrium, and the concept of stability cannot be understood without the concept of crisis. What we ought to search for is not a better apprehension of each of these conditions alone, but of their interpenetration. Stability and crisis ought not to be seen as negative and positive, but as mutually dependent, though contradictory conditions that only in their dialectical conjunction make development possible at all.

B. Contradictions and Development

Previously I have criticized the equilibrium model of development (Riegel, 1973b, 1975; see also Hogan, 1974; Rychlak, 1972, 1975; Wozniak, 1975) and in particular Piaget's theory of cognitive development as insufficient to account for changes during adulthood and aging (Piaget, 1972). Piaget emphasizes the removal of conceptual contradictions as the child's most essential development task. Similar arguments have been made for moral development by Kohlberg (1969). The young child will be, at first, quite at ease when making contradictory judgments, for example about the amounts of two clay balls; at one instance he might say that they have the same amount, at the next, that they have not. But eventually the child begins to feel uncomfortable with these contradictions; he experiences a disequilibrium. If he succeeds in resolving the contradictions in a consistent manner, he thereby lifts himself to the next higher level of cognitive operations, toward a new equilibrium.

This development continues, according to Piaget, until the period of formal operational thought is reached. By now the child's thoughts have become logically consistent and he cannot any longer be caught easily making contradictory judgments. But while scientific or scholastic debates among adults continue to aim at detecting contradictions in the opponent's statements, mature operations and thoughts cannot be based on such academic gamesmanship alone. The mature person needs to achieve a new apprehension and an effective use of contradictions in operations and thoughts. Contradictions should no longer be regarded as deficiencies that have to be straightened out by formal thinking but, in a confirmative manner, as the very basis of all activities. In particular, they form the basis for any innovative and creative work. Adulthood and maturity represent the period in life during which the individual knowingly reappraises the role of formal, i.e., noncontradictory thought and during which he may succeed again (as the young child has unknowingly succeeded in his "primitive dialectic") to accept contradictions in his actions and thoughts ("scientific dialectic").

C. Contradictions and Crises

The confirmation of contradictions, in contrast to their denial by cognitive and mentalistic psychologists, enables us to propose an alternate interpretation of crises and catastrophes. For the individual, contradictions, doubts, questions, and inner dialogues represent the very basis of his actions and thoughts. His social development likewise is founded upon and finds expression in conflicts, disagreements, debates, and dialogues. Both these inner and outer interactions are functional and beneficial for both the individual's development and that of the social group. Occasions may arise, of course, when the interactions are blocked or when the opposing forces are so strong that the individual or the group is unable to cope with them. Instead of constructive developments they might become subdued and the dialectic interaction thus destroyed. These conditions should be called crises or catastrophes in the proper senses of these words. They represent pathological deviations from normal development.

The normal course of life is partially determined by inner–biological factors that find expression in the normative age-grading system of any society (Neugarten & Datan, 1973). Thus, the individual becomes ready for leaving his parents' home and establishing his own career, for marriage and for having children. Physical maturation determines the boundaries of these normative events (Neugarten & Datan, 1973). None of them can properly be called crises, and even if they have such implications for the individual, the consequences are predominantly social in nature. Inner–biological crises do occur, however, in form of accidents or illnesses at any time in the life cycle, and in form of increasing sensory–motor deficiencies during the later years of life. Unless these events lead to gross incapacitations or death, and even though his chances for success may not always be very bright, the individual will always attempt to overcome them through his psychosocial adjustments.

Besides inner–biological determinants, the occurrence of some outer–physical events such as earthquakes, floods, and droughts may create catastrophes for the individual and society. Most of the efforts of society can be regarded as reactions against such catastrophes, trying to control or at least to predict them, and thereby to improve the security and welfare of its members. Indeed, events become catastrophes or crises only in their interaction with social groups or individuals. Outer–physical events that strike an organism and, in the extreme, destroy his existence cannot be considered as crises or catastrophes unless they are experienced by the psychological individual or recorded by the sociological group. In particular, the recognition of crises and catastrophes is brought about by asynchronies between some or all of the four major planes of progression: (1) the inner–biological, (2) the individual–psychological, (3) the cultural–sociological, and (4) the outer–physical. In my discussion, I shall focus primarily upon developmental stratifications that are determined by psychological or sociological conditions rather than by biological or physical factors and their temporal synchronization or lack of it.

D. Preview

After the general development through the adult years has been described, I consider the special case of a scientist. This progression, although it is not offered as a model of normative development, is of interest because the scientist's development is closely dependent upon the concurrent development of a social group, representing his particular research orientation or discipline. Distinct developmental stratifications can be described for such a group, first, by determining specific participatory roles for the scientist at different stages in his development, and second, by comparing major revisions brought about through confrontations between various groups representing different paradigmatic orientations in the history of the scientific discipline. The first component determines individual changes in a specific manner, and thereby may provoke the occurrence of crises in the individual. The second component affects the group as a whole, and may provoke conflicts or, in the extreme, the breakdown of the group. In particular, most individuals affiliate with only one group or paradigmatic orientation during their lifetimes and thus benefit during its recognition and suffer during its decline or rejection; only a few exceptional individuals might actively participate or even initiate the formation of several paradigmatic orientations during their lifetimes. The summaries of the life histories of two such persons, Piaget and Wundt, represent almost ideal cases of the structural coordination between individual and societal progressions.

The history of conflicts between different paradigmatic orientations leads to the discussion of historical progression in general and of its crisis-generating impact upon the individual. As for the scientific paradigms, cultural and political progression is brought about by the sequential effectiveness of various subgroups. Through competition as well as cooperation they exert a dominant influence for limited periods of time only; soon afterward they are replaced by other subgroups. The model to be presented applies to groups of scientists representing different paradigmatic orientations, to artists representing different styles, to individuals representing different political and economical interests, and, ultimately, it applies to groups of groups, that is, to whole nations and civilizations. But it applies also to different cohorts or generations within any one and across all of these social groups. The resulting interactions of age strata and social groupings in their historical progressions determine crises in the development of society. The interactions in the developmental progression of one particualr individual with the generational and historical changes in society determine the crises in his individual life.

II.   Contradictions and Crises in Adult Life

A. *Former Interpretations*

Occasionally attempts have been made to describe the progression during adulthood in terms of developmental stages, most often determined by psychosocial factors. These interpretations have frequently imposed an over-systematized order upon the life cycle. Although stages were described in eloquent terms, all too often convincing arguments have been lacking on why a particular age span, e.g., 7 years, should receive exceptional attention and what would trigger the switch into more advanced forms of psychosocial interactions. But in this regard these interpretations are just as fallacious as Piaget's interpretation of early cognitive development.

One of the earliest attempts to describe the progression through the adult years was made by Charlotte Buehler (1933; see also 1968). Relying on biological and psychological investigations, on production and performance records, and, most important, on autobiographical or biographical descriptions, Buehler subdivided the life cycle into distinct phases that were mainly determined on an intraindividual basis and remained rather flexible. She was primarily interested in describing different styles of progressions, and thus, corresponding to the three types of material relied on, Buehler distinguished progressions that were dominated by biophysical performances (e.g., those by manual workers and athletes) from those that led to productions and achievements (e.g., by businessmen, scientists, and artists) and from those that revealed contemplative integrations (e.g., by philosophers and writers). Her approach, though with a lessened emphasis upon developmental styles, has been applied by Kuhlen (1959, 1964) and is retained in the extensive work by Lehman (1953).

One of the best known recent proposals of developmental stages for the human life span has been made by Erikson (1963). Of the "eight ages of man" described in contrastive pairs, the last three cover adult development and aging.

> Basic trust versus mistrust
> Autonomy versus shame, doubt
> Initiative versus guilt
> Industry versus inferiority
> Identity versus role confusion
> Intimacy versus isolation
> Generativity versus stagnation
> Ego integrity versus despair

Erikson's theory as well as Clayton's (1975) modified interpretation (which is especially devoted to the elaboration of the eighth stage) regard development as constituted by the interaction of inner and outer forces.

> Each successive stage and crises has a special relation to one of the basic elements of society, and this for the simple reason that the human life cycle and man's institutions have evolved together. . . . This relation is twofold: man brings to these institutions the remnants of his infantile mentality and his youthful fervor, and he receives from them—as long as they manage to maintain their actuality—a reinforcement of his infantile gains [Erikson, 1963, p. 250].

For Erikson the dualistic determination implies

> (1) that the human personality in principle develops in steps predetermined in the growing person's readiness to be driven toward, to be aware of, and to interact with, a widening social radius; and (2) that society, in principle, tends to be constituted as to meet and invite this succession of potentialities for interaction and attempts to safeguard and to encourage the proper rate and the proper sequence of their enfolding [1963, p. 270].

But it remains insufficient to explain the development from within by postulating a "predetermined" order of enfolding. We need to know the determinants of the shifts constituting this order.

In place of such an explanation Erikson introduces the concept of "crisis" or "conflict," which he elaborates in the following manner:

> We claim only that psychological developments proceeds by critical steps—"critical" being a characteristic of turning points, of movements of decision between progress and regression, integration and retardation. . . . This indicates (1) that each critical item of psychological strength discussed here is systematically related to all others, and that they all depend on the proper development in the proper sequence of each item; and (2) that each item exists in some form before its critical time normally arrives [1963, p. 270–271].

While all these statements strike a reasonable balance. they fail to explain *why* the organism grows and moves from stage to stage. Again they merely describe a proper order of development.

In summary, Buehler has provided us with the notion of individual styles in progression through the human life cycle Erikson has emphasized the interdependence of individual and cultural development, but neither of the two has succeeded in giving us a deterministic, systematic interpretation of why the human being develops and ages. Neither the individualistic notions of achievement, power, creativity, and self-actualization as implied in Buehler's theory (1933, 1968) and elaborated by Kuhlen (1964) nor Erikson's concept of "critical time" and "critical steps" provide appropriate explanations. Most recently, at a time when this chapter was being completed, Kimmel (1974) elaborated an interpretation of development and aging on the basis of George Herbert Mead's symbolic interactionism (1934). The present outline resembles in several respects this interpretation. It considers the occurrences of asynchronies as the singular cause of development. But in contrast, it gives stronger emphasis to the developmental synchrony (and asynchrony) along four and not only two planes of progression. In addition to the individual–psychological and the cultural–sociological, the lack of synchronization with inner–biological and outer–physical progression is being regarded as the major cause for individual crises and cultural catastrophes.

B. Temporal Stratifications of the Life Span

1. Adult Development.

In following the earlier interpretations by Buehler (1933, 1968), Erikson (1963), and Kimmel (1974), a sequence of events can be described. These events, some of which might have crisis character, are codetermined by inner–biological and outer–physical conditions. While the occurrences of the latter can be explicated to some extent, we know much less about biological determinants. Since, at the present time, biological shifts can neither be pinpointed nor their sequential order explained with precision, most of our attention has to be directed to the outer–physical and cultural–sociological determinants. Such emphasis has the advantage that it might lead to modifications. Although the possibilities for constructive changes have rarely been implemented, their discussion will be directive for future designs and planning.

In considering various conditions affecting the individual during his adult life, a list like Table 1 can be derived. This list shows separately those changes that occur gradually and those that occur suddenly. The former are separately given for males and females.

After leaving school or college, males will enter their first occupational careers; at the same time they may get married. The attendance rates of colleges by females is still lower than those for males; subsequently, females are more likely to accepy their first jobs at an earlier age than males. The attainment of an occupational role is primarily dependent on social conditions, which in turn are the reflection of cultural standards at a particular historical time. The marital role, on the other hand, requires sexual maturity of both partners. But in all these instances the separation of biological from sociological determinants is hard if not impossible to draw. Nevertheless, I have listed the former event in the left-hand column and the latter in the right, thus indicating their differential determination by psychosocial and biophysiological factors. Most notable, the birth of children will have a strong biological effect upon the mother; the father, however, will be mainly socially affected.

As determining events at the second developmental level, I have listed the birth of other children coupled with a complete or partial loss of the wife's job and a possible change in the job of the husband. A child cannot be born unless a social or at least biological marriage has taken place; a job cannot be lost or changed unless it has been held before. As obvious as these conclusions may seem, they need to be emphasized because they represent the very markings that structure the progression of the adult's life. They play an important role for the recollection of minor events at a later date, such as an accident, the purchase of a household item, a birthday, or a party, as well as for the temporal markings of what the individual might perceive as a crisis in his life.

The determining events at the third developmental level include the execution of specific parental roles during the children's school years (especially by the mother), promotion of the father, move to a larger house or to a different community. Of course, the delineation of a developmental level corresponding to and determined by the children's school years is possible only for families with single or very few children narrowly spaced by birth over a short time period. This limitation indicates, once more, the cultural–sociological determination of distinct periods in the adult life. Most of them can be identified only for members of small nuclear families in industrial-

Table 1

Levels and Events in Adult Life

Level (years)	Males		Females		Sudden changes
	Psychosocial	Biophysical	Psychosocial	Biophysical	
I (20–25)	college/first job marriage first child		first job/college marriage	first child	
II (25–30)	second job other children children in preschool		loss of job children in preschool	other children	
III (30–35)	move children in school	promotion	move · without job children in school		
IV (35–50)	second home	promotion departure of children	second home second career departure of children		
V (50–65)	unemployment isolation grandfather head of kin	incapacitation	unemployment grandmother head of kin	menopause	loss of job loss of parents loss of friends illness
VI (65+)	deprivation	sensory–motor deficiencies		widowhood incapacitation	retirement loss of partner death

ized settings. Agricultural societies with elaborated kinship traditions do not allow for subdividing the life span into distinct periods founded on determinants other than biological ones. As described, for example, by Margaret Mead (1928), large kingroups experience closely spaced arrivals of children, which do not allow for the sectioning of the life span by generational shifts or career alterations.

In contrast to the events marking the two preceding levels, the following ones are spread over longer and more variable time periods. During the fourth developmental level, the children have departed from home in preparation or in search for their own adult development and careers. Thus, the mother may begin her second career. Few changes except those of promotion or shift in assignments may be experienced by her husband. Undoubtedly, the departure of the children profoundly affects their parents. If these departures are accompanied by—as is becoming increasingly likely—the death of one or both members of the older generation, the status of the adult is even more drastically altered. Both husband and wife may now attain the top position among the living members of the extended family with their own children ready to marry and grandchildren to be expected. At the fifth developmental level, the individual, especially the husband, becomes increasingly vulnerable to dismissal, unemployment, and chronic diseases. Not only the death of the parents, but of the partner, friends, and relatives may create personal crises. These incidents are now occurring with greater frequency and in greater number.

While most of these events are brought about by uncontrollable outer–physical circumstances or are due to unavoidable inner–biological changes in the aging organism, one of the most decisive final affronts, retirement, is not caused by increasing inner or outer deficiencies but by conventional regulations. Mandatory retirement provides the last insult to the adult person and initiates his progressive social deterioration.

2. Career Development

The preceding discussion has been based on a review of some literature and on intuition. Supportive evidence is available from census statistics and has been reported by Kimmel (1974). Our discussion delineated a general sequence of levels in adult development which are partially influenced by cultural–sociological and partially by inner–biological and outer–physical conditions. Development occurs either in form of gradual changes or suddenly in form of crises and catastrophes. Throughout, the interdependence of the various determinants and of the forms of changes was emphasized (most often gradual changes are triggered by sudden alteration, e.g., when entering college, when being drafted, when a child is born, etc.). Because of the possibility for constructive modifications, special attention was paid to

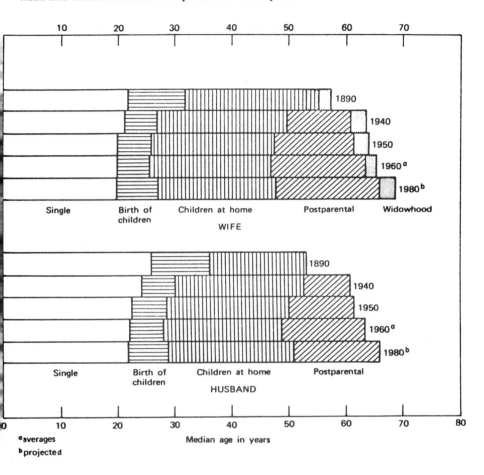

Fig. 1. Median age of husband and wife at critical stages of the family cycle. [Adapted from Duvall, 1974, Table 5-1.]

the cultural–sociological determinants of events and episodes in the adult life. The summary shown in Figure 1 also attends to the interactions of the sequence of events in the life of both males and females and cultural–sociological changes.

In pursuing this topic further, an ideal sequence of structural changes is to be described in the present section, which might suggest a more effective use of the adult's knowledge and abilities, and subsequently enable him to lead a more successful and gratifying life. Since few records are available on this topic, I retreat to the description of career development in an area best

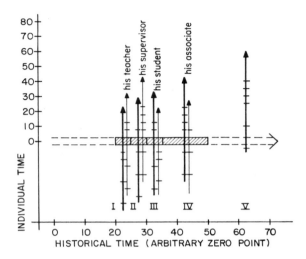

Fig. 2. The changing roles of a scientist participating in one paradigmatic orientation at different historical times. Each heavy vertical line represents one developmental level in the individual's career, i.e., I: from 20 to 25: II: from 25 to 30; III: from 30 to 35; IV: from 35 to 50; V: from 50 to 65 years. The thin vertical lines represent the careers of persons with whom he is affiliated (see also note to Figure 3).

known to me, to academic careers. As shown in Figure 2, the progression is described in form of five distinct developmental levels corresponding to all but the last discussed in the preceding section and shown in Table 1.

The foundations of an academic career are laid during the undergraduate and graduate years at the first developmental level. Although teachers may not always be convinced of the impact of their teaching, and students may not always be convinced of the sense of learning and its influence upon their future career, there can be little doubt that fundamentals are laid and formative directions are established. This result might not be achieved so much through the specific content of lectures, discussions, and readings but through the impact of the basic mentality and theme exhibited at a particular institution at a particular time. Through this influence, the philosophic–scientific images of the young cohort of scholars are formed and a paradigmatic orientation (in the narrowest sense of Kuhn's term, 1962) is created which the new cohort will implement by failing to question it any further and by using it as a basis from which the explication of a new orientation can proceed during the coming years.

One could select many examples for demonstration purposes. Let us consider the conception of life-span psychology with its recognition of the interdependence of individual and societal changes as recently promoted at the West Virginia conferences. This selection does not imply a disregard for similar suggestions made at earlier times by other persons. In particular, we recognize two earlier movements, one led by Charlotte Buehler (1933, 1968) in extension to her research on children and adolescents during the late 1920s and 1930s in Vienna, the second with a base in Chicago and led by Burgess, Havighurst, Neugarten *et al.* Among many other issues, their work led to the rediscovery of the concepts of generation and generational shifts in general, and of Mannheim's theory in particular (see Neugarten & Datan, 1973; Riley, Johnson, & Foner, 1972).

Those of us who have lectured on the topic of individual and social changes and have tried to implement these ideas through their presentations at scientific meeting will often have felt a sense of helplessness when recognizing the sluggishness with which new issues are apprehended by the listeners, for example, by child psychologists. Undobtedly the audience was often enthusiastic, but as soon as they returned to their routine jobs, their enthusiasm seems to have disappeared rather quickly. Occasionally there was active resistance to the new conception. After all, the life-span concept raises questions about many past achievements by demanding that they be placed in a much broader conceptual framework, namely a framework that takes account not only of individual changes but also of historical and social changes. No wonder, therefore, that members of the dominating older cohorts failed to listen or became resistant.

The reactions, at the *first developmental level,* of the students were quite different. While some of the older graduates, by the time of our teaching, might have been already too firmly committed to an antiquated conception, the younger students accepted the new viewpoint without much quarrel, quite matter-of-factly. Their attitude may even have raised doubts in the mind of the teacher whether he did not emphasize the issue too repetitiously, causing boredom among his listeners. When the new conception was stated in a confirmative manner, the younger students accepted it and, on this basis, were ready to implement it as a self-evident form of thinking, and eventually to go beyond it. For their teachers, in comparison, the apprehension and realization of this conception was the result of a long struggle that, at the time of his lectures, was still not completed.

The activities of young scientists at the *second level* of their academic career aim at their establishment as instructors and researchers. The demands upon them are heavy. They will have to teach a variety of courses, not all of which are close to their own interests. They may join an existing laboratory and use facilities made available to them, thereby engaging in work that is not necessarily to their own liking. Nevertheless, through their teaching, research, and writing they will try to reveal their unique orientation in confrontation to the existing one and in cooperation with the cohort of young scientists who have entered the field with the same paradigmatic conviction. This orientation might be based, for example, upon the life-span conception. They do not *propose* this orientation but rather *presuppose* it, develop it further, and thereby establish it firmly within behavioral sciences in general and developmental psychology in particular. Only the application of a paradigmatic orientation by subsequent cohorts of scientists leads to its full acceptance and victory.

At the *third level* of their academic career, our psychologists are well established, most likely, as associate professors. They have become effective teachers lecturing on topics close to their fields of specialization. They have published a number of papers explicating their unique orientations, though many of them have not received the attention that they feel these publications deserve. They have obtained research grants and succeeded in establishing their own laboratory sections with a few students, assistants, and doctoral condidates. These are the most effective years in the young scientist's careers, during which they propose and explicate their own paradigmatic orientations in deviation from the one to which they were exposed during their undergraduate and graduate years.

At the *fourth level,* our scientists have firmly established themselves. They are full professors, have their laboratories and research teams, are nationally known and often sought speakers at colloquia and conventions. They mainly lecture in advanced seminars but continue to teach undergraduate classes because these efforts assist them in writing advanced texts on the topics of their specializations. Through textbooks, their scientific themes become confirmed and accepted outside the narrow professional quarrels and debates. They serve on governmental, professional, and university boards, are chairpersons of their departments or of scientific committees. Their recognition is widespread and their influence is strong.

At the *fifth level,* our scientists have slightly retreated from their research activities. They still run their laboratories or programs but devote most of their time to administration. If they write, they contribute chapters to specialized books or prepare new editions of their texts. They might continue to serve as chairpersons of their departments or have accepted other administrative duties in the university or professional organizations. Their activities have not decreased but are rather channeled into managerial tasks. Their influence continues to remain strong and might even have increased within the administrative structure. They have become more remote from their original activities, e.g., of teaching and research. They see students less often and even their assistants will not interact with them directly, but through intermediaries.

Their role and status remain unchanged until their retirement. But even this event does not affect them as strongly as it does most other persons. They continue to serve on committees and accept honorary assignments. Although rarely found in the laboratory, they continue to write and might even increase the volume of their production in both amount and scope. While thus the scientists continue to fulfill gratifying roles throughout their later years, their lives are, of course, affected by all those gradual or sudden events listed in Table 1, which place a heavy burden upon the aging individual. Before they die, they might have completed their *Reminiscence,* as indeed Wilhelm Wundt did when he was 88 years old.

C. Breaking of Paradigmatic Crises by Exceptional Individuals

This sketch of the scientist represents a structural progression of a fortunate person in order to show an ideal coordination of the individual's progression and the changes in the social group. The sketch has been intuitive since records and systematic interpretations are lacking. These shortcomings are still more serious if one were to describe the structural progression for other careers, especially those with fewer opportunities for promotion and variation. In most of these cases, once a particular occupational role has been accepted, the holders remain tied to it for the rest of their lives or until their retirements, with gradual increases in their salaries being the only benefit that they can expect. Of course, each occupation allows for some changes. These possibilities ought to be elaborated more forcefully, and once structural alternatives have been recognized, they ought to be implemented through programmed job arrangements in order to generate the most gratifying career development for the participating members.

Thus far I have considered a developmental sequence in which the individual fulfills, essentially, only one basic theme, i.e., the attempts of scientists to build a new paradigmatic orientation upon that of their teachers, and thus to serve as historical catalysts of generational consciousness in their scientific discipline (Neugarten & Datan, 1973). In comparison to the one-paradigm scientists, persons may have the vision and power to embrace more than one orientation. They may, for example, quickly depart from the original paradigm that was imprinted upon them during their student years and lead the successive cohort of young scientists to a new orientation. But a few years later they may already aim at the development of another paradigmatic orientation, thereby alienating themselves from their former friends, colleagues, and students. Still later, they might develop a third orientation. There are at least two well-known psychologists whose careers can be described in terms of multiparadigmatic progressions: Piaget and Wundt.

The careers of both of them give dramatic demonstration of how the individual's generativity catalyzes a new paradigmatic consciousness and how in the further course of their own progressions the very orientations that they have created in society prevent them from moving successfully ahead. Society is being changed by the individual, but as it is changed it also changes the generativity of the individual. This holds for both the common and the exceptional persons. I focus upon the latter because their contributions, especially in sciences, are move visible. The former's participatory actions are mainly expressed by their conforming or nonconforming in particular roles, attitudes, and values. Any deviation from them represents a step, though a small one, in generating a new mode of living and a new historical consciousness.

1. Piaget

As shown in Figure 3, three periods can be distinguished in Piaget's career and work. After receiving his training as a biologist and deciding to direct his intellectual efforts to the study of the growth of knowledge, he settled upon child psychology as a pragmatic route for investigating these problems. The first period in his career can be denoted as *functional* and is best represented by his book entitled *Language and Thought of the Child* (1923). In contrast to his later approaches, he analyzed intellectual development in close conjunction with the child's acquisition of language, stressing the lack of communicative functions in the language of young children. This interpretation led to the well-known controversy with Vygotsky (1962; see also Piaget's separate preface to Vygotsky's book, 1962) about the social basis of language and cognitive development as well as to excessive research in the United States (see, for example, McCarthy's review, 1954) which through mechanistic distortions brought the first wave of enthusiasm for Piaget to an early end.

In the meantime Piaget had further developed his perspective. He deemphasized the functional and social aspects of language and elaborated his theory of stages in cognitive development. These activities covered the late 1930s, 1940s, and 1950s and aimed at structural descriptions of the child's logical operations at successive developmental levels. Beginning with interpretive–clinical observations covering the six stages of the sensory–motor period (Piaget, 1936), considerable experimental attention was given to preoperational (2 to 7 years) and concrete operational intelligence (7 to 11 years) (Piaget, 1947). The fourth and last period, formal operational thinking, has been explored in theory but less thoroughly in his research investigations. Here, and to a lesser extent for the earlier stage, Piaget's work culminated in theoretical constructions of how the child's thought ought to operate. Piaget's work during the second period in his own development

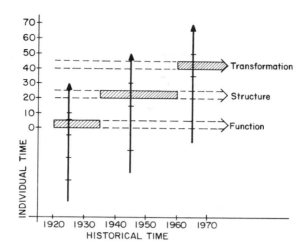

Fig. 3. The changing roles of one eminent scientist, Jean Piaget, participating in three paradigmatic orientations at different historical times. This figure corresponds to a two-dimensional time representation occasionally used in physics (see Cohen & Riegel, 1972). The vertical vectors represent "world lines" for the individual at different historical times; the horizontal vectors represent "world lines" for society at different individual times (see also note to Figure 2).

can appropriately be called *structural.* It has been supplemented by extensive studies of perception and perceptual development which have not yet received the full attention of American investigators, since only a few have been translated into English (see Piaget, 1961).

In pursuing further his theoretical analyses, Piaget has since then moved forward to what might be called his *transformational* period. While previously he maximized the differences between the "logics" of children at successive developmental levels, he became more profoundly concerned with the changes from one into the other, with the problem of invariances in transitions, with transformations. His interpretations—oddly enough published in a book entitled *Structuralism* (1968)—have attracted considerable attention, but it is doubtful whether they will influence psychology as deeply as his earlier work. In part, this expected lack of broad success is determined by the difficulty in translating his ideas into operational routines for the American psychological laboratory and by Piaget's disinterest in providing such translations.

Conceivably, Piaget might still enter into another stage of his career. He might integrate, perhaps from a developmental–historical perspective, much of his former work and lend it an authoritative and *absolute* character. In part, this is indicated by his growing concern with "genetic epistemology"

(1950, 1970) during the preceding period. But primarily my speculation is based upon biographical reports about developmental changes of famous philosophers, for example, Schelling and Aristotle (see Jaeger, 1923). It finds further support in Lehman's (1953) comparisons between the intellectual productivity at various periods during the life span and between various disciplines and art forms that show a general shift from creative achievement and empirical work to theoretical analyses, logic, history, and metaphysics.

2. Wundt

A better documented case for a scientist's constructive participation in several paradigmatic orientations as well as for the collective disregard of his progressing contributions is that of Wilhelm Wundt. As shown in Figure 4, Wundt was born in 1832 and in 1851 entered the University of Tübingen where he stayed for 1 year only before he moved to Heidelberg for 4 years. Part of his last year of study, 1856, was spent in Berlin, where he was influenced by Johannes Mueller, Magnus, and du Bois-Reymond.

The following decade centering around 1860 is described by Boring (1957) as "presystematic." Nevertheless, Wundt laid the foundation for his later work during this time. Between 1857 and 1864 he was *Dozent* (assistant professor) in Heidelberg, at the same time as Helmholtz was there and presumably under his influence. In 1858 Wundt published the first section of his book entitled *Beiträge zur Theorie der Sinneswahrnehmungen,* which was completed in 1862 and has been regarded by Titchener as a blueprint of his lifetime work. Also during this period he published in 1863 his *Vorlesungen über die Menschen and Thierseele.* This book includes a brief outline of his "Ethnopsychology," a topic and program of investigation that was to lie dormant for several decades until Wundt started extensive writings on this topic at the beginning of the twentieth century.

Wundt revealed his first paradigmatic orientation during the period from about 1865 to 1880. He elaborated and presented his work on perceptual–motor processes with an emphasis on sensory elements and their compounding into complex units. Although much broader and more comprehensive than later critics have made us believe, Wundt was never able to shake off the impressions that he created during these years, i.e., the impressions of promoting psychophysiological elementalism. This paradigmatic orientation is most distinctly represented by his two-volume work entitled *Grundzüge der physiologischen Psychologie,* which appeared between 1873 and 1874. Also during this period he became *Ausserordentlicher Professor* (associate professor). In 1874 he moved for one year to Zürich and in 1875 to Leipzig, where he opened his psychological laboratory in 1879.

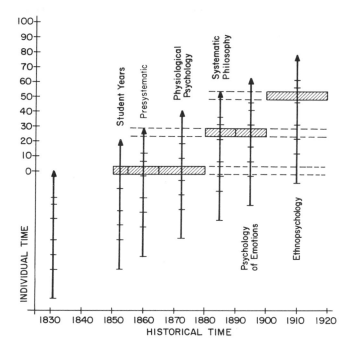

Fig. 4. The changing roles of one eminent scientist, Wilhelm Wundt, participating in three paradigmatic orientations at different historical times (see notes to Figures 2 and 3).

The following decade was almost exclusively devoted to philosophical writings. In 1881 he started the journal *Philosophische Studien* (although it included predominatly psychological reports and was later renamed in this sense). Between 1880 and 1883 he published two volumes on logic, in 1886 one on ethics, and in 1889 a book entitled *System der Philosophie.* He concluded the decade by serving as the rector of the University of Leipzig.

The 1880s can be regarded as a preparatory period for the expounding of his second paradigmatic orientation. This work led to his three-dimensional theory of feelings, first elaborated in his *Grundriss der Psychologie* of 1896. In contrast to the earlier psychophysiological and psychophysical theorizing, Wundt tried to establish psychology systematically on a more independent basis. Although the extensive theorizing and research on his theory of emotions or feelings created a considerable stir during Wundt's time, later psychologists (at least of the post-Titchener period) paid little attention to his work. Wundt remained branded as an introspective elementalist.

A similar disregard was shown by psychologists for his very extensive writing in ethnopsychology during the first two decades of the twentieth century until his death in 1920. This approach, as already outlined in his *Vorlesungen* of 1863, was to supplement the experimental methods promoted by the two earlier paradigmatic orientations. By analyzing the customs, habits, and languages of society as objectifications of the human mind, a second route for the study of psychology was to be provided. Experimentation is analyzing the mind from within; enthnopsychology analyzes the mind (more precisely, its products) from without. Both approaches are necessary and supplement each other. But in spite of the significance that Wundt assigned to it and in spite of the extensive debates and controversies that ethnopsychology created amont anthropologists, linguists, and historians, present-day psychologists are hardly aware of this contribution and of Wundt's two-pronged attempt for a comprehensive integration of the behavioral and social sciences. Only renewed historical interest in Wundt's work during the most recent years (see Balance, 1973; Blumenthal, 1970, 1973; and Brinkmann, 1973) has given him some delayed recognition.

3. Conclusions

Undoubtedly the lives of Piaget and Wundt have been subjected to the same alternating conditions and constraints that affect the individual's life cycle and which I have elaborated in the preceding section for a person less productive in scientific or intellectual affairs. Wundt, for example, moved steadily through all the administrative duties of a scientist establishing himself. He founded and directed his laboratory, served as chairman, dean, and rector of the university, participated actively in various scientific organizations, and even ran for and held a political office. Thus, both sequences, that of Wundt as a creative, ever–moving scientist and that of Wundt as a skillful researcher and administrator, ought to be integrated to provide a comprehensive picture of his career and the criterial points in its development.

The descriptions of these two scientific careers were introduced to indicate how, in exceptional cases, the individual may break out of the paradigmatic orientation that is imposed upon and restricts the development of the "normal man," including the "normal scientist." This comparison enables us to elucidate the interactive progression of the individual and society in the following manner: Historical progression is constituted by generational shifts and by the substitution of one cohort of leading individuals by the next. The individuals, through their life-span developments, change, but they make their main contributions during a limited time period only, most likely around or just before mid-adulthood. During the other periods, they either prepare themselves or rigidify their paradigmatic orientation, the scientists, for example, by writing textbooks and chapters and by their administration of laboratories and departments. The shifts in roles and, in particular, the experienced lack of success to continue in contributing in modes of earlier developmental periods might be considered as crises in adult life. Only a few exceptional persons, e.g., Piaget and Wundt, succeed in providing an array of different conceptions to the community.

The individual, especially the creative individual, produces social changes; but as they are brought about, the modified conditions change the individual. The individual might have been the spokesman for a new paradigmatic orientation; as this conception becomes obsolete or is substituted by a newer orientation, a crisis is generated reflecting qualitative shifts in the interactions between the individual's and society's development. Crises generated by the individual might become a revolution in society, e.g., scientific revolutions. Crises generated in society are, in all cases, traceable to individuals' actions; they might be experienced as catastrophes. In the preceding sections I have looked at the individual and, finally, at his interaction with the social group. In the following section, I analyze cultural–sociological changes and catastrophes.

D. Structural Stratifications in History.

In several recent investigations (Riegel, 1972b, 1973c, in preparation) I was struck by the apocalyptic view of the past exhibited by most individuals. When students were asked to recollect the names of historical figures, they produced many more names of persons who were instrumental in coping with major historical catastrophes, i.e., revolutions and wars. Few names were given for the more peaceful interludes although many of them produced important changes in economic, social, educational, and scientific domains. These findings are depressing, but one will have to realize that they give adequate expression of events decisive for the contemporaries who suffered through them as well as for later generations of individuals who merely heard about these events but were nevertheless influenced because their parents feared their repetitions.

In my earlier interpretations (Riegel, in preparation) I emphasized perceptual–constructive aspects in historical progression. Human beings through their actions generate events that might converge into catastrophes; in their perception of history, they focus upon these events rather than upon the tranquillity of intermediate stages. Similarly for the development of individuals; through their participatory actions, they create changes, e.g., accept jobs, marry, have children, move to another location. When they reflect about their development in retrospect, they perceive their pasts as structured sequences marked by these "disruptive" events. Unless seen as an object, neither historical progression nor individual development is experienced as a process of continuous and smooth changes but always as a progression in qualitative leaps. These leaps, experienced as crises or catastrophes, are brought about by the asynchrony in either inner–biological, individual–psychological, cultural–sociological, or outer–physical progressions.

1. The Family

Considering first the smallest subunit, the family or kin, I disagree with the traditional view expressed, for example, in Galton's study of *Hereditary Genius* (1869). By analyzing the family trees of famous people, Galton tried to show that superior productivity is genetically inherited since it occurs disproportionately more frequently within certain well-known families than others. Disregarding the likelihood that this observation is determined by cultural–sociological factors of upbringing, education, and intellectual milieu rather than inner–biological, genetic components, the domination of such families or kin groups is temporally restricted. Although strong supportive data do not seem to be available except from family biographies such as *Buddenbrooks* by Thomas Mann, different clans replace each other in the course of history of growth, stability, and decline. These changes in significance create crises for its members as much as its competition with other clans cause conflicts in society. Major catastrophes arise if a particular clan succeeds in dominating others and the society in general for an extended period of time. In these cases of aristocratic or monopolistic dominations, only warfare or revolutions succeed in restructuring the society for the benefit of other subgroups and its individual members.

The present discussion of historical progression regards the family or the clan as an extended cohort with an internal history that becomes significant for society during a limited period of time only. Overall progression is brought about by the replacements of different cohort clans during historical time. These families and clans represent subgroups of larger social, political, and geographical units, which in turn have their own internal history and replace each other in historical time. Finally, the analysis leads to the histories of states and nations.

2. The Nation

Different social groups or nations undergo profound changes generating upward and downward trends with peaks at different historical periods. The political–cultural history of Western Europe can be written, for example, as a sequence in which different political groups attained their domination in ordered succession. The late Middle Ages were dominated by the remnants of the Frankish empire, especially in western and southern Germany. Their influence was replaced by the Italian city–states during the early Renaissance of the fifteenth century, and by Spain and the Netherlands during the later periods up to the sixteenth century. In the meantime, France gained increasing recognition and became the dominating power during the seventeenth century even though several other nations, mostly notably England, Austria, Russia, and Sweden, entered into ambitious conflicts. England dominated the European scene of the nineteenth century until in renewed competition with Germany and France all of these nations began to lose out to the United States.

The sequence described might appear as simplistic. It depicts alternations in political domination that are not necessarily synchronic with cultural progression, e.g., in arts and sciences. Indeed, cultural progression often seems to lag behind political advances. During the height of the Spanish empire, for example, artists, craftsmen, and scientists had to be recruited in foreign countries in order to express the power and prestige of the state through their creations. During the eighteenth and early nineteenth century, on the other hand, when Germany was everything else but a political power, music, writing, and painting reached never achieved heights, and sciences began to make decisive advances.

3. The Arts

While political history attains its consistency by the geographical cohesion of the supportive groups, arts and sciences have always broken through these barriers and cannot be firmly tied to particular places, groups, or nations. What provides cohesion to these domains of human activities are the common mentality of the participants, the universality of their theme, and the accumulative advances in knowledge and technology. In the history of arts, for example, it is only sensible that during the early periods the main activities centered upon architecture. Only after basic needs for shelter and storage were secured did it become possible to add decorative refinements and sculptures. The art of painting required further technological advances and fulfills basic biological needs of the individuals to a lesser extent. Materials, tools, and media had to be developed before painting could become a dominating mode of artistic expression. The history of painting, when studied in some greater detail, reveals a close dependency upon scientific conceptions, going as far back as the planar murals of the Egyptians. During the Renaissance the history of painting can be described as a sequence of advances in projecting the three-dimensional space defined by scientists and philosophers upon the two-dimensional canvas. Boring (1957) described how, step by step, all the perceptual cues were mastered until, during the Baroque, the artists were engulfed in dynamic overrepresentation of space in action, and until modern art both playfully and compulsively began to deny the very cues laboriously acquired during centuries of artistic traditions. Finally, music, first created for ceremonial and devotional purposes, later realized in concrete performances at the stage, still requires a higher degree of abstraction and the development of sophisticated instruments and refined transcription systems until it could become a dominant mode of artistic expression.

4. The Sciences

Although artistic styles differ widely, there exists an intrinsic logic that determines their historical progression. Cohesion of this type is still more characteristic for scientific efforts. In the history of physics, for example, the study of mechanics had to precede that of thermodynamics, which had to precede that of electromagnetics, which, finally, had to precede that of nuclear physics. Although I do not wish to promote an accumulative model of growth (guided by the conception that the more you do, the closer you get toward the detection of "the truth"), sciences are founded upon the ceaseless efforts of many individuals over many generations contributing step by step to the stock of universal knowledge. But in Kuhn's sense (1962), development of sciences is also determined by changes in style (e.g., experimental versus clinical analysis), breakthroughs in technology (e.g., the measurement of the speed of nerve conductivity, the development of microelectrodes), and confrontations of scientific paradigms (e.g., behaviorism versus cognitive psychology). Finally, not only does scientific knowledge progress by paradigmatic leaps, but the various orientations are related in structurally complex manners reflecting coexisting competition and progressive differentiation and integration (see Riegel, 1969, in preparation).

5. Conclusions

The example from the history of three-dimensional representation in painting has demonstrated the interdependence of arts and sciences. This interdependence prevails throughout history: All arts are also sciences, and all sciences are also arts. During history this relationship changes in a systematic manner. Following Spengler's (1918–1922) provocative analysis, during the early periods of the history of a civilization, art dominates over science. Later on the relationship is reversed. At the point of reversal, arts and sciences find both balanced and dichotomized expressions; this condition typifies the "classical" period of a cultural–historical progression.

In concordance with these historical shifts, society demands different kinds of persons to represent different historical times. Early in history the artist and craftsman will outweigh the scientist and technician; during the classical period a balanced orientation is demanded; later in history the preference goes to the scientist–technician. Groups that fulfill the required conditions best prevail as leaders; all others fade into the background until their time arrives. Individuals who do not fulfill the demands of their time attain lesser significance and may experience their lot as personal crises. But individuals can change their affiliation. By taking such action they may create history. And even though these steps may be experienced as crises, they lead to a new consciousness and a new sense of freedom.

III. Conclusions

A. *Extrascientific Bases of the Concept of "Crisis"*

The contrastive distinction between continuous and discrete models of growth (Riegel, 1969, 1972b; van den Daele, 1969) redirects our attention towards issues raised in the early parts of this chapter. If we look at the history of sciences as a continuous accumulative growth process, crises are offensive disturbances; if we look at the history of sciences as a progression through discrete leaps, crises are necessary steps in the advancement of knowledge. Both interpretations fail to detail the reasons and causes of crises, and thus we need to extend our interpretation further. By arguing that crises are generated at the interface between different planes of progressions—especially through interactive changes along the individual– psychological and the cultural–sociological ones—we specify the advancements not only in sciences but in political history as well. Thereby we are also able to return to the discussion of crises in the life of common man.

The concept of crisis and its significance for human and societal developments are culturally determined. In Western philosophy and sciences at least two orientations can be distinguished. One conceives development as a progression by qualitative leaps and structural reorganizations. It represents the continental European way of thinking and, since Cuvrier, has been represented in the interpretations of development by Rousseau, Pestalozzi, Spranger, Piaget, and, most recently, in the writings by Velikovsky (1950, 1955). The other orientation interprets development as a continuous accumulation of bits of experience or information and deemphasizes structural reorganizations. In the words of a modern exponent of the theory of evolution: "Present continuity implies the improbablity of past catastrophism and violence of change either in the lifeless or in the living world; moreover, we seek to interpret the changes and laws of past time through those which we observe at the present time [Osborne, 1917, p. 24]." This orientation originated in Britain through the works of Lyell, Darwin, and

Galton and gained a dominant influence in the United States both in biology and in the social sciences. As I have argued elsewhere (Riegel, 1972a), the origin of these two orientations can be traced to different political and economic ideologies and need to be extended by a third or dialectic viewpoint that subordinates both as one-sided interpretations.

For the Western conceptions of continuous growth, crises do not seem to play a significant role for individuals' achievements and developments. Although the directions of their changes are not always clear individuals strive toward greater success by accumulating information in the same way as the merchant accumulates wealth. However, crises are significant in a deeper sense. More than in any of the other two interpretations, they appear as shocks and unpredictable interruptions of the process of steady expansion and enrichment. Crises are unpredictable in this case because neither inner–biological nor cultural–sociological structural sequences are interactively considered. There is only one predictable crisis for such a conception, namely, the final shock when individuals realize that they do not compete effectively any longer with younger persons; when they recognize that they are losing the struggle for survival in competition with the younger persons, the fittest.

In contrast to this orientation, the continental European viewpoint gives positive recognition to "crises" that thereby lose their deleterious character. In Piaget's theory of cognitive development, for example, the transitions from earlier periods of cognitive operations to the following ones can be considered as constructive crises. The forms of operations at different levels are not compared as one being qualitatively better or worse than the other; all of them serve their appropriate function at appropriate developmental time. Especially when extended into cross-cultural and cross-generational comparisons, such conceptions could provide a positive interpretation of actual or potential crises. Unfortunately, such extensions have been rarely proposed with theoretical rigor. In particular, Piaget's interpretations have not been successfully extended into adulthood and cross-generational comparisons. If this were attempted, serious considerations would have to be given to cultural–sociological changes as determinants of stages in adult life. At the present time, few such extensions have been proposed.

Erikson (1963) was one of the first modern writers to emphasize the codetermination of crises by inner–biological and cultural–sociological forces that initiate distinct periods in adult life. In my own extension— following the interpretations by S. L. Rubinsteijn (1958, 1963; see also Payne, 1968; Riegel, 1973a, 1975; Wozniak, 1975)—I studied the double interaction of individual-psychological conditions with inner–biological and with cultural–sociological determinants. According to such a dialectic interpretation crises are brought about by the discordance between the inner–biological order and individual–psychological development; catastrophes are brought about by the discordance between the outer–physical and the cultural–sociological progressions. While thus the concepts of crises and catastrophes attain well-defined positions, this theory also eliminates the pathological and fatalistic features so often attached to these concepts. Recognizing discordance enables us to correct it (especially by inducing changes on the individual–psychological or on the cultural–sociological plane). Under concordant conditions, crises represent steps of constructive changes aiming toward better synchronization along the different planes of progression. Crises in the constructive sense are the "knots" that tie together structural changes on the biological, psychological, cultural, and physical levels; they are also opportunities for change, and provide meaning to change.

B. Integration

The careers of common man and woman often represent deficient forms of structural developmental progressions. The major events affecting individuals are arbitrarily induced upon them by social and legal regulations, e.g., departure from school, recruitment into military service, job appointments and dismissals, and ultimately retirement. Other changes are brought about by cultural–sociological or outer–physical catastrophes, e.g., economic depressions, inflations, revolutions, and wars, or droughts, floods, fires, and earthquakes. Only the inner–biological determinants seem to follow some predictable order, first revealing the individual's maturation, the birth of children, and later his increasing proneness to incapacitation, illness, and death. Most of these events appear as crises to the individual and as catastrophes to society. They reflect a lack of synchronization between the biological, psychological, cultural, and physical event sequences. The fatalistic viewpoint, in turn, is generated by our failure to consider these progressions simultaneously, and thus to reach a more comprehensive understanding that enables us to program and coordinate them more effectively.

Among the few favored individuals, the life span of an academic scientist allows for greater structural variations and for more sensible structural transformations during his developmental progression. Since also the structure of the scientific community and its historical changes are more variable and better understood than those of most other groups, I devoted much attention to the interactive development of scientists and their scientific disciplines or subdisciplines.

Scientists in the development of their careers tentatively explicate their paradigmatic orientation through their teaching and their affiliation with a few like-minded colleagues and students. As they advance, they establish their own "scientific communes" and disseminate their ideas through reports and papers until crystallized in research routines and textbooks. The small team with which scientists affiliate represents the basis for their activities and success. But the more they advance, the more they will find recognition from other groups, which, though geographically remote, become attached to one another by their shared knowledge and technology. Eventually, the larger group might come to represent a distinct paradigmatic orientation that through its achievements creates a new constructive interpretation of a scientific theme.

As one scientific cohort succeeds, it forces others into opposition and rejects earlier ones as insufficient. The resulting conditions create conflicts for coexisting orientations and crises for the preceding ones. These discrepancies exist between the groups but are created by individuals. They affect the individual members of coexisting groups who find themselves in competition. The ideas expressed by representatives of former paradigms are regarded as outmoded and obsolete, although the individuals who represent them are not likely to accept such a judgment. If they do, they are faced with a personal crisis. For a while they will find some like-minded colleagues to lean on, but these persons might more successfully adjust to the changing conditions by moving forward in their individual careers and retreating from the laboratory into organizing and administrative duties. Finally, only the staunchest supporters are left, and they are left in a state of crisis.

Crises can be resolved by structural transformations of the individual's life in concordance with social progression. Ideally, one should outline a structural progression, as I have tried to do for the career of an academic psychologist, and implement such a model through the proper selection of assignments and allocation of resources. Such a design can be prepared only through careful observations of the changes within the scientific–social system. Therefore the study of historical progression has to be linked with the analysis of individual developmental patterns. One can depict a healthy individual progression only if one also describes the historical progression within which it takes place. And what holds for the scientist holds for any other woman or man in the array of other activities and occupations. Unfortunately—because their life styles provide lesser structural–developmental differentiations—their forms of operations are more difficult to describe. This should only induce us, however, to search harder and to become more determined to change their fate. Only when individual and societal changes are transformationally synchronized can the individual succeed in happiness and society in achievement.

REFERENCES

Balance, W. The Grundzüge revisited: A review for contemporary psychology. Paper presented at the 81st Annual Convention of the American Psychological Association, Montreal, Canada, 1973.

Blumenthal, A. *Language and psychology.* New York: Wiley, 1970.

Blumenthal, A. Wundt's psycholinguistics. Paper presented at the 81st Annual Convention of the American Psychological Association, Montreal, Canada, 1973.

Boring, E. G. *History of experimental psychology* (2nd ed.). New York: Appleton, 1957.

Brinkmann, W. The background: Wundt at Heidelberg. Paper presented at the 81st Annual Convention of the American Psychological Association, Montreal, Canada, 1973.

Buehler, C. *Der menschliche Lebenslauf als psychologisches Problem.* Leipzig: Hirzel, 1933.

Buehler, C. The developmental structure of goal setting in group and individual studies. In C. Buehler & F. Massarik (Eds.), *The course of human life.* New York: Springer, 1968.

Clayton, V. Erikson's theory of human development as it applies to the aged: Wisdom as contradictive cognition. *Human Development,* 1975, **18** (in press).

Cohen, D., & Riegel, K. F. Time as energy: On the application of modern concepts of time to developmental sciences. (unpublished report) Univ. of Southern California, Gerontology Center, 1972.

Duvall, E. M. *Family development.* (4th ed.). Philadelphia, Pennsylvania: Lippincott, 1971.

Erikson, E. H. *Childhood and society.* New York: Norton, 1963.

Galton, F. *Hereditary genius: An inquiry into its laws and consequences.* London: Macmillan, 1869.

Hogan, R. Dialectic aspects of moral development. *Human Development,* 1974, **17**, 107–117.

Jaeger, W. *Aristotles: Grundlegung einer Geschichte seiner Entwicklung.* Berlin: Weidemann, 1923.

Kimmel, D. C. *Adulthood and aging.* New York: Wiley, 1974.

Kohlberg, L. *Stages in the development of moral thought and action.* New York: Holt, 1969.

Kuhlen, R. G. Aging and life-adjustment. In J. E. Biren (Ed.), *Handbook of aging and the individual.* Chicago: Univ. of Chicago Press, 1959. Pp. 852–897.

Kuhlen, R. G. Developmental changes in motivation during the adult years. In J. E. Birren (Ed.), *Relations of development and aging.* Springfield, Illinois: Charles C. Thomas, 1964. Pp. 209–246.

Kuhn, T. *The structure of scientific revolution.* Chicago: Univ. of Chicago Press, 1962.

Lehman, H. C. *Age and achievement.* Princeton, New Jersey: Princeton Univ. Press, 1953.

McCarthy, D. Language development in children. In L. Carmichael (Ed.), *Manual of child psychology.* New York: Wiley, 1954. Pp. 492–630.

Mead, G. H. *Mind, self, and society.* (C. W. Morris, Ed.) Chicago: Chicago Univ. Press, 1934.

Mead, M. *Coming of age in Samoa.* New York: Morrow, 1928.

Neugarten, B. L., & Datan, N. Sociological perspectives of the life cycle. In P. B. Baltes & K. W. Schaie (Eds.), *Life-span developmental psychology: Personality and socialization.* New York: Academic Press, 1973. Pp. 53–69.

Osborn, H. F. *The origin and evolution of life.* New York: Scribner, 1917.

Payne, T. R. *S. L. Rubinstein and the philosophical foundations of Soviet psychology.* New York: Humanities Press, 1968.

Piaget, J. *Le langage et la pensee chez l'enfant.* Neuchatel: Delachaux & Niestle, 1923. (*The language and thought of the child.* New York: Harcourt, 1926.)

Piaget, J. *La naissance de l'intelligence chez l'enfant.* Neuchatel: Delachaux & Niestle, 1936. (*The origins of intelligence in children.* New York: International Universities Press, 1952.)

Piaget, J. *La psychologie de l'intelligence.* Paris: Armand Colin, 1947. (*The psychology of intelligence.* London: Routledge & Kegan Paul, 1950.)

Piaget, J. *Introduction a l'epistemologie genetique.* (3 vols) Paris: Presses Universitaires de France, 1950.

Piaget, J. *Les mechanisms perceptifs.* Paris: Presses Universitaires de France, 1961. (*The mechanisms of perception.* New York: Basic Books, 1968.)

Piaget, J. Comments. Supplement to Vyotsky, L. S. *Thought and language,* Cambridge, Massachusetts: MIT Press, 1962.

Piaget, J. *Le structuralisme.* Paris: Presses Universitaires de France, 1968. (*Structuralism,* New York: Basic Books, 1970.)

Piaget, J. *Genetic epistemology.* New York: Columbia Univ. Press, 1970.

Piaget, J. Intellectual evolution from adolescence to adulthood. *Human Development,* 1972, **15,** 1–12.

Riegel, K. F. History as a nomothetic science: Some generalizations from theories and research in developmental psychology. *Journal of Social Issues,* 1969, **25,** 99–127.

Riegel, K. F. The influence of economic and political ideologies upon the development of developmental psychology. *Psychological Bulletin,* 1972, **78,** 129–141. (a)

Riegel, K. F. Time and change in the development of the individual and society. In H. W. Reese (Ed.), *Advances in child development and behavior,* Vol. 7, New York: Academic Press, 1972. Pp. 81–113. (b)

Riegel, K. F. Developmental psychology and society: Some historical and ethical considerations. In J. R. Nesselroade & H. W. Reese (Eds.), *Life-span developmental psychology: Methodological issues.* New York: Academic Press, 1973. Pp. 1–23. (a)

Riegel, K. F. Dialectic operations: The final period of cognitive development. *Human Development,* 1973, **16,** 346–370. (b)

Riegel, K. F. The recall of historical events. *Behavioral Science,* 1973, **18,** 354–363. (c)

Riegel, K. F. (Ed.) The development of dialectical operations. Basal: Karger, 1975.

Riegel, K. F. Fifteen essays on the psychology of development and history. London: Plenum (in preparation).

Riley, M. W. Johnson, W., & Foner, A. (Eds.). *Aging and society, Vol. 3: A sociology of age stratifications.* New York: Russell Sage Foundation, 1972.

Rubinsteijn, S. L. *Grundlage der allgemeinen Psychologie.* Berlin: Volk und Wissen, 1958.

Rubinsteijn, S. L. *Prinzipien und Wege der Entwicklung der Psychologie.* Berlin: Akademie Verlag, 1963.

Rychlak, J. F. The multiple meanings of dialectic. Paper presented at the 18th Annual Meeting of the American Psychological Association, Honolulu, Hawaii, September, 1972.

Rychlak, J. F. (Ed.) *Dialectic: Rationale for human behavior and development.* (Contributions to Human Development, Vol. 2.) Basel: Karger, 1975 (in press).

Spengler, O. *Der Untergang des Abendlandes.* München: Beck, 1918–1922. (The decline of the West. New York: Knopf, 1946.)

van den Daele, L. Qualitative models in developmental analysis. *Developmental Psychology,* 1969, **1,** 303–310.

Velikovsky, I. *Worlds in collision.* New York: Macmillian, 1950.

Velikovsky, I. *Earth in upheaval.* New York: Doubleday, 1955.

Vygotsky, L. S. *Thought and language.* Cambridge, Massachusetts: MIT Press, 1962.

Wozniak, R. H. Dialecticism and structuralism: The philosophical foundation of Soviet psychology and Piagetian cognitive developmental theory. In K. F. Riegel & G. Rosenwald (Eds.), *Structure and transformation: Developmental and historical aspects.* New York: Wiley, 1975. Pp. 25-45.

CHAPTER 7

Crises: An Abstract Model versus Individual Experience

JAMES F. CARRUTH

WEST VIRGINIA UNIVERSITY
MORGANTOWN, WEST VIRGINIA

ABSTRACT

Adult life crises may be a continuous dialectic between individual, group, and cultural development, but Riegel's model may not illuminate the possibilities for the individual to be lost or thwarted by insufficient support or antagonism from subgroup development or cultural change. Some experiences of today's college students, women students in particular, are used to illustrate adult development frustration.

Riegel's model of adult development has outlined for us a triple interaction effect among strata of individual, biological, and psychological development; progressive patterns within social subgroup development, and the dialectic influence of historical and cultural changes. The task of the individual—and of the group—is to achieve synchrony at each challenging discordant interface of individual, social, and historical change.

I support Riegel's thesis that "crises" are too often viewed as unwanted catastrophes or conflicts. He prefers to view crises as creative development challenges with socially determined characteristics that may be studied and

perhaps modified by social scientists. In addition to giving us a broad overview of cognitive models for individual adult development, Riegel has, in
effect, extended his continuous model to deal with the complex of challenges for adult development.

Unfortunately, some of us take the first step in judging the validity of a
theoretical model in the general area of personality theory by applying it to
ourselves for "goodness of fit." Even Riegel may have fallen victim to this
when he illustrated his own model with the academic scientist in search of
new paradigms, giving me a model that I appreciate, that recognizes I am
not only dealing with biological aging, loss of self-esteem, and role changes
in my family, but also making vigorous efforts to keep abreast of my profession and working on my cosmic consciousness to relate to an aging, if not
dying, civilization. In Riegel's model, the tensions along the "interfaces" of
my triple interaction conflicts are painful but *normal* concomitants of rees-
tablishing personal synchrony and, I hope, a creative renewal of me. In
short, it is not catastrophe, just growing pains: That has a nice youthful
ring.

But has the model some utility in explaining or describing the experiences
of other individuals than oneself? Will it contribute to social modifications
that are facilitative to individual personality development? I do not claim
such prescience, but as a clinical psychologist working at a counseling center with developmental problems of college students, I cannot help but put
content in the model and ask questions of application.

To me, today's graduating college students illustrate the impact of social
and historical developmental progressions. These students also demonstrate
that Riegel's model does not eliminate the possibilities of real crises and
catastrophes. Our middle class young men and women, conditioned to affluence and perhaps the pleasure of prolonged adolescence, are now facing
severe asynchrony. Graduate programs do not welcome them. Employers
are not seeking them. Economic agony and hard times are upon us. Culturally, monogamous pairing is under severe attack and children are not
wanted. The interaction of adolescent self-actualization goals, the economy,
and people pollution do not support parenting: Increasingly, developmental
psychologists focus on adults.

In the broader cultural context, faith in family, school, and church are
long gone. Faith in corporation and government are disappearing over the
horizon.

Women are being pressed to experience sex like men and, in fact, develop
machismo. Men are encouraged to experience their "feminine" needs. Ra-
cial and cultural differences are being alternately revived or denied. Gueril-
la violence or cynical apathy seemingly increase. How do these phenomena
fit Riegel's optimistic model of development?

Riegel has reaffirmed that frustration, whether derived from individual or social change, leads to new problem-solving efforts and learning, and therefore is developmental. Conflict may lead to new levels of complexity and maturity, and this is a positive alternative to withdrawal behaviors or some other form of developmental arrest. Riegel is trying to help us toward a mature level of theorizing by looking at interaction effects but has of necessity overlooked the actual content of our personal, social, and historical time.

Use of the academic scientist pattern as an illustration has some limitations. The developmental challenge is not only a cognitive one, as in the creation of new paradigms. There is also a more general identity change for the individual as well as the group, which is changing as universities change. Both personally and professionally, the male professor traditionally moved from youthful challenges to productive father to wise and perhaps creative grandfather. It is questionable whether ex-academic Benjamin Spock is more interesting for his contributions 20 years ago or for his social action against the Vietnam war. Spock, as a grandfather, has created a new paradigm but has also left the medical profession and become political.

As I have indicated, Riegel's theoretical model has been illustrated as if it were a masculine model with little application to women. However, additional considerations arise through the study of conflicts women experience in psychosocial development within the changing group norms of today's culture. My own clinical observations of women clients and nonclients in a counseling service for a relatively conventional state university population might be illustrative. Our experiences reflect that the developmental tasks of women undergo increasingly severe crises at the college and postcollege levels.

Dana Farnsworth (1966) outlined some important developmental tasks for college students in general, including autonomy, competence, and self-esteem. The changing interpretations of these objectives for women students appear to me to be causing special problems in resolving these tasks with real personality growth. These observations are based on my work with female college students, which suggests that up to the time of university entrance perhaps 80% have been reinforced directly and indirectly during school and family experiences to base primary self-esteem on male admiration. Other competencies are insufficient to maintain full self-esteem. As a corollary, the counseling center staff anticipates that women's anger at dependency on parents and males and at their own helplessness is increasing.

Nevertheless, many women students appear still vulnerable to interpreting male controlling behavior as strength. Thus seeking a strong (i.e., controlling) male to pair with and respect leads to baffling and severe disappointment. Increasingly women students appear to be seeking to satisfy relationship, dependency, and affectional needs through sexual relationships. In short, young women are having more trouble than ever in shifting to genuine adult role relationships from the detested childlike dependency they feel trained for. The apparent "adult" behaviors—e.g., rejecting any dependency and seeking casual sexual freedom and assertive careers—are often frightening and potentially unsatisfying.

These observations were partially supported by a random sample of interviews with nonclient students we accomplished as part of a larger study (Morrill, Oetting, & Hust, 1974), and by an unpublished replication done by students (Koppelman, Toothman, Porterfield, & Stark, 1974).

Perhaps the shock wave of change has come and gone and the dialectic process is now at work. In a survey of graduating students at West Virginia University in May, 1974 there may be some evidence of change as well as an underlying stability. There are still significant sex differences operating in favor of males. Out of our total sample of 900 graduating men and women at all degree levels, women were mainly represented at the bachelor's and master's level and practically nonexistent in professional degrees, law, medicine, dentistry, engineering. More women were uncertain about their job futures, or looking for work. None were planning on self-employment, professional practice, or small business. Only 15% were expecting to make $10,000 or more, whereas 41% of the males were planning on larger incomes. However, only 1% of women planned only for marriage and family.

In our total sample, 67% were engaged or married, and it was primarily in this marriage-oriented subsample that signs of change might be found. Seventeen percent of the women responded that their jobs were going to determine where both worked. For those couples without jobs, 57% of women said location of work would be determined by first spouse getting a job and 58% of men said it would not. Fifty-eight percent of women said they expected to work in different communities, if necessary, and 58% of men said they would not.

Of course, these data can only be suggestive because they are based on a general return from 38% of graduating students in a state university. Furthermore, the questions were limited and the answers speculative. However, they do reflect that even though the individual crises may be severe, the group is resistant to rapid change.

Women in particular may be struggling to change personal and interpersonal identity, and failing to modify their views about marriage, jobs, and incomes. The dilemma may be illustrated by women's responses in a developmental seminar conducted by Phillip Comer of the counseling center staff. Comer reports the students as bright, assertive women who completely endorsed autonomy, career, deemphasis on family, and equal competition with men. However, they also endorsed pairing—only with more independent, stronger, higher salaried men they could look up to!

We might speculate that the majority of our women are not confronted with groups and cultural change until they are already young adults, having received little modeling or direct reinforcement in the past. Perhaps they receive little even after the shock wave of change. However, we can hope for glimpses at Riegel's dialectic process at the group and individual level, even as we are concerned about the developmental tasks of identity, competence, and self-esteem. Group developmental changes may meet interactions with individual resistances as well as resistant social structure.

The problem for the individual adult is that he is continually attempting to apply laboriously acquired personal values to a constantly changing set of problems and interpersonal and group relationships. Possibilities for progress or peril derive from the fact that nothing progresses in synchrony. We may be tempted to resist forward movement, and to cling to consistencies in the face of new psychological situations so that we can say, "Here we are!" Adult crises may be magnified when individuals are poorly prepared by their social structure, whether it be family, school, or socioeconomic organization, or when they are poorly supported as adults by our institutions.

Furthermore, the developmental phases of childhood may be modified by changing cultural patterns. We can overprotect our children, and fail to teach them delay of gratification because of recent affluence. We can teach them there is no tomorrow of adult responsibility because they remain adolescents in school: Perhaps these factors have shaped recent trends toward the rejection of parenthood.

I have stressed my fears in this exploration of Riegel's thoughtful overview and model. I hope Riegel is correct in his optimism and stress on the positive dialectic patterns of adult development. I too am an optimist, but a frightened one; and my work with individuals who are struggling not only nurtures my hope but also fuels my concern. In my opinion, Riegel's model is an attractive view of the complexities of adult development, incorporating the developmental patterns of individual, group, and culture. It is a sophisticated attempt to reconcile internal and external events in the growth of persons. However, it also may be applied to the destructive interactions between an individual's stage of developmental changes within his major subgroups and historical forces. Riegel's perspective of a continuous model does not exclude the possibilities for Eriksonian polarities at critical phases (Erikson, 1963). We may hope that the majority of individuals and groups will respond to interactive developmental conflicts with some levels of synchronizing growth. But, as one who has developed through shame, guilt, inferiority, role confusion, and, so far, avoided despair, I am forced to remind my readers that there are individual and group crises and failures to resolve them positively.

REFERENCES

Erikson, E.H. *Childhood and society* (2nd Ed.) New York: 1963.
Farnsworth, D.L. *Psychiatry, education and the young adult.* Springfield, Illinois: Charles C Thomas, 1966.
Koppelman, D., Toothman, M., Porterfield, M. S., & Stark, R. *Outreach by structured interview: Follow-up by student pollers.* Student Counseling Service Reports, Vol. II, No. 4, West Virginia Univ., 1974 (unpublished).
Morrill, W. H., Oetting, E. R., & Hust, J. C. (Eds.) *Nine outreach-developmental programs in college counseling centers.* Final Report submitted to National Institute of Mental Health, Applied Research Branch, MH 18007, Colorado State Univ., 1974.

CHAPTER 8

Adaptive Processes in Late Life

MORTON A. LIEBERMAN

THE UNIVERSITY OF CHICAGO
CHICAGO, ILLINOIS

ABSTRACT

This chapter presents a model for predicting adaptational success/failure of the elderly under crises. The predictive framework examines the elderly from the perspectives of resources, current functioning, social support, life stress, crises management techniques, degree of threat, threat and loss management strategies, and amount of current stress. The framework is used to examine the question: Why do some individuals adapt better than others to the crises associated with the last phase of life? The nature and effects of two central crises are empirically assessed: loss and adaptive demands. Findings from four studies representing 870 elderly before and after they underwent radical shifts in living arrangements (the stress situation) are discussed in regard to: (a) differential effects of loss-related crises and crises generated from situations demanding change in previous coping strategies and life styles; (b) differences between successful adaptive strategies of the aged contrasted to those of younger populations; and (c) the relative predictive power of the various social and psychological indices in predicting failures of adaptation.

To begin with a simple question does not necessarily ensure that investigation will yield a simple answer. I initiated studies of old people with what I thought to be a simple question: Why do some people adapt better than others to the crises associated with the last phase of life? The course of human life can be described by a series of events or crises that require adaptive effort. Examples of such "life crises" are legion; they include the entrance of the young child into school (Lindemann & Ross, 1955; Kellam & Schiff, 1967; Kellam, 1969; Klein & Ross, 1965), adolescence (Barthell & Holmes, 1968; Melges, Anderson, & Tinklenberg, 1969; Marcia, 1966, 1967; Brosin, 1964; Musgrove, 1964; Remmers, 1962), college entrance (Silber, Coelho, Murphey, Hamburg, Pearlin, & Rosenberg, 1961; Silber, Hamburg, Coelho, Murphey, Rosenberg, & Pearlin, 1961; Coelho, Silber, & Hamburg, 1962; Stern, Stein, & Bloom, 1956; Levin, 1967), serious illness (Visotsky, Hamburg, Goss, & Lebovits, 1961; Janis,1958; Abram, 1965; Andrew, 1967; Chodoff, Friedman, & Hamburg, 1964), marriage (Raush, Goodrich, & Campbell, 1963), parenthood (Caplan, 1960; Kaplan, 1965), migration (Bower, 1966; Gfzi, 1965; Levine, 1966), natural disasters (Clifford, 1956; Perry, Silber, & Block, 1956), institutionalization in old age (Lieberman, Prock, & Tobin, 1968), and so forth. Our everyday observations about people suggest that no matter what the stage of life or what the event, we can always point to some individuals who seem to grow as a result of the crisis, other individuals who appear to handle the situation without showing any marked effects, and still others who wither—who cannot cope, who experience severe psychological distress or become somatically impaired.

Although many investigators have examined adaptive,or coping, processes, it is not easy to delineate the boundaries of this area of inquiry. My own interest in adaptation, or coping, processes has led me to ask myself who are my relevant colleagues, on whose work do I attempt to build, what theories may I salute. The fact of the matter is that in current day psychology, interest in coping is so broadly conceived and so variously studied that it is difficult to label it as a distinct area of inquiry.

Are the massive number and varied types of empirical studies of coping examining similar questions? Indeed, that is where my simple interest in adaptation has led me and where I find myself still more groping than coping. Is the investigator who is interested in how well a person adapts to a benign new situation—be it the Peace Corps, kindergarten, college, a new job, or whatever—exploring the same question as one who studies people in severe crises—the parents of fatally ill children, victims of natural disasters, people undergoing widowhood or other major losses? The literature (Coelho, Hamburg, Moos, & Randolph, 1970) would suggest that they are not. Even when examining similar life events, some investigators have taken adaptation to mean growth, that is, heightened ability or effectiveness to operate in a new set of circumstances; others have measured coping by asking whether the individual has maintained homeostasis, has not broken down; still others have associated capacity to cope with the individual's ability to expand his own inner sense of worth and satisfaction. Some examples may help to illustrate the diversity of orientations toward the meaning of adaptation or coping.

Wolff, Friedman, Hofer, and Mason (1964) studied parents of fatally ill children. Parents were considered to be effectively defended if (1) they demonstrated little or no overt distress; (2) they showed little or no impairment in everyday functioning; and (3) they demonstrated the ability to mobilize their defenses further against superimposed, acutely stressful experiences. In other words, effective coping was the ability not to be overwhelmed by tension and to be able to function adequately. In studying parents' efforts at coping with delinquency in their children, Hurwitz, Kaplan, and Kaiser (1965) used the criterion of whether the families acted constructively or destructively in court appearances related to the delinquency of their children. These two studies are examples in which successful adaptation is defined as a response to a negative event. For Wolff *et al.* successful coping was defined as maintenance of homeostasis; in the other study, role performance under crisis. Other investigators have examined situations that are not so clearly negative. Smith (1966), for example, in his study of Peace Corps volunteers, addressed himself to the issue of competence in job performance.

The concepts of competence, effectiveness, mastery, subjective experience of well-being, and homeostasis recur throughout the vast and varied theoretical and empirical literature on adaptive processes. Two major themes are apparent. One theme assesses the adaptive process in terms of such concepts as mastery and competence. The person responds to the demands created by the event or condition at issue by meeting them above the level he had heretofore achieved. A simple example might be a study of children entering school for the first time. Successful adaptation is more likely to be viewed in terms of the child's ability to meet the demands of the situation by employing behaviors that may not have been in his repertoire before. He is expected to act or behave above the level required in the home situation. He must "learn" new mechanisms to cope with a more complex social system, to relate to larger groups of people, to deal with peers, unfamiliar adults, and so forth. Competence, in a situation of this order, implies more than the ability not to break down (regress, withdraw, be emotionally upset). Investigation of such events tends to be directed toward the identification of behaviors that were not previously in the individual's repertoire. The second way adaptive processes are often assessed in the coping literature is in terms of the absence of breakdown. Here the usual concern is with whether a person meets the demands of the new condition without showing signs of psychological distress or functional inability. The person is considered to adapt if he deals with the new set of demands by maintaining a homeostatic level.

This diversity of perspectives for examining adaptation is particularly important to those interested in personality over the life span, for it raises the question of whether it is possible to develop unified concepts that would allow fruitful investigation of adaptation over the life span. If coping or adaptation has thus far been so diversely defined, can successful adaptation at different stages of life be compared? Can general criteria of coping adequacy be determined which would allow different stages of life to be studied in a uniform way? The investigator who attempts to generate broad criteria that permit comparisons across life stages finds himself faced with the problem that his assessment criteria become less accurate for situation-specific prediction.

A second problem facing the investigator interested in adaptational processes is to decide under what conditions he will study such processes. Even if we limit such study to people in real-life situations (rather than in controlled laboratory experiments), the investigator still must choose which life situations or events he will use to study coping processes. Perhaps the initial choice must be made with reference to base rates. Life events such as retirement, widowhood, migration, menopause, "empty nest" can be surveyed to estimate how many individuals are likely to be affected by them. One of course might say: Choose events that happen to everyone. This would make sense if we were only interested in general patterns of adaptation to such common life events. The problem is that though such events all may elicit coping behavior, they are likely to differ radically with regard to the number of individuals who will show signs of failure to cope. The next approach might be to look for a situation in which there are reasonable base rates of failure. Such a decision raises other conceptual and strategic issues, however. Situations that produce such large numbers of adaptive failures are, to introduce another still relatively unspecified concept, situations of high stress. Is it reasonable to assume that the ability to adapt successfully to everyday life issues is related to the ability to adapt to extreme situations? Does the individual who is able to cope successfully with the exigencies of combat, for example,use the same processes with relatively the same degree of success to cope with more common transitional crises, such as parenthood? *Are the same traits, processes, or qualities of the person of equivalent value in all coping situations?*

A third problem faces the investigator who wishes to account for the vast individual differences in adaptive success. What characteristics of the person and social circumstances will he study in order to predict such individual differences? If we sidestep for a moment the obvious response of adopting extant theoretical models (which are plentiful in the field) and turn rather to the status of investigative findings, they can be summarized quite easily. The prediction of successful coping or adaptation has met with limited but consistent success by large groups of investigators using different theoretical models, different measures, and different views about what constitutes successful coping (Moos, 1974). In other words, the empirical base in this area is broad and marked by numerous limited successes, if we take success to mean prediction of individual differences. Thus, selection of person characteristics for study of stress adaptation represents another source of complexity when examining current knowledge in the field with a view to life-span comparisons.

I On the Nature of Crisis

By and large adaptive processes have been studied under conditions of high stress rather than in everyday life. One consequence of this research strategy is that it limits the response repertoire observed. Crises can be defined as highly demanding situations in which the individual must adjust his behavior to a new set of circumstances. Crises are events that elicit in the person subjective experiences of control and loss. Generally, most of those events considered crises are of two major types: events associated with *loss,* a subjective experience associated with a break in previous attachments to persons, places, or things; and situations that *disrupt the customary modes of behavior* of the people concerned, which alter both their circumstances and their plans and impose a need for strenuous psychological work. They present the individual with the opportunity and obligation to abandon many assumptions and to replace them with others, thereby constituting a challenge. The bulk of studies in the area of adaptive processes concern such crises. The division of crisis situations into these two broad classes of loss and accommodation to significant change in circumstances has some important analytic implications, but it must be emphasized that in real life they are usually inextricably intertwined. Perhaps the best example of their interdependence can be found in studies of reaction to widowhood. The processes defining loss are most clearly seen and studied in bereavement.

> In any bereavement, it is seldom clear exactly what is lost. The loss of a husband, for instance, may or may not mean the loss of sexual partner, companion, accountant, gardener, baby-minder, audience, bed-warmer, and so on, depending upon the particular roles normally performed by this husband. Moreover, one loss often brings other secondary losses in its train. The loss of a husband is usually accompanied by

a considerable drop in income, and this often means that the widow must sell her house, give up her job, and move to a strange environment. The need to learn new roles without the support of the person upon whom one has come to rely, at a time when others in the family, especially children, are themselves bereaved and needing support, can place a major burden on a woman over and above the fact of bereavement itself. . . .

Apart from grief, two other factors that always play a part in determining the overall reaction to a bereavement are *stigma* and *deprivation*. By *stigma* I mean the change in attitude that takes place in the society when a person dies. Every widow discovers that people who were previously friendly and approachable become embarrassed and estranged in their presence. Expressions of sympathy often have a hollow ring and offers of help are not followed up. It often happens that only those who share the grief or have themselves suffered a major loss remain at hand. It is as if the widow has become tainted with death in much the same way as the funeral director. . . .

Deprivation implies the absence of a necessary person or thing as opposed to loss of that person or thing. A bereaved person reacts to both loss and deprivation. Deprivation means the absence of those essential "supplies" that were previously provided by the lost person [Parkes, 1972, pp. 7–9].

Even in such a clear situation as bereavement the nature of the stress or the crisis is complex and not only involves the loss of a significant other, but also entails numerous other sources of stress or strain on the person requiring adaptive behavior. Although they may be analytically distinct, loss and other sources of strain are often intertwined in real life. Our attempt in the studies to be discussed has been, however, to examine adaptive processes in circumstances where they can be analytically distinguished.

My work on adaptive processes has been related to identifying those that older people use to cope with two central forms of crisis: loss and radical changes in life space. The question is whether the adaptive processes involved in both these types of stress (stress associated with loss and stress stemming from new adaptive requirements) can be examined through the same framework. Are generalizations about adaptive processes possible, or must one consider the particular nature of the stress before one can talk intelligently about the processes by which people cope? Underlying such a question is the issue of whether it is reasonable to conceptualize about personality over the life span in terms of individuals who possess good adaptive characteristics and others who do not. Can one look at humans this way or are the abilities to cope successfully more specific to particular circumstances, making efforts to arrive at explanations across various life crises a fruitless search? To examine adaptive processes, my colleagues and I have, over the years, studied a total of 870 old people before and after they underwent radical shifts in living arrangements and concomitant additional dimensions of their life space. This choice of life stage and of type of crisis was predicated on three considerations:

1. That radical changes confront the vast majority of aged with a stress of enough severity to affect a significant portion of the sample.

2. That it was possible to study the individuals in depth prior to the stress—an important consideration inasmuch as many studies of coping or adaptation involve the examination of individuals only during or subsequent to the stress event, making it difficult to differentiate stress reaction from characteristics of persons that can predict adaptive processes.

3. That changes represent the crucial elements involved in all crisis situations—loss and the demand to adapt to an altered set of circumstances.

In all, we have conducted four major studies of elderly persons who underwent radical changes in their life spaces.[1] One of these studies included an examination of healthy elderly persons moving into top-quality institutional facilities; another involved sick, highly debilitated human beings moving into circumstances that would delight a muckraker. Two of the four studies examined aged persons who were mentally and physically comparable to the elderly living in the community; two involved populations of aged persons who were still or had formerly been mentally ill. The range of psychological and physical resources in the four populations studied is considerable, as is that of the conditions under which the environmental changes occurred. In the initial *transfer study*, physically healthy and psychologically robust elderly women were studied when they were forced to move from a small, hotel-like institution to a larger, quasi-military institution for the aged. In the *institutionalization study*, community-dwelling aged persons were studied as they voluntarily entered homes for the aged, to meet physical or social needs. In the *therapeutic transfer study*, a highly selected group of geriatric patients were studied as they were prepared for discharge from a mental hospital to a variety of community-based institutional and semi-institutional settings. The *mass transfer study*, finally, examined 470 geriatric patients who were relocated en masse from a state mental hospital to a variety of other institutional settings. Some of these cases were ready for therapeutic discharge; others were relocated only because the

[1] The empirical research described in this chapter is based upon four studies: The Old Age Home Transfer Study (Wilmington-Quincy), Morton A. Lieberman, principal investigator, and the Institutionalization Study, Morton A. Lieberman, principal investigator, and Sheldon S. Tobin, project director; both were supported by a Public Health Service Research Grant, #HD–00364, from the National Institute of Child Health and Human Development. The Therapeutic Transfer Study (Manteno State Hospital), Morton A. Lieberman and Sheldon Tobin, co-principal investigators, and Darrell Slover, project director, was supported by a Department of Mental Health, State of Illinois, grant, #17–328. The Mass Relocation Study (Modesto State Hospital), Morton A. Lieberman and Roberta Marlowe, co-principal investigators, was supported by a grant from the Department of Mental Hygiene, State of California.

institution was to be closed down. Although the last two studies both involved mental hospital patients, in the first case the subjects were highly selected, physically healthy "therapeutic discharges." The final study involved the total population of a state mental hospital, including both physically and mentally deteriorated individuals, as well as others who were to be therapeutically discharged to community residence.

The basic design in all four studies was similar. Individuals (and in the mass transfer and institutionalization studies, matched controls) were examined up to a year prior to being moved from one home to another and studied again one year after environmental change. In one study (institutionalization), individuals were also examined during the transition period, that is, a month before and a month after environmental change. Although the techniques of measuring successful or unsuccessful adaptation to the crisis varied from study to study, they were all directed toward answering the same question: whether the individual, subsequent to being moved, departed in major ways from his prior physiological, behavioral, and psychological status. Was his level of competence—his ability to adapt—reduced (or enhanced)? A preview of the general findings reaped from all four studies may provide appropriate background for the framework we are about to suggest for viewing questions of this nature regarding the adaptive process. Marked declines, major changes in the homeostasis of the individual—behaviorally, physically (including death), socially, or psychologically—ranged from a low of 48% to a high of 56%. The frequency of adaptive failure was consistently high no matter what the particular populations studied or the particular conditions under which the person altered his life circumstances. The rate of change for controls, individuals not involved in major environmental upheavals, was considerably lower—for example, in the mass transfer study, which had the best control group situation, death rates for those involved in environmental change were triple those of matched controls who did not undergo environmental upheavals.

How then do we understand why it is that some of those studied were able to cope adequately with a situation that appears to be a major crisis while others were not?

II.   A Framework for Looking at Hypotheses Relevant to Discriminating between Successful and Unsuccessful Adaptation

I have organized my thinking about people under stress into a series of interrelated questions that provide a framework for examining characteristics of the person and the situation that are relevant to predicting differences in adaptation to crises. What will be portrayed in this framework is a series of interrelated and overlapping "templates" for examining individual differences. Although these are static templates, alternative ways of looking at people, the model is asymmetric in that processes later in the chain are assumed to be dependent on those appearing earlier. Figure 1 shows a schematic overview of the framework.

A. Resources

The model begins with the notion that individuals differ in their psychological and biological resources and that when confronted with situations that require major adaptive effort, differences in success will depend upon the resources available to the person in the face of the situational demands. The resources available to a person set limits on the processes the person can employ for coping. This orientation implies that there is no point to examining a process such as threat appraisal without examining whether the person has the cognitive resources required to appraise the situation. The inability of a person to differentiate among environmental stimuli limits his ability to assess the possible constraints and opportunities within the environment for adaptation, thus limiting the range of coping strategies he is likely to develop. Or, to cite another example, if one can speak of various coping strategies as requiring certain levels of energy expenditure, before one could ask about various consequences of different coping or defense strategies one would have to know something about the capacity of the person to mobilize energy.

When individual capacities have been discussed with regard to stress and adaptation, two concepts have recurred throughout the literature: ego strength and impulse control. Ego strength has been conceptualized as an indicator of capacity for perceiving external reality as well as for dealing with internal impulses and pushes. It reflects the ability to integrate internal needs and external reality so that the executive capacities of the ego are freed for coping with demanding events. Closely related to ego strength as a construct is impulse control, which has been used, for example, by Werner's students (Schaib, 1962) to characterize the level of coping ability. Such studies assume that those individuals who have arrived at higher levels of cognitive development as assessed by impulse control capacity have more resources for coping with stressors in the environment. Our own approach to the resource issue has been to fractionate these rather broad concepts into more specific functions that serve as underpinnings to the concept of ego strength, a notion that is more specifically assessed when considering the current functioning of the individual.

In our own studies of the elderly, three basic resource areas were as-

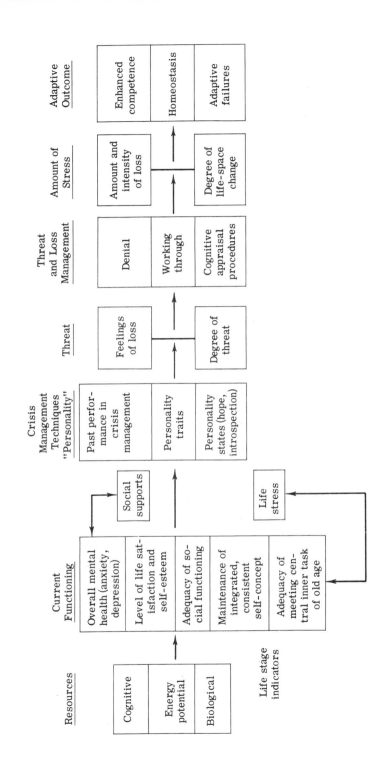

Fig. 1. Predictive framework.

144

sessed: the cognitive, physical, and energy outputs of the individual. The ability to take in, process, store, and recall information; the ability of the person to orient himself in time and place and to organize complex information; the ability to accomplish cognitive shifts—all these are probably abilities that are required to appraise threat accurately and realistically, so that coping strategies can be organized and carried out. In this sense, the level of cognitive functioning probably sets the floor or lower limit on coping. Poor cognitive functioning should be related to inability to adapt to stress; adequate cognitive functioning would not, on the other hand, necessarily ensure adequate coping. The decrements associated with aging with regard to the processing and particularly the speed of processing information, however, suggest that for old people cognitive capacity would become central in ability to adapt to stress.

Health status is not ordinarily considered in most human stress studies. Those who have considered psychological functioning in response to stress adaptation have viewed adaptation in relation to specific psychological mechanisms, or they have examined adaptation relative to differences in physiological types. How the physical status of the individual affects or is affected by psychological processes is still, after so many years, an open question. In the area of aging, however, one can hardly ignore the question of physical capacity. As Selye has suggested, the ability to maintain physical integration is rapidly exhausted as the organism ages. Although we may not understand the processes, it seems reasonable to think the physical capacities of the aged person set a limit on his ability to adapt. Previous findings such as those of Birren, Butler, Greenhouse, Solokoff, and Yarrow (1970) suggest that although psychological and social functions are largely unrelated to somatic functioning in relatively healthy aged persons, greater interrelationship of these functions is observed when some critical limiting level of physical capacity is reached. Like cognitive functioning, physical capacity is seen in our framework as a limiting condition. For the older person who is relatively adequate in physical capacity, the question of predicting the effects of stress must be related to other, more complex processes. At the lower limits the physical capacity, at least for older people, may be the most important and perhaps the only salient predictor of adaptive failure.

Popular conceptions of the aging process assume diminished energy during the last phase of life. Such a simple observation might of course relate to several perhaps more discrete aspects of the aging process. The observation may reflect actual decrease in physical energy or the increase in depressive affect that so often accompanies the aging process. As a psychological concept, energy has been primarily employed in psychoanalytic theory and ego psychology. The concept of psychological energy has been varyingly fash-

ionable in psychology, possibly because it has been peculiarly unresponsive
to measurement. Despite the serious limitations of measurement technology, three measures (which were of limited value) were developed to assess
this potentially important aspect of human functioning in relation to stress
adaptation.

Three simple conditions underlying adaptive capacity have been discussed: the physical, cognitive, and energy potentials of the person. Our
model would suggest that in our attempt to understand the adaptive process
these three capacities of humans form the floor that defines how and if
other more complex processes will be employed. In other words, limitation
in any one of these three capacities would be predictive of inadequate adaptation or unsuccessful adaptation, but sufficient capacity would not predict
successful adaptation.

B. Adequacy of Current Functioning

Predictions about ability to cope with future stress are facilitated by
knowledge of how well an individual functions in the absence of stress,
since such information affords some clues about what resources the individual possesses. The assessment of how well someone normally functions in
turn requires information about whether his current environment is harmo-
nious or stressful. Thus in order to answer with any degree of accuracy how
well a person is currently doing, both the stress on the person and the social
resources around him must be gauged.

The contextual issue becomes clearer if we look at the various forms
responses to the question of how well the person is functioning may take.

An operationalized concept of psychological health offers one general
perspective for calibrating overall functioning. In order to make such an
assessment of our elderly respondents, individual differences in psychological health/psychological maladjustment were assessed using the Block Q-
Sort (1961). This measure is akin in many ways to the concept of ego
strength, which has been found by many investigators to be a proven predictor of adequacy of stress coping. The items in the Q-Sort represent a
wide range of feelings, attitudes, interpersonal characteristics, symptoms,
and moods. Underlying these various behavioral descriptions are the essential ingredients of a concept of psychological health which involves impulse
control, flexibility, meaningful relationships to other human beings, positive
view of self and others, and the absence of incapacitating symptoms. Two
other indices were used to obtain an assessment of the individual's mental
health. Measures of anxiety and of depression have been shown by several
investigators to be relatively precise indicators of current functioning as
well as predictors of future adaptation to crisis.

No matter how broadly the concept of mental health is defined, it certainly does not offer the only perspective for assessing how well people are doing. Many investigators contend that the most reasonable way of assessing how well a person is functioning at any given time is to ask him. The concepts of gratification or satisfaction and the related concepts of happiness and positive self-view were also operationalized in our assessment procedures.

A third approach to examining how well an individual is functioning is to look at the extent, range, and quality of his interpersonal relationships. It should be emphasized that both the nature of the person's interpersonal relationships and the level of happiness and self-esteem are in general ways included in the more inclusive concept of psychological health. Thus one would expect overlap but not identity in these different assessment perspectives.

There is no dearth of approaches for assessing adequate functioning. Measures of performance, be they in school or at work, are obvious and often-used criteria. Other perspectives articulate a developmental model and base assessment on how well the person is able to meet psychological issues central to particular life stages. In contrast to the other perspectives on adequate functioning—psychological health, happiness, self-esteem, and social interaction—developmentally based criteria do not require the assumption of absolute levels without respect to life stage. Some of the normative changes associated with aging—lowered status, income reduction, and physical limitations—pose a crucial problem for the aged, maintaining an acceptable and consistent self-image. In our framework it was assumed that people need to maintain a consistent and recognizable self-concept despite such changes. How well a person is able to maintain such a stable self-image and how he accomplishes this task were taken as an index of adequate functioning.

Some theorists have posited reminiscence to be a central process in psychological functioning during old age. Erikson (1963) has proposed that the acceptance of one's own life history is a primary task if he is to age successfully and come to terms with death. A useful approach to answering the question of how well a person is functioning is to provide a developmentally based perspective on the central psychological inner task associated with the last decade of life.

These five perspectives on the adequacy of functioning—mental health, happiness, social interaction, maintenance of a coherent and consistent self-concept, and how the person responds to the central task of old age (reminiscence)—are closely tied to social context. To assess realistically the predictive power of these indices of current functioning the predictive framework must also take into account the characteristics and qualities of the social supports around the person, for they are factors that most assuredly affect the measurement of many, if not all, five indicators of successful functioning. The ability to maintain a consistent, coherent self-image, for example, depends to some degree on what kind of feedback (or how much) the person is getting from his social environment. Or, to cite another example, inherent in the definition of psychological health are implications about the nature and kind of relationships the person establishes with others. Yet to say that social supports affect measures of psychological health does not guarantee that cause–effect relationships between adequacy of psychological functioning and social supports can be isolated.

Degree of stress—the other end of the social pole from support—is another aspect of a person's social context which affects the psychological well-being of the person. Clearly, both current and anticipated life events are crucial social determinants of the current psychological functioning of the person. How well a person is doing may depend upon the particular stresses and strains he is currently experiencing. Accordingly, assessments of current stresses on the person, the number and kind of life changes during the past several years in a person's life, and the cumulative life stress experienced over the life span are entered into the prediction framework. Considerable work by many investigators on life change as a stressor has indicated the predictive utility of such measures in assessing subsequent adaptive failures.

C. Procedures for Managing Crises

So far we have discussed the resources a person can bring to bear on the adaptive process and have outlined ways for examining current functioning which include characteristics both of the person and of his life context. We have not as yet considered how the person typically copes with crises. Individuals differ immensely in their preferred coping modes. These differences among people mean that the prediction of adaptive capacity must take into account variation in personal processes or styles people bring to bear under crisis conditions. We must ask, in other words, what characteristic methods the person uses to handle both the alloplastic and autoplastic adjustments required by the crisis. We are asking how the individual deploys his resources, how he acts upon himself and the world around him when he must accommodate to crisis conditions.

The underlying reason for assessing crisis management is to determine what procedures a person is likely to bring to bear in meeting a future crisis. The literature on coping and adaptation suggests that investigators have employed several strategies for such an assessment. In general, a person's relevant past behaviors tend to be the best predictors of his future behavior in similar situations. It is increasingly evident that even simple, crude demographic indices of an individual's past behavior and social competence predict his future behavior at least as well as, and sometimes better than, personality tests or clinical judgments. Such a perspective, of course, implies that reasonable continuity of personality exists, so that future crises are likely to elicit the same response pattern a person has used in the past. The crucial task is the determination of equivalents of crises in the environmental context, for predictions of long-term outcomes for persons in heterogeneous and completely uncontrolled environments have been shown to be especially poor.

Another strategy is to assess traits or states of the person. This approach begins with asking the question: What sorts of dispositions exist in the person with regard to traits assumed to be relevant to crisis management? Both approaches—examining the person's history of crisis management and examining relevant current dispositions—assume that the person is likely to utilize similar processes to manage future crises. We have studied a variety of personality traits—generalized dispositions to behave in particular ways—as well as several processes hypothesized to be crucial in crisis management. Among the traits assessed were dominance, submissiveness, and narcissim. Several processes such as hope and introspection were examined. Hope is conceived of as a process of time-binding, a crucial asset in stress adaptation. Similarly, introspection was identified as the propensity of people to utilize inner state informational cues that can lead to increased mobilization of resources for stress adaptation. These generalized dispositions are predictions about what resources and what processes a person might bring to managing a crisis situation; they do not provide information on how the person will manage a specific crisis.

D. Threat and the Management of Threat

Many recent studies of stress adaptation focus on the psychological reactions of the person toward the impending crisis or threat. In order to explain and predict individual differences in reaction to crisis, we examined anticipatory processes used to cope with threat. We asked what meaning the crisis had for the person, to what extent he was experiencing threat and anticipating loss, and how he handled these issues. We attempted to separate the processes the person brought to bear in managing threat from the intensity of the threat itself. Although obviously intertwined, analytic methods were developed that could, in part, distinguish the coping procedures from the intensity of the threat; one set of procedures was addressed to loss, the other to general effects of anticipated change.

The degree of loss was assessed through direct questions about the person's phenomenological experience, through indirect measures of the degree to which the person was imbedded in a meaningful social network (where we assumed that degree of imbeddedness implied high loss), and through projective measures of early memory themes. (This last measure has been partially validated as a measure of intensity of loss; repeated use of the instrument over time demonstrated that early memory themes of loss increase as a person approaches entrance into an institution and become higher once he actually enters the institution.)

Threat themes associated with the anticipated relocation were assessed through a discrepancy measure based upon performance criteria in response to two sets of TAT cards, the standard Murray set and a specially constructed TAT depicting older people in situations associated with moving or with aspects of the new environment assumed to be problematical. The respondent's ability to deal with the institutional TAT cards was compared to his ability to deal with the Murray series of TAT cards. Poor performance in the former was interpreted to indicate relatively high levels of threat. This measure was partially validated by examining community elderly who achieved similar mean scores for both sets of cards.

Similarly to the examination of personality dispositions, we asked, for example, to what degree the individual attempted to master the threat, to what degree he succumbed to the threat, and what coping or defense strategy he brought to bear in managing the threat situation. Did he, for example, deny or shut out of awareness the impending event, as constrasted with what has been called a "working through process"? Some but not complete overlap between general personality dispositions and, for example, the tendency to use denial as a preferred coping strategy toward the threat might be anticipated. The difference is, of course, that general personality dispositions are unrelated to particular events, whereas management of the threat is specifically tied to the person's attempts to manage a particular future crisis and the attendant current psychological state subsumed under the word "threat." Thus three general questions were asked: (1) How much threat was involved? (2) How much loss was involved? (3) What procedures did the person bring to bear in managing the threat and resolving the experience of loss?

In general, then, it can be seen in the overall framework that as we move from left to right along the continuum shown in Figure 1, the questions become more specifically related to the particular situation, the crisis under study. In this sense one would anticipate that measures of threat management, for example, of the particular crisis under study should produce better predictive results because such measures represent a narrower band and are directly related to the way a person is managing a particular crisis.

General dispositions would less likely be predictive than specific procedures a person is applying to a particular situation. As we move out along the continuum back to resources, it seems likely that these general qualities of people, although they may be as crucial as specific dispositions in dealing with a particular threat, would yield lower order correlations.

E. Intensity of Stress

Up to now, the characteristics used to define the predictive system have implied that all individuals are stressed equally by a given crisis. This is a common assumption of most investigations of stress adaptation. In the present case, however, because radical changes in life space constituted the experimental condition, it was theoretically and methodologically possible to distinguish the degree of stress actually encountered by the individual from responses to the stress. In most human stress studies, stress intensity is associated with response to the stress, making it impossible to separate person characteristics associated with coping processes from the crisis itself. In the present model, intensity of experienced stress is considered to be dependent upon the degree to which an individual is required to make new adaptations associated with environmental change. The assumption is that the greater the difference between the Time 1 life space and the Time 2 life space, the higher the degree of stress and consequent adaptive requirements; conversely, the smaller the difference for the person, the lower the degree of stress and number of adaptive demands.

III.　Empirical Illustrations of the Predictive Framework

Let me now turn to the four life-space change studies and examine their findings within the framework offered for predicting reactions to crisis. Selective findings germane to the theme of this conference and to the issue of coping will be emphasized. Does a reasonable framework exist for a life-span perspective on crisis management? Is it sensible to talk about continuity of coping processes or of individuals over the course of their lives in terms of processes that predict success or failure under crisis?

The appropriate question to start with would seem to be whether the sum of empirical observations justifies the examination of stress-inducing episodes or events under a unitary framework. Without such a coherent framework it is unlikely that specific processes that are inherently productive or counterproductive in crisis management across the life span can be identified. Recall that investigators have examined a wide variety of events over the life span in their attempt to study reactions to and management of stress. Major transitional states from early childhood on have been examined. Many of the events studied involve high levels of life threat—surgery, combat, incarceration. Still others imply losses of highly significant others—widowhood, fatal disease of children, and so forth. Most crises involve three basic elements: loss, the demand to change previous patterns of behavior and adopt new ones, and the particular subjective meaning a person places on a specific event we label as a crisis. This last point is in many ways the crux of the matter in determining how worthwhile a life-span view of crisis management will become. That a person places meaning on any event is of course a truism, but the central question is whether events become crises primarily because of the meaning placed on them.

Findings from our studies bear directly on this issue. The general conclusion that I will draw from our findings is that *the central element in defining crisis is the degree of change and not the meaning a person attaches to the particular event, or even the amount of loss involved*.[2] This suggests that it may be possible to examine developmentally various transition states and other events, for inherent in all of them is the requirement for new behaviors, the requirement to engage in adaptive behaviors. Such a view means that it is reasonable to study crisis management processes across the life span, for if most crises make similar demands on the person, it would seem reasonable to assume that a generalizable management process is involved.

Let me briefly review some of our findings that have suggested this perspective. Our evidence suggests that the particular meaning that radical change in life space had to the person was not associated with how well or how poorly he was able to cope with the change. These four studies involved a broad range of conditions, from voluntary, and perhaps even desired, relocations to moves that were decidedly unwelcome. Various aspects of the meaning such changes had, such as positive and negative expectations, realism, and degree of control, were measured. Despite vast differences in the meaning of the event for the four populations, the frequency of maladaptive responses to relocation did not relate to these differences as one would expect if the definition of an event as a crisis were dependent on the phenomenological experience persons attached to such an event. Furthermore, looking now at the populations within any one study, we see that whether the person saw the upcoming relocation as a self-enhancing, self-

---

[2] A similar point is made by some investigators who have examined life crisis events (Dohrenwend, 1973). The evidence presented by investigators representing an event-type research strategy supports the change hypothesis; a meaning and/or loss hypothesis is by no means accepted by all. At best, it serves to raise the question.

controlled event or whether he perceived it as an externally controlled event leading to dire consequences (e.g., a "death house") did not predict subsequent adaptation.

On the contrary, it can be shown that the degree of environmental change was the crucial element in determining whether or not the event was a stressor for the person. Two sets of findings support this statement. Across the four studies there was a rough ordering between frequency of breakdown and amount of environmental discontinuity. More important, within any one study one of the strongest predictors of subsequent adaptation/maladaptation was the similarity/dissimilarity between a person's Time 1 and Time 2 environments. In other words, the amount of change and the adaptive demands required for change varied from person to person, depending upon the particular characteristics of each and the specific environment from which he originated and to which he moved. It is but a small step to make the assumption that degree of change is associated with degree of stress. People whose adaptive pattern fits or matches a new environment are less likely to need to make new adaptations and hence less likely to be stressed; conversely, when the person's adaptive pattern or style in the prior environment is ill matched to the new environment, high stress and frequent failures in adaptation may be expected.

The salience of this observation is given added weight because of the variety of methods used to assess environmental match in the four studies. In the institutionalization study, fit profiles were determined by analyzing personality characteristics of individuals who had lived in and made good adjustments to various institutional environments. When community aged had personality characteristics that matched those of individuals already well adapted to the institution, their ability to adapt to being institutionalized could be predicted.

In the therapeutic transfer study, need patterns were examined prior to relocation. The new environments were rated according to the degree to which they would satisfy specific need patterns. This approach for assessing person–environment fit led to a similar conclusion: Degree of similarity was a crucial element in determining degree of stress.

In the mass transfer study, macro- as well as micro-aspects of both the old and new environments were examined. *Macro-* refers to the characteristics of the environment, and *micro-* to the specific interpersonal environment surrounding each person. The individuals who remained stable or unchanged following relocation were those for whom the Time 1 and Time 2 environments were most similar.

That loss is a salient feature of most crises is not, I think, a matter of disagreement. Our data left no question that the experience of loss—uprootedness and disintegration of important attachments both to persons and to things—is part and parcel of an event that is elevated to crisis proportions. Yet the findings did establish that intensity of loss is not the crucial element in determining how well or how poorly people adapt. Loss was measured from an external perspective, the degree to which the individual had important attachments that were severed, as well as subjectively, through direct questions and projective data. Considerable variation in degree of actual and experienced loss was apparent among our subjects. Degree of loss, however, was not related to failure (or success) in adaptation. Clearly, loss entails human suffering, but our examination of the adaptive process suggests that it is possible to distinguish between such suffering and the crucial elements that make a difference among individuals in subsequent adaptation to a specific crisis. The finding that person characteristics predicted adaptation added weight to this view of loss, since the same person characteristics did not predict ability to deal with loss. Processes associated with coping with loss, that is, ability to manage an aspect of their emotional life, were not the same processes that predicted successful coping with crisis. Furthermore, individuals who successfully coped with stress, who were able to maintain homeostasis, were not necessarily the same individuals who dealt successfully with loss.

The main thrust of our findings about person characteristics suggests a major discontinuity in the processes used by the elderly in crisis management as compared to people in earlier life stages. Characteristics or processes shown by numerous investigators to predict adaptation at other life stages appear to be irrelevant in predicting adaptation in old age. Characteristics of people and processes employed for successful adaption at other stages of life in fact may be nonadaptive characteristics among the elderly.

The findings further suggest that adaptation among the elderly is dependent upon the cognitive and physical resources a person can bring to bear on crisis management. Those who were cognitively or physically impoverished could not adapt. The magnitude of this fact is well illustrated in one of our studies, in which a multivariate analysis of several cognitive and physical characteristics accounted for 73% of the variance predicting breakdown. Of equal importance, however, is that although the resources a person brings to a crisis situation are intimately associated with adaptive failures, the reverse is not true. Inadequate resources predict maladaptation, but adequate resources do not necessarily predict successful adaptation. The resources set the floor on the adaptation process. The individual below a certain level cannot mobilize the processes that might lead to adaptive success, but when an individual possesses resources above the minimal level, other more complex psychological characteristics become critical. For those elderly who possessed adequate physical and cognitive resources, predictions of subsequent adaptation were contingent upon (1) certain aspects of *current functioning*, (2) *specific personality characteristics*, and (3) processes they used for *threat appraisal*.

We have considered a number of alternate concepts for examining adequacy of current functioning: psychological health or ego strength, social functioning, issues of happiness and positive self-esteem, the maintenance of a coherent and consistent self-image, and finally ability to accept one's own life history. Only one of these conceptual tools for assessing adequacy of current functioning proved to be an incisive predictor of subsequent adaptation: This one exception was that the adequacy of the processes used to maintain a coherent and consistent self-image was positively associated with the maintenance of homeostasis.

Perhaps the single most important aspect of such findings is that they are contrary to those of most studies of stress adaptation in younger people. That such person characteristics as ego strength and impulse control proved not to be predictive, and in fact in one of our studies even showed a small negative association with positive adaptation, should alert us to the need for a reexamination of our theories about old people. It appears that the processes for adequate coping with crises, crises that we believe can be defined as having essentially the same demand properties across the life span, may be life-stage specific. The replication of this finding in several of our studies of the elderly in which the intensity of crisis and the characteristics of the populations differed distinctively adds weight to this consideration.

An examination of the personality traits associated with coping lends further support to this general conclusion. Those who were *aggressive, irritating, narcissistic,* and *demanding* were the individuals we found to be most likely to survive crisis. They certainly were not the most likable elderly. It would seem that the thought of "growing old gracefully" is more a comfort to the young than an adequate guide to surviving generally inescapable stresses of longevity. Being a good guy—having qualities associated with passive acceptance—was a trait we found in old people most likely not to survive the crisis of environmental change. A poignant illustration occurred in conducting one of our studies, when we asked the staff of an institution to predict which newcomers would best adapt to that institution. We found a very high negative association between their predictions and actual adaptation. When we examined the data more closely, it was obvious that those whom the staff liked—who were not troublemakers, who were easy to relate to—were those they expected to be more likely to adapt. Quite the contrary. Unpleasant and neurotic old people adapted quite well in this case and in the other three. The traditional views of psychological health are of no help in determining crisis management in old age. A certain amount of magical thinking and perceiving oneself as the center of the universe, with a pugnacious stance toward the world—even a highly suspicious one—seemed more likely to insure homeostasis in the face of a severe crisis.

It is also of interest that the only indicator of current adequate functioning that predicted subsequent reaction to crisis was a measure related to developmental stage. Those elderly who were able to support consistent and coherent self-images remained intact in the face of radical environmental change despite major changes in the social system sources of evidence normally supportive of their self-images. Those who could not find meaningful ways of maintaining their self-images showed significant deteriorative decline. This ability or lack of it appears to be a critical issue for the aged, because those unable to experience a situation as supportive of their self-images and unable to develop alternative strategies for maintaining their senses of selfsameness might be open to a second crisis. Since they are unable to maintain the sense of selfsameness which we believe to be a necessary condition in adequately coping with aging, they may be required to turn toward energy-depleting processes of constructing fantasies about the self. It almost seems as if this crisis around the self-image, which is by some elderly met by distorting processes, depletes their ability to mobilize resources for the task of making the numerous adaptations confronting them in the altered life space.

Two other personality processes did prove to be predictors of subsequent adaptation in the face of crisis: the person's *level of hope* and his ability to *introspect*. Both these processes have special significance for the elderly. *Hope* is fundamentally an index of the ability of the person to bind time and to extend his sense of time into the future as well as into the past. Amount of introspection has been shown to be one of the few psychological variables associated with chronological age from age 65 to age 95 (Gorney, 1969). Introspection decreases with age and may be a relevant indicator of a diminishing function associated with the aging process.

The processes identified in our studies which the elderly use for threat appraisal and coping with threat were consistent with those identified in other studies of coping at other life stages and under other conditions. Those aged who did not grossly deny the emotional impact of threat and who were able to engage in appraisal processes consistent with the realities of the impending threat fared much better than those who did deny both the affect and in some cases even the acknowledgment that the critical event was near at hand.

These selective findings from our studies suggest some points of correspondence with those of other investigators who asked what characteristics predict adaptation/maladaptation under crisis conditions. Yet our findings were sufficiently distinct from those rendered in studies of younger populations to raise an issue about the consistency over the life span of similar processes and their role in the adaptive cycle. The personality portraits of the elderly who adapted do not incorporate characteristics that would ordinarily be expected to be signs of adjustment or predictors of adequacy in the face of crisis. If, as we have assumed on the basis of our analysis, the core issues presented by crisis are similar across the life span, then the question of life-stage-specific processes becomes all the more crucial for those who wish to examine human functioning from a life-span perspective. Our findings raise numerous questions regarding developmental issues. Aged populations are, of course, highly selected; it is unlikely that longevity is randomly distributed relative to person characteristics. This natural selective bias involved in studying the aged makes it more complex to examine life-span processes, of course. Are the characteristics associated with adaptation in the aged those that predict adaptation for younger people? Such a question, and many others, are not even worthy of speculation at the stage we are yet at in life-span psychology.

REFERENCES

Abram, H. S. Adaptation to open heart surgery: A psychiatric study of response to the threat of death. *American Journal of Psychiatry,* 1965. **122,** 659–667.

Andrew, J. M. Coping styles, stress relevant learning, and recovery from surgery. Ph.D. dissertation, Univ. of California at Los Angeles, Los Angeles, California, 1967.

Barthell, C., & Holmes, D. Highschool yearbooks: A non-reactive measure of social isolation in graduates who later became schizophrenic. *Journal of Abnormal Psychology,* 1968, **73,** 313–316.

Birren, J. E., Butler, R. N., Greenhouse, S. W. , Solokoff, L., & Yarrow, M. R. *Human aging.* Public Health Service Publication, Number 986, 1970.

Block, J. *The Q-sort method in personality assessment and psychiatric research.* Springfield, Illinois: Charles C. Thomas, 1961.

Bower, E. M. American children and their families in overseas communities and schools: Problems, programs, and possibilities. Unpublished paper, National Institute of Mental Health, June 1966.

Brosin, H. W. Adolescent crises. *New York State Journal of Medicine,* 1967, **67,** 2003–2011.

Caplan, G. Patterns of parental response to the crisis of premature birth. A preliminary approach to modifying the mental health outcome. *Psychiatry,* 1960, **23,** 365–374.

Chodoff, P., Friedman, S. B., & Hamburg, D. A. Stress, defenses, and coping behavior: Observations in parents of children with malignant disease. *American Journal of Psychiatry,* 1964, **120,** 743–749.

Clifford, R. *The Rio Grande Flood: A comparative study of border communities in disaster.* Disaster Study Number 7. Washington, D. C.: National Academy of Sciences—National Research Council, 1956.

Coelho, G. V., Hamburg, D. A., Moos, R. E. and Randolph, P. *Coping and adaptation: A behavioral sciences bibliography.* Public Health Service Publication, Number 2087, 1970.

Coelho, G. V., Silber, E., & Hamburg, D. A. Use of the student-TAT to assess coping behavior in hospitalized normal and exceptionally competent college freshmen. *Perceptual and Motor Skills*, 1962, **14**, 355–362.

Dohrenwend, B. S. Social status and stressful life events. *Journal of Personality and Social Psychology*, 1973, **28**, 225–235.

Erikson, E. *Childhood and society*. New York: Norton, 1963.

Gfzi, K. I. Factors associated with student adjustment in cross-cultural contact. *California Journal of Educational Research*, 1965, **16**, 129–136.

Gorney, J. Experiencing among the aged. Ph.D. dissertation, University of Chicago, Chicago, Illinois, 1967.

Hurwitz, J. I., Kaplan, D. M., & Kaiser, E. Designing an instrument to assess parental coping mechanisms. In H. J. Parad (Ed.), *Crisis intervention*, New York: Family Service Association of America, 1965. Pp. 339–348.

Janis, I. *Psychological stress*. New York: Wiley, 1958.

Kaplan, D. M. Predicting outcome from situational stress on the basis of individual problem-solving patterns: A study of maternal coping patterns in the psychological stress situation posed by premature birth, 1965.

Kellam, S. Adaptation, mental illness and family life in the first-grade classroom of an urban Negro community. Paper given at conference on Coping and Adaptation, Palo Alto, California, March, 1969.

Kellam, S., & Schiff, S. Adaptation and mental illness in the first-grade classroom of an urban community. American Psychiatric Association, *Psychiatric Research Report*, 1967, **21**, 79–91.

Klein, D. C., & Ross, A. Kindergarten entry: A study of role transition. *Orthopsychiatry and the school*. New York: Family Service Association of America, 1965. pp. 140–148.

Levin, S. Some group observations on reactions to separation from home in first-year college students. *Journal of Child Psychiatry*, 1967, **6**, 644–654.

Levine, M. Residential change and school adjustment. *Community Mental Health Journal*, 1966, **2**, 61–69.

Lieberman, M. A., Prock, V. N., & Tobin, S. S. The psychological effects of institutionalization. *Journal of Gerontology*, 1968, **23**, (3).

Lindemann, E., & Ross, N. A follow-up study of a predictive test of social adaptation in pre-school children. In G. Caplan (Ed.), *Emotional problems of early childhood*. New York: Basic Books, 1955. pp. 79–93.

Marcia, J. E. Development and validation of ego identity status. *Journal of Personal and Social Psychology*, 1966, **3**, 551–558.

Marcia, J. E. Ego identity status: Relationship to change in self-esteem, "general maladjustment," and authoritarianism. *Journal of Personality*, 1967, **35**, 118–133.

Melges, F., Anderson, R., & Tinklenberg, J. Identity and temporal experience. Unpublished manuscript, Stanford Univ. Stanford, California, 1969.

Moos, R. H. Psychological techniques in the assessment of adaptive behavior. Unpublished manuscript, Stanford Univ. School of Medicine, Stanford, California, 1974.

Musgrove, F. Role-conflict in adolescence. *British Journal of Educational Psychology*, 1964, **34**, 34–42.

Parkes, C. M. *Bereavement: Studies of grief in adult life.* New York: International Univ. Press, 1972.

Perry, S., Silber, E., & Block, D. *The child and his family in disaster: A study of the 1953 Vicksburg tornado*. Washington D. C.: National Academy of Sciences—National Research Council, Disaster Research Group, Disaster Study Number 5, 1956.

Raush, H. L., Goodrich, W., & Campbell, J. D. Adaptation to the first years of marriage. *Psychiatry*, 1963, **26**, 368–380.

Remmers, H. H. Cross-cultural studies of teenager's problems. *Journal of Educational Psychology,* 1962, **53,** 254–261.

Schaib, K. W. A field-theory approach to age change in cognitive behavior. *Vita Humana,* 1962, **5,** 129–141.

Silber, E., Coelho, G., Murphey, E., Hamburg, D., Pearlin, L., & Rosenberg, M. Competent adolescents coping with college decisions. *Archives of General Psychiatry,* 1961, **5,** 517–527.

Silber, E., Hamburg, D., Coelho, G., Murphey, E., Rosenberg, M., & Pearlin, L. Adaptive behavior in competent adolescents. *Archives of General Psychiatry,* 1961, **5,** 354–365.

Smith, M. B. Explorations in competence: A study of Peace Corps teachers in Ghana. *American Psychologist,* 1966, **21,** 555–566.

Stern, G., Stein, M., & Bloom, B. *Methods in personality assessment.* Glencoe, Illinois: Free Press, 1956.

Visotsky, H., Hamburg, D., Goss, M., & Lebovitz, B. Coping behavior under extreme stress: Observations of patients with severe poliomyelitis. *Archives of General Psychiatry,* 1961, **5,** 423–448.

Wolff, C., Friedman, S., Hofer, M., & Mason, J. Relationship between psychological defenses and mean urinary 17-hydroxycorticosteroid excretion rates. I. A predictive study of parents of fatally ill children. *Psychosomatic Medicine,* 1964, **26,** 576–591.

CHAPTER 9

Adaptation and Survival:
New Meanings in Old Age

MARTIN B. LOEB

UNIVERSITY OF WISCONSIN—MADISON
MADISON, WISCONSIN

ABSTRACT

Evidently new skills based on new knowledge will have to be developed which will help old people adapt to necessary changes in the living environment. Living conditions such as long term care institutions can be designed both physically and socially which reduce the demand on adaptation capabilities.

My approach to life crises takes several perspectives—as a social worker, a social scientist, and perhaps as an expert on aging trained to take a life-span perspective. Lieberman deals with the nature of crisis. I shall present a similar, though perhaps simpler, model, which incorporates some of the features of Riegel's model.

Let us construct such a model by first assuming that there are physical environments and sociocultural contexts as surrounds, or external determinants. There are also biological or inner determinants derived genetically, developmentally, and traumatically (such as losing the sense of sight or hearing). The interaction of these two sets of determinants produces means of dealing with ordinary and expected conditions of life.

Each individual also has met extraordinary conditions and has coped to one extent or another. In so doing he has added to his store of skills for mediating between his biological capacities and his environmental demands. The goal of adaptive behaviors is, first, survival, and second, a comfortable existence. Each person develops a unique repertoire of adaptive behaviors from a pool of socially acceptable responses. That pool of responses is shaped by the cultural context. When an individual style or pattern is generated in the adaptive process, it may be called personality.

I think it necessary to postulate, as does Selye, that the magnitude of effort directed at adaptation depends on available energy, which is biologically determined. Available energy diminishes over the life span as part of the aging process. So we have biological determinants interacting with environmental determinants as well as with learned coping techniques. The adaptive responses that are the outcome of this interaction are used not only for crises, but for everyday experiences as well.

We know relatively little about the limitations on the ability of the aged to learn new coping techniques, however. We also do not know whether or not the loss of available energy obliterates coping techniques that were learned earlier. It is possible that the strength of earlier learning affects the maintenance of coping behavior in later life. For example, the child of an army officer who learned to cope with moving often in his early life may have more success in moving once he is an adult. But we really do not know the answers to these questions.

Lieberman tells us that adaptation to stress is not the same among older people and among the young. I would add that adaptation is a matter of survival. In young people there is a high degree of inherent concern for survival of the species and for reproduction. These concerns are both personal and social. In older people, personal survival is of the greatest importance. Therefore, it is no surprise that "those who were *aggressive, irritating, narcissistic,* and *demanding* were the individuals we found most likely to survive crises." This suggests that the older person relies less on group or social strengths learned earlier than do young people facing crises, and is forced inward, to his own resources. It may also mean that those who have not learned a great deal about personal survival have difficulty coping with crisis in the later years.

The foregoing observations are intended as background to my role as a social worker: I am interested in the application of Lieberman's findings in the service of older people. Do the studies of adaptation to stress tell us anything about helping people cope when we know they are going to face a crisis? I believe they do.

Any behavior, including adaptive behavior, may be seen as a component of a role. In any role, a person musters his resources, inherent and learned, in order to interact with other recognized roles in a manner that is satisfying to himself and also within the range of expectations of others. In new and stressful situations, the person must (a) develop a role and (b) muster his resources to enact that role. In a crisis, because of decreased elasticity and energy, the response to these two tasks may be impaired. The reaction may be diffuse or disorganized.

However, if we know what crises may come, there may be ways in which we develop a pattern of roles or role sets, developing appropriate behaviors for those roles, and so help individuals use their past experiences to enhance their functioning in new roles. That is what the modern social worker is equipped to do—not only with individuals but with groups and communities as well. If the crisis is generally expected by a larger group or by a whole community, the social worker can develop techniques for intervention at the preventive level, before the crisis.

The social worker can prepare the individual or group or community for the crisis and can help them learn useful coping techniques. At the time of the crisis, the social worker can help the client mobilize energy, rather than expend it diffusely. After the crisis, appropriate behaviors can be reinforced and inappropriate behaviors discouraged.

Lieberman's subjects, persons in transition, were adjusting to a social prosthesis. They could no longer stay in one social setting and needed to move to another that was designed to compensate for deficiencies in adaptive capacity. Accommodating to a prosthesis, whether it is a hearing aid, bifocals, false teeth, an artificial limb, or an institution, is difficult for all who use them. There are people specially trained to help others in making these accommodations. Assistance in this transition is no less important to psychosocial prosthetics than to the more obvious physical prosthetics. Analogous advances are possible in the field of social prosthetics. We need to do much more in the design of living situations that can reduce the demands on the adaptation skills.

Social workers essentially help people develop and learn coping techniques. They can also contribute to the design of new social institutions that minimize the need for adaptive responses. I am certain this can be done with the aged as well as with younger people, if we draw upon the new knowledge about aging presented to us by Lieberman and others who have studied the aged and their needs.

NORMATIVE LIFE CRISES
IN THE FAMILY LIFE CYCLE

CHAPTER 10

Parenthood: A Key to the Comparative Study of the Life Cycle

DAVID GUTMANN

UNIVERSITY OF MICHIGAN
ANN ARBOR, MICHIGAN

ABSTRACT

Transcultural regularities in sex-role training, in the male and female response to the "chronic emergency" of parenthood, and in the phasing out of parental responsibilities all suggest that sex distinctions have an instrinsic basis, and that they are organized around the vital requirements of young children. It is further argued that parenthood constitutes the pivotal stage of the human life cycle, organizing the form and content of the stages which lead up to it, as well as those that succeed it. Accordingly, study of the common denominators and requirements of human parenthood could be an important first step in developing a comparative psychology of the human life cycle.

I. Adulthood and Parenthood: Neglected Topics in Psychology

As a field, psychology is in its untidy adolescence; perhaps as a consequence we have no dynamic psychology of adulthood. Psychologists now hunt for the independent variable as alchemists once hunted for the philosopher's stone, and in this search we have by-passed the later stages of the life cycle in favor of the formative years, when certain maturationally linked independent variables of human development are most easily observed. The investigation of adulthood is left by default to the clinicians, who may study an unrepresentative sample of patients, or it is left to the sociologists, who ignore the internal organization of their subjects, and confine their attention to the external order of social norms and institutions. Because they study adults who are still mired in their earliest conflicts, clinicians develop personality models that infantilize adulthood. Because they fix their attention on the mutable norms, the sociologists relativize adulthood: In their vision, the adult individual is a rather accidental by-product of the various and shifting socioeconomic and sex-role pressures to which he is exposed. Although much adult behavior—particularly public behavior—is indeed role-determined, there is still room for the psychologist's question: Why is it that mature adults, more than the young, and more than the aged, are *particularly* motivated to maintain and respond to social norms? Questions of this sort might help us to identify some distinctive features of adult personality, of the sort that distinguish it from the initial (as well as the terminal) periods of the life cycle.

The individualistic bias of psychologists also compromises our study of adulthood, as it leads us to overlook the evolutionary basis of this period of the life cycle. Thus we tend to think of adulthood as the time when the individual is most self-actualizing, moving via self-developed resources toward self-defined goals. But if adulthood is a product of human evolution, and more than an arbitrary division of the life cycle, then it is tied to species survival, as well as to individual enhancement. Perhaps, by identifying the *species* meanings of adulthood, we will also identify those personality features that are *singular* to adulthood, those that distinguish it from other portions of the life cycle, and which make this period comparable, both dynamically and structurally, across individuals, across cultures, and across historical periods.

The species perspective is useful; it does highlight a central feature of adulthood: namely, that it is essentially coextensive with a crucial piece of species business—parenthood. If there are defining regularities in adult life, then these are likely to be revealed through the comparative study of human parenthood.

Like adulthood, parenthood is a relatively neglected topic in psychology. Dynamic psychologists have usually focused on the consequences for human development of being *parented*—of being the child of parents. But we do not, as a rule, study the effects of parenthood on *parents* themselves. Thus, we study the routes whereby an infant may come to develop basic trust in the good intentions and continuity of the parent; but we do not study the equally crucial process whereby a new mother, a primapara, comes to trust her own capacity to keep an infant alive, after it has been turned over to her care.

A. Transcultural Themes in Parenthood

My own interest in parenthood developed as a kind of startle reaction. I was personally surprised by the strength of my own reaction to becoming a father; and I was further surprised, in my cross-cultural studies, by the central role that their fatherhood played in the lives of the subsistence agriculturalists that I have interviewed in various parts of the world—the Maya of Mexico, the Navajo of Arizona, and the Druze of the Middle East. The resulting ideas concerning the keystone role of parenthood in the normal human life cycle have helped me to understand and organize certain age and sex regularities and variations that show up in my data, across sites.

I did not initially go to the field with a primary interest in parenthood. I interviewed men aged 35–95, and I was chiefly interested in the postparental periods of life in diverse cultures. However, the field always surprises us, particularly if our methods are open enough to permit surprise. Fortunately, I kept my procedures relatively unstructured; the interviews were based on my training as a clinical psychologist, and were aimed at helping my subjects teach me what questions I should be asking them. Though I kept the conversation focused on the informant's subjective life—his memories, his pleasures, his pains, his remedies, his motives, and his fantasies—he was free to develop these topics as he saw fit. Accordingly, since I could not predict the data, I was in a position to be instructed by my subjects. One thing they taught me was the vital importance of parenthood in their lives; and they also taught me that this concern, and their responses to it, took fairly standard forms, across a variety of cultures.

It can be truly said that, as regards parenting, nothing human is strange. My subject and I might not agree as to which child-rearing method is best; but, despite our ethnic, linguistic, and regional differences, we *do* agree as to the range of possible child-rearing styles, from harsh physical discipline to laissez-faire permissiveness. Furthermore, illiterate and even preliterate peasants are not surprised by a psychologist's interest in such topics as weaning, toilet training, sibling rivalry, and the impact of a stepmother. They already know a good deal about the effects on the child's feelings, the family's mood, and the child's later development of these contingencies.

I was particularly surprised by the strong effect that paternity seems to have on men. We readily assume that parenthood stimulates powerful "maternal" instincts leading to unselfish nurturance in normal women; but we also tend to believe that the male response is less reliable, less instinctually based, and that men even have to be coaxed and coerced into accepting parental responsibilities. On examination, matters prove to be more complex. Men in various cultures, particularly stable cultures, have told me that their character following marriage and particularly after fatherhood shaped dramatically toward greater responsibility, selflessness, and moderation: "I used to hell around, I didn't care for myself or anybody else. . . ." (What happened?) "I got married; I had kids . . ." by the same token, the degree to which younger men define both their pleasures and their pains in terms of their family's welfare is striking. Thus, for younger Mayan peasants, happiness is defined as a full belly and good health—not for themselves, but for their children. As with women, parenthood seems to mobilize profound motives and sentiments in men, and these find standard expression across disparate cultures.

B. The Parental Imperative

In sum, many of the qualities that are currently ascribed to masculine power and achievement motives seem to be aspects of the predictable male response to what I would call the "parental imperative." These responses are not, as is fashionably assumed, in the service of male chauvinism, nor do they register the malignant effects of capitalist socialization. Rather, it appears that such traits are developmental and even evolutionary outcomes; and as such they are in the service of family and ultimately species survival rather than male prestige. And indeed, for both sexes, parenthood seems to represent the point at which individual satisfaction intersects with species needs. For most adult humans, parenthood is still the ultimate source of the sense of meaning. For most adults the question "What does life mean?" is automatically answered once they have children; better yet, it is no longer asked.

To repeat, I am a psychologist, trained to look at adulthood as the most individualized and self-determined portion of the life span, the outcome of individual history, individual experience, and self-directed education. However, repeated observations of the sort cited earlier urge me toward the conviction that supraindividual or species factors, mobilized by our parental bonds to children, organize much of our adult lives—just as our relations to our adult parents organized much of our life as children. Furthermore, I now believe that parenthood, as a vital species activity, and as a period of chronic emergency, exercises a pivotal and controlling role over the entire life span, shaping the events that precede the onset of parenthood as well as the later periods of the life cycle which follow it. In this view, the child is not only father to the man; rather, the child is already, through his intense relations with his own parents, brought into mutual regulation with the father that he will one day be. This parent-centered perspective has helped me to make sense of yet another set of empirical findings dealing with age changes in male and female sex-role patterns. I shall briefly describe these changes, and then discuss their possible meaning in relation to the parental imperative.

C. Sex-Role Changes in Later Life: Transcultural Findings

The data pertaining to psychological change in middle and later life for both men and women have been reported in detail elsewhere (Gutmann, 1964, 1969, 1974). Briefly, as estimated from various measures, there are some important age changes in the psychological stances of both men and women, changes that are possibly developmental in nature, since they occur in predictable sequence across disparate cultures. Thus, the transcultural data make it clear that, by contrast with younger men, older men are on the whole less aggressive: They are more affiliative, more interested in love than in conquest or power, more interested in community than in agency. The younger men see energy *within* themselves, as a potential threat that has to be contained and deployed to productive purposes. But the old men see energy as outside of themselves, lodged in capricious secular or supernatural authorities. For older men, then, power must be manipulated and controlled in its external form through postures of prayer and other forms of supplication and accommodation.

Consistent with this age-graded switch to a more dependent and affiliative position, there is also in later life the turn toward diffuse sensuality. In the main, younger men are businesslike; they do not go out of their way to seek pleasure, nor do they avoid necessary discomfort. They mainly seek pleasure in sex, at night, when work is done; and even their sexual acts may have a rational goal: They are in the service of procreation, the production of sons who will aid the father in his work and who will be his social security in old age. The "phallic" organization of personality does not lead to productivity, but is its consequence. Older men, by contrast, are more diffusely sensual, more sensitive to the incidental pleasures and pains of the world. Unlike the phallic younger men, the older men seek pleasure in the pregenital direction: They become particularly interested in food, pleasant sights, sounds, and human associations. Where younger men look at the world instrumentally, older men take some incidental bonus of esthetic pleasure from their daily routines.

We also find, across a wide range of cultures, that women age psychologically in the reverse direction. Even in normally patriarchal societies, women become more aggressive in later life, less sentimental, and more domineering. They become less interested in communion and more turned toward agency. Thus, over time and across sex lines a massive transcultural involution takes place: During the earlier parental years the husband comes to be more dependent on the wife; and he tends to defer to her wishes and requirements, acting toward her as he does toward other sources of security in his life. The older wife becomes something of an authority to the husband; and through these various sex-role changes, there is ushered in the normal unisex of later life.

These intersexual developments are best illustrated through reviewing some representative age differences and age changes in our subjects' interpretations of the Thematic Apperception Test (TAT) stimuli that have been used in various cultures. Starting with the American respondents, middle-majority subjects (men and women) from Kansas City have delineated such age differences in their response to the "family" card specially designed for the Kansas City Study of Adult Life. The card depicts four figures, an older man, an older woman, a younger man, and a younger woman, usually seen as a family group dealing with some problem or crisis that has been initiated by the younger couple—they wish to marry, to leave home for career or educational reasons, etc. To a significant degree, younger respondents, both men and women, see the older man figure as the authority in dealing with the situation facing the family. He is an "ego" representation: He wisely sponsors the younger people's drive toward one or another version of autonomy, while in effect holding off the impulsive older woman, who generally objects to their maturity. However, for subjects over 55 the older woman, though she occupies the least space as a stimulus, becomes increasingly active and dominant, even as the older man increasingly retires into his shell: Older respondents usually see him as "thinking" about the situation that confronts the group, without, however, taking any decisive action. If he does relate to others, it is in nurturant rather than authoritative ways, in distinct contrast to the now "masculinized" older woman figure: "Look at that bull neck. . . ." "She runs the show; she wears the pants in the family. . . ."

The age trends developed across cultures by the "heterosexual" card of the standard TAT set tend to replicate the Kansas City findings in regard to sex-role change with age. This card, which shows a young man half turned away from a young woman who reaches toward him in a restraining or pleading manner, provides further evidence of the shift from exuberant and outward-directed male aggression toward more security-seeking, receptive stances. Thus, as Table 1 indicates, younger men—urban Americans, Maya, Navajo, or Druze—propose that the young man brushes aside a beseeching or timorous woman and forges out into a dangerous but exciting world of combat, carouse, and mistresses. Thus, for younger men, the sexes are sharply distinguished: The young man pushes toward some extradomestic periphery without much regard for consequences; inhibition and timidity are mainly located in the woman. But to the *same stimulus* older men propose more anergic, constricted, or "pregenital" themes. In their version the young woman tends to domineer; or the male protagonist retreats back to her consolation, and away from a world in which he has known danger and defeat. In either case, initiatives and strength have migrated away from the young man toward the young woman. Finally, for many older men, the male protagonist does not reject the nurturance offered by the young wom-

Table 1

The "Heterosexual-Conflict" Card:
Distribution of Stories by Age, Culture, and Theme

		35–49	50–59	60+
1. Male initiative and dominance:	Kansas City	21	12	10
Young man's intrinsic sex, ag-	Navajo	9	7	9
gression, and autonomy needs con-	Lowland Maya	4	1	2
stitute a problem for a gentle,	Highland Maya	2	–	–
nurturant young woman and po-	Druze	20	13	7
tential danger for himself.		56	33	28
2. Domestic problems: Conflict	Kansas City	1	3	–
centered around young man's	Navajo	4	4	4
aggression; but direction,	Lowland Maya	7	5	7
scope, cause, or outcome of	Highland Maya	–	2	1
this aggression is unclear.	Druze	8	8	8
		20	22	20
3. Female initiatives and domi-	Kansas City	6	5	6
nance: Young man's anger is	Navajo	–	3	9
reactive to young woman's re-	Lowland Maya	7	5	7
jection of him, or dominance	Highland Maya	–	2	1
over him.	Druze	5	4	8
		18	19	31
4. Rationalized male succorance:	Kansas City	–	1	4
Menaced by external forces, or	Navajo	–	1	12
defeated in his outer-world	Lowland Maya	–	1	2
achievement strivings, the	Highland Maya	1	–	2
young man looks for or accepts	Druze	18	5	22
female nurturance and control.		19	8	42
5. Untroubled affiliation (or	Kansas City	–	–	–
syntonic dependency): mild,	Navajo	1	6	6
untroubled affiliation be-	Lowland Maya	3	7	12
tween relatively undifferen-	Highland Maya	8	3	3
tiated young man and woman.	Druze	11	9	32
		23	25	53

Kansas City	N = 69	N+	136	107	174
Navajo	N = 75				
Lowland Maya	N = 70	+Chi square (of cell totals) = 42.165,			
Highland Maya	N = 125	df = 8, $p < .001$			
Druze[a]	N = 178				
Total	N = 417				

[a] Druze group includes Golan (Syrian), Galilean, and Carmel (Israeli) Druze.

Table 2

*Longitudinal Changes in TAT Imagery of Navajo and Druze Subjects
Elicited by the "Heterosexual-Conflict" Card*

	Number of passive images discarded in favor of more active imagery after Time 1[a]			Number of passive images appearing only at Time 2		
	Navajo	Druze	Total	Navajo	Druze	Total
Male aggression is in reaction to female dominance	3	1	4	8	8	11
Man is inactive; woman is active and/or dominant	2	2	4	4	7	11
Man and woman react similarly to troubling or pleasant scene	3	2	5	5	7	12
Man is sick; woman is his nurse, or is concerned about him	1	3	4	6	4	10
Man is tired, or old (woman may be his daughter)	1	2	3	2	5	7
Man and woman like or love each other. No conflict or role distinctions.	1	9[b]	10	8	4	12
	Total number of passive images discarded by Time 2 30			Total number of new passive images by Time 2 . . . . 63[c]		

[a]Time 1 – Time 2 interval is 4 years in the Navajo case and 5 years in the Druze case. The Galilean and Carmel Druze, but not the Golan Druze, were reinterviewed for the Time 2 study.

[b]Two-thirds of the Druze reversals in this category toward more "active" imagery occur among men younger than age 65; three-fourths of the new perceptions of an affiliative and undifferentiated couple occur in men aged 65 and over.

[c]These are not independent entries. A single story may be entered under more than one heading.

an, but instead dwells with her in happy, seamless harmony. Potential trouble comes from outside, not within the dyad, and menaces the young man and woman equally. These age shifts appear to be developmental rather than secular in nature. Thus they appear with some predictability across a panel of disparate cultures where the drift of generational, cultural change

Fig. 1. Male Druze Card.

has been different in each case; and, within cultures, these changes in sex-role perceptions show up in longitudinal as well as cross-sectional data. Thus when the same heterosexual card is shown after a 5-year lapse to the panel of Navajo and Druze respondents who first reacted to it at Time 1, the results are as shown in Table 2: Though some "passive" interpretations of the heterosexual card have dropped out by Time 2 in favor of more active images of the younger man figure, a far greater number of passive images and themes have appeared *for the first time,* replacing more active imagery, by Time 2. Clearly, then, the original age X theme distributions of responses to this card were produced by psychological changes within individuals, and not by intercohort differences having to do with generational changes in the various cultures. Thus, as they age, men are increasingly prone to assign dominance to the female figure, and to see the younger man as her satellite; and this intraindividual change proceeds independently of culture.

This same sex-role turnover is dramatically captured by another card, used only among the Druze, which, for most subjects, elicits concerns around intergenerational and intermale relations and lines of authority (see Figure 1). Almost invariably, Druze men below age 60 see the card as depicting relations between an executive or advisory older man, and usually compliant boys, or younger men. However, a number of men over 60 see the older man as a beggar, asking for food or money from a *woman,* who may or may not indulge him. Again, the tendency to turn a compliant young man into a dominant woman and to turn an authoritative old man into a beggar is not a cohort phenomenon, limited to a particular generation of Druze men; longitudinal studies with this card reveal that nine Druze, all but one over 60, who saw the older man as an authority at Time 1 see him as a beggar by Time 2.

These findings in regard to age shifts in fantasy are in general confirmed by anthropologists, by those who study more overt and public behaviors. Thus Gold (1960) asked some 26 anthropologists, varied in their theoretical interests, and students of culturally diverse societies to report on any age-related changes in sex role in the groups that they had worked with. Fourteen out of 26 reported a shift, in most cases not registered in the formal rules of the society, toward greater female dominance in later life. The remainder reported no change; but in *no* case did the balance swing toward greater male authority over the wife with advancing age.

II. Sex Differences and the Parental Emergency

Thus, there appears to be a comprehensive developmental event of middle and later life, involving strongly bonded mates, that acts to reverse or at least equalize the domestic status of the partners, and that tends to redistribute the so-called masculine and feminine traits among them. There is no use speculating which partner initiates this sex-role involution. The total event takes place simultaneously within two individuals who comprise a unified field in regard to this comprehensive developmental sequence. To repeat, we are not speaking of related but separate developmental events in men and women; in this case, each partner is the context for the developmental change within the other. Moreover, just as the sharp sex-role distinctions of young adulthood are bonded to the early years of parenthood, so are the sex-role reversals captured in our data coordinated with the twilight of parenthood. There appears then to be some relationship between sex distinctions and the fluctuating demands of parenthood.

But how do we understand the seeming covariance between stages of parenthood and sex-roles? Here, the idea of the parental imperative, of parenthood as a period of chronic emergency, becomes useful, particularly after a necessary digression to spell out the ways in which the sexual potentials and sex-role training of parents intersect with the protracted and often desperate needs of the infant for physical and emotional security. Having exited from the sheltering womb, the infant immediately required alternate sources of warmth, insulation against shock, and nutriment; and the parent's own need to provide physical security is responsive to this emergency. However, though these needs are less dramatically evident, the infant also requires comforting and predictable presences to replace the lost physical tie to the mother: He requires emotional as well as physical security. Parents soon learn that the infant is much more responsive to physical care that is provided in a tender manner than he is to offhand, impersonal care. Certainly, Harlow's experiments with chimps raised on terry-cloth "mothers" and Spitz's observations on the marasmic depressions in hospitalized infants demonstrate very clearly that physical security alone does not ensure the survival of the human or the primate infant. The infant who is adequately cared for physically, but who is not given a loving welcome to the world, will probably not thrive; he will be terribly vulnerable to diseases that normally reared babies can shrug off, and he will not grow in turn to be the adequate parent of viable children. Just as physical and emotional security are to some degree independent of each other, so are the providers of these two aspects of security. Given the condition of relative scarcity and danger under which our species evolved its generally successful child-rearing practices, the *same parent* could not adequately meet the physical and emotional requirements of the young and vulnerable child. The provider of physical security had to range far in the search for food, in the pursuit of enemies, or in the defense of the group's perimeter. Clearly, he could not pack a vulnerable and cumbersome child with him on these forays; and he could not perform these vital tasks adequately and yet stay within range of the child's cry, close enough to give the kind of assurance on which basic trust is founded. By the same token, the parent charged with assuring emotional security was severely limited regarding the provision of physical security. Efforts in that direction had to be restricted to the domestic zone, within the sight and sound of her children. Her maintenance activities were necessarily confined to the cooking fire, the household garden, or any other relatively safe setting to which the child could be transported with a minimum of discomfort and risk.

Thus, marked sexual distinctions have evolved, most clearly seen among young parents, which correspond to the child's need for distinct forms of physical and emotional sustenance. The more expendable parent, with the larger muscles and the greater innate fund of aggression, is generally assigned to provide physical security: to hunt large game and to guard against human and nonhuman predators. The parent with the breasts, with the milder nature, the parent who grew the baby in her own body, is generally assigned to supply the experiences that foster emotional security. This basic division of responsibilities is recognized by most subsistence-level human groups. Thus, Murdock's (1935) tables, based on data from 224 subsistence societies, indicate that any activity requiring a protracted absence from the home—hunting, trapping, herding, fishing (particularly deep-sea fishing).

and pursuit of large sea mammals—is almost exclusively performed by males. Activities carried out close to home—dairy operations, erecting and dismantling shelters, harvesting, tending fowl—are in some cultures the province of men; in some, they are the province of women; and in some cultures they are performed by both sexes. However, activities carried out within the house itself, particularly those having to do with preserving and preparing food, are, regardless of culture, almost exclusively the province of women. Clearly, it is not the capacity for hard labor that discriminates the sexes, but the *site* at which the labor is performed. Women can work, often harder than men, at labor that does not require their absence from the hearth; but activities that call for extradomestic forays are almost exclusively the province of men.

These sex-linked proclivities, to forage beyond the home range in the case of men, to stay within it and close to children in the case of women, are more than built-in, instinctive responses to parenthood. Intrinsic action and attitudinal potentials that distinguish the sexes are necessary but not sufficient bases for the sex roles and sex differences that have species and social utility. Male aggression, for example, is intrinsic, the bases for it laid down prenatally; but it can have destructive or productive consequences depending on the cultural surroundings in which it emerges and is shaped. Thus, the aggression of young men in disorganized ghettos, *barrios* and *favellas* does not serve parenthood, but instead takes murderously antisocial or self-destructive forms. An organized society, based on a moral and traditional consensus, is necessary if male aggression is to achieve protective and productive forms. It is only an organized (though not necessarily literate) society that can provide men with strong moral incentives—registered in the sense of personal identity and personal *meaning*—to tame their narcissistic or murderous potentials, and to respond to the parental emergency in responsible ways. In effect, culture exists in order to provide, both to males and to females, the larger meanings that make it possible for them to submit to the socialization practices whereby their aggressions and sex-role potentials are trained, exercised, and *structuralized*, long before parenthood, into ego executive capacities vital to adult parental roles.

Since genderhood implies innate potentials as well as parental roles congruent with these potentials, socialization pressures from childhood on have to take account of sex-differences. Thus, Barry, Bacon, and Child (1957) have abstracted socialization data from ethnographic reports of 110 separate subsistence societies, and here again we find a striking transcultural consensus: Societies may differ greatly in cultural terms; but they consistently recognize the female responsibility for emotional security and the male responsibility for physical security; and with great unanimity they sponsor, through their socializing practices, the psychological traits that underwrite successful performance in these assignments. Thus, the central themes in female socialization are nurturance, responsibility, and, to a lesser degree, obedience, while male children are almost universally (and exclusively) socialized toward achievement and self-reliance. Girls are confirmed in the psychological counterparts of the mothering role, while boys are confirmed in the drive for achievement and exploit that will impel them beyond the home, and in the self-reliant qualities that will sustain them in their extracommunal sorties. Masculine attainment in these terms is frequently tested in puberty rites, in *rites de passage*. These vary in content across cultures, but seem to have a common aim: to test whether the boy has developed the psychological structures that are fundamental to the far-ranging life of the adult male. In one form or another the young candidate for manhood is subjected to an ordeal. If he endures it with grace, dignity, or at least silence, then he has made it as a man; if he shows weakness, if he in effect cries for his mother, then he has not. Thus, each sex is trained to amplify, to transform into executive capacities, and to *enjoy* the emotional potentials that are declared off limits for the other sex. Men are groomed to take pleasure in prowess, action, and endurance; women are groomed to the cultivation of their emotional sensitivity, their sensuality, and even their obedience. At least in the first half of the life cycle, each sex may appear to the other as a representation, a metaphor of the potentials that have been denied and stunted in the self.

These sex-role divisions are sharpened by entry into the period of parental emergency. Prior to marriage, and despite their continuing training toward distinct sex roles, young men and women are allowed some freedom to indulge their full and overlapping range of psychic potentials. Thus, unmarried girls can be tomboys, while young men can live out the extremes of their nature, toward violence on the one hand and passivity on the other. They can be offhandedly daring one day, lazy and self-pitying the next. However, marriage and parenthood bring, especially for men, a clear mobilization or energizing of the structures that were laid down in the course of their earler socialization. For young fathers there takes place a kind of instrumentalizing of the self: They tame the extremes of their nature, deploying aggression toward production, curbing passive tendencies, and generally accepting, even with good humor, the responsibilities and sacrifices that come with the productive stance. During the period of early parenthood, younger men strive toward creating and controlling the sources of security for themselves and particularly for their dependents: They work very hard to increase flocks, fields, or business clienteles; and they do not indulge the "softer" yearnings toward comfort and pleasure that could interfere with their effectiveness in productive roles. Thus, by forcing out of their consciousness the longings for pleasure and security that might distract them from the role as provider and defender, they divest themselves of the passive dependent traits *that might prove lethal to their children.* These dangerous promptings are repressed, and they are further handled by conceding them to a relatively indulged and dependent wife, by living them out vicariously through her. The wife and mother becomes an external representation of the "passive" yearnings that the husband and father must give up in order to provide physical security to others. By the same token, the wife concedes to her husband—figuratively sends out of the house with him—the more assertive potential of her own nature. Her aggression, if openly displayed, could destroy the relationship with the husband, on whom she and her children must rely. Furthermore, if mothers indulged a quite understandable anger toward continually demanding but also vulnerable infants, they might do them irreparable damage. On both counts, female aggression is ruled out as being potentially lethal to the mother, and to the children who look to her for love rather than hate. Consequently, female aggression is repressed, and lived out vicariously, through identification with the prowess of the husband.

In sum, the needs of vunerable children seem to be a formidable stimulus to younger fathers as well as to mothers, and the standard reaction for each sex is to surrender to the other the qualities that would interfere with the provision of their special form of security. Men, the providers of physical security, give up the need for comfort and dependency that would interfere with their courage and endurance; and women, the providers of emotional security, give up the aggression that could alienate their male providers or that could damage a vulnerable and needful child. Again, the traditional sex-role distinctions are not male chauvinist inventions; among other things, they are ways of getting dangerous *male and female* aggression out of the family, away from the vulnerable children, by deploying it, through men, against enemy, prey, or natural forces on the frontier of the community.

III.   The Normal Unisex of Later Life

While both sexes are sensitive, under culturally stable conditions, to the parental imperative, there is no denying that men are less easily domesticated, and that they are more ready than women to abandon their own homes and to destroy the homes of others. However, contemporary attacks on the *idea* as well as the institution of sex distinctions have most recently been propagated by radical feminists who claim that sex roles are a social invention, in the service of the male rather than the parental imperative. The radical feminists' resentment partially expresses a defiance of fate: If they can depict sex roles and characteristics as a trick played on them by men rather than by nature, then their resentment of existential limitations can be justified, and channeled into the politics of protest. But the anger that the radical feminists feel against the idea of clear sex distinctions is also founded on their ignorance (which they share with men) of the sexual staging of the life cycle. They fear that by conceding the inevitability of sex differences for the earlier years, they concede it for the entire life span. But our transcultural data show that as regards sex differences the past is not prologue. Particularly for women, aging paradoxically brings new beginnings. As parents enter middle age, and as children take over the responsibility for their own security, the chronic sense of parental emergency phases out, the psychological structures established by men and women in response to this crisis condition are in effect dismantled, and the sex-role reversals that shape our transcultural data occur. The general consequence of this period of mid-life relaxation is that both sexes can afford the luxury of living out the potentials and pleasures that they had to relinquish early on, in the service of their particular parental task. A massive turnover of sex roles takes place, wherein men begin to live out directly, to own as part of themselves, the passivity, the sensuality, the tenderness—in effect, the "femininity"—that was previously repressed in the service of productive instrumentality. By the same token, we find, transculturally, the opposite effect in women, who generally become domineering, independent, and unsentimental in middle life. Just as men reclaim title to their denied "femininity," women repossess the aggressive "masculinity" that they once lived out vicariously through their husbands. The consequence of this internal revolution is that the sharp sex distinctions of earlier adulthood break down, and each sex becomes to some degree what the other used to be. With their children grown, wives become less needful and admiring of male assertion, more ready to recognize and enjoy such energies in themselves. They take over some of the drive toward dominance that up to then had been almost exclusively the hallmark of the male. By the same token, men are free to recapture the hidden duality of their own nature: They become more hedonic, more dependent, and also more irritable. That is, they again live out the extremes of their nature, but in later life their aggression is biologically reduced, and takes a peevish rather than a murderous form.

Thus, neither sex is the final custodian of the qualities that we choose to call "masculine" and "feminine." These qualities tend to be distributed not only by sex but also by life period. Men are not forever "masculine"; rather, they can be defined as the sex that shows the trait arrangement that we call "masculine" *before* they show the arrangement that we call "feminine"; and the reverse is true for women (although older women do not by and large acquire the murderous aggression that is biologically available to young men). In sum, the particular constellations that we associate with maleness and femaleness do not pertain to biological sex as much as they pertain to parenthood; and they lose their distinctness and gender specificity as the psychic structures predicated on parenthood are phased out, with varying consequences for men and women.

In effect, this parent-centered perspective allows us to regard the average expectable human life cycle as a coherent psychological event, composed of substages in systematic relationship to each other. From this perspective, the earlier stages of life not only determine the nature of later development, but also are shaped by the oncoming stages, whose future requirements in part organize childhood experience. Thus, the early phases of life, involving the inculcation of trust in others, joy in competence, reliable inner controls, and the capacity for intimacy, can be viewed as necessary preparations for later parenthood. The period of adulthood can be seen as the time when the psychic structures laid down in childhood are energized in response to the parental emergency, along gender-specific lines. Middle and later life can be seen as the period during which the psychic structures predicated on the parental emergency are deenergized, in part dismantled, such that previously disowned behavioral and emotional potentials can be lived out, with varying consequences, depending on biological sex and cultural sponsorship. If we think of parenthood as a pivotal and common human denominator, then we may have a basis for a comparative psychology of the life cycle.

IV.   New Life Styles and the Parental Imperative

An important question still remains: Namely, what significance can this model have for us, who do not live in scarcity societies, and who are not required by necessity to partial out sex roles according to the formula outlined here? Lacking the sense of clear and present danger, we find less and less rationale for the sex differences that impose so much inner restriction on young adults of both sexes. As the sense of emergency ebbs, the privatist critiques of sex distinctions—indulged by men as well as by women—seem more justified, and we are increasingly tempted to undo them in favor of early unisex. Women put aside cosmetics and bras, wear jeans, and go off in search of their manhood. Young men wear their hair long, put on beads, and cultivate their sensitivity and receptivity—their femininity.

Of course we cannot continue to portion out parental responsibilities as though we were still living in the jungle, but we should also remember, as we consider the new versions of marriage that are promoted in contemporary media, that the parental imperative and the parental emergency have not ended with the reduction in infant mortality. The affluent classes tend to confound physical and emotional security, thinking that they have accounted for all their children's needs because they have invested money in child care. This error is revealed too late by bills from their children's psychotherapists, which dwarf whatever was previously paid out for orthodontia and immunization. While physical security is now more predictable (though not guaranteed), urban children in the nuclear family need, perhaps more than ever, the assurance of emotional security. Accordingly, when we consider the unisex marriage, the open marriage, the group marriage, we must ask if these formats continue to ensure the emotional security of young children. Men have been accused, most recently by feminists, of being chauvinists toward nature, of thoughtlessness wrecking fragile ecological balances in the pursuit of profit. But the radical feminists may be equally reckless when they consider demolishing, with only an angry ideology as guide, the species ecology of sex roles and sex differences. Thus, when we view revisions of sex roles now proposed by radical feminists from the comparative perspective, we see how revolutionary they really are. The proposal is to insert unisex, in effect a postparental life style, directly into the pivotal years of young parenthood, the period when sex distinctions are normally sharpest. We do not yet know the consequences of this massive revision of the species-typical life cycle, but it is certain that there will be consequences—I believe that there already have been—and there is a fair chance that they will be disastrous.

After all, while necessity may be the mother of convention, established conventions may also create their own necessities. Sex distinctions may or may not have arisen long ago, in reaction to the conditions of outer necessity and danger that have—at least temporarily—diminished; but we do not know to what extent our contingent accommodations to necessity have become, in their turn, the very necessities to which new adaptations must be fitted. What were once ad hoc adaptations can become fixed features of the internal environment, linked in intricate and irreversible ways with our psychic constitution, even though the original, sponsoring conditions have subsided or disappeared. Thus, while we no longer need to raise boys to be hunters, we do not know to what degree our own or our children's psychic health is predicated on a clear sense of sexual identity, and the presence in the home of two parents, each of whom stands for, *and enjoys,* a distinct sexual nature.

We should not ask innovators to cease experimenting with the forms of human association, but we *can* insist that they be careful, and that they monitor and be accountable for the outcomes that they have helped to bring about. To repeat, sex roles and parental responsibilities cannot remain static, but they should not be blithely changed without first considering the requirements that the parental imperative still sets for our time. Otherwise, as part of the new gluttony, parenthood becomes just another "experience" to be consumed, a piece of adult "self-actualization" for which children pay the ultimate price.

REFERENCES

Barry, H., Bacon, M., & Child, I. A cross cultural survey of some sex differences in socialization. *Journal of Social and Abnormal Psychology,* **55,** 372–432.

Gold, S. Cross-cultural comparisons of role change with aging. *Student Journal of Human Development* (Committee on Human Development, Univ. of Chicago), No. 1, Spring, 1960.

Gutmann, D. An exploration of ego configurations in middle and later life. In B. Neugarten (Ed.), *Personality in middle and later life.* New York: Atherton, 1964.

Gutmann, D. The country of old men: Cross-cultural studies in the psychology of later life. *Occasional Papers in Gerontology,* No. 5, Institute of Gerontology: Univ. of Michigan–Wayne State Univ., April, 1969.

Gutmann, D. Alternatives to disengagement: The old men of the highland Druze. In R. LeVine (Ed.), *Culture and personality: Contemporary readings.* Chicago: Aldine, 1974.

Murdock, G.P. Comparative data on the division of labor by sex. *Social Forces,* 1935, **15,** 551–553.

CHAPTER **11**

The Further Evolution of the Parental Imperative

PATRICIA A. SELF

WEST VIRGINIA UNIVERSITY
MORGANTOWN, WEST VIRGINIA

ABSTRACT

Limitations of Gutmann's parental imperative (Chapter 10, this volume) are discussed in this paper. Although Gutmann is concerned with the impact of changing sex roles upon species survival, it could be argued that these same changes are essential for survival and are occurring out of necessity. The task then becomes recognition of the unique contribution that each person can make, irrespective of expected sex roles. Gutmann also regards the parental imperative as an important focus for explaining adult development. However, the parental imperative is only one of many important influences on the adult. Others might include career development and acquisition of property and stature. All of these theorectical explanations, however, remain to be tested by researchers; until then, Gutmann's model of the parental imperative provides a useful focal point.

Gutmann's model of parenthood and the parental imperative (Chapter 10, this volume) requires additional focus on and elaboration of two issues. The first issue is that parenthood and sex roles, as seen in the past, are necessary components for species survival. The second issue concerns parenthood as the important focus for explaining adult development and behavior.

185

I. The Parental Imperative: Directions for Future Change

At the outset, let me state that I am much more optimistic about the changes occurring in the tradition of parenthood than Gutmann is, and I can only look forward to the "price that children have to pay for their parents' self-actualization." My argument, in essence, is that in order to ensure the survival of the human species, changes must come in the manner in which children are taught, or not taught, sex roles.

In the early days of our species' history, and even today in some parts of the world, it may have been true that one parent could not provide both the physical and emotional security necessary to ensure the survival of its young; however, this seldom seems the case in our modernized society. Not only are there more and more conveniences for both the worker and the homemaker, but now we have machines replacing workers and soon we may see robots maintaining households. At any rate, much of modern society has evolved to such a degree that many of the earlier sex roles (such as father as the hunter and mother as tender of the home fires) are now completely out of place. Our society now demands that persons be much more flexible with regard to the duties required by virtue of being parents. Now fathers are often seen changing diapers or taking the children to the park, and mothers may have obligations outside of the home setting and may often work. In spite of their early sex-role training, or evolutionary determinants if you wish, many persons seem to have been able to adapt successfully to this transition in sex roles.

This successful transition makes one suspect that sex roles are indeed trained and not innate. Literature appearing ever more frequently in the area of infancy substantiates that claim For instance, a study with newborns done by Thoman, Leiderman, and Olson (1972) indicates that mothers, particularly primaparas, respond differently to their infants on the basis of sex. This differential responding was also recently shown in a study done at West Virginia (Will, Self, & Datan, 1974). One 5-month baby was used as the stimulus, dressed alternately as male and female, and maternal responses to the "baby boy" or "baby girl" were measured. It was found that different toys were presented to the infant on the basis of its perceived sex. As well, mothers tended to smile more at the infant when it was dressed as a female and comment more about its appearance than when it was dressed as a male. Will interprets this differential treatment as a consequence of the maternal expectations attributed to sex and not to cues inherent in the infant's behavior. If any degree of infant learning is acknowledged (and we have an ever increasing body of knowledge that the infant is capable of processing considerable environmental information shortly after birth), it is small wonder that 12, 15, or 18 years later males and females differ in such traits as aggression and emotionality To those who argue that there are genetic determinants that cause sex role differentiation in later life, information available from studies of the environmental impact on genetic determinants has shown that the rearing environment can influence the later learning behavior of the same strain of rats (Cooper & Zubek, 1958); it seems unlikely that many years of training would not have considerable impact on sex roles in humans.

Current society is becoming increasingly technological; sex roles that were so useful in the past are now becoming less and less important to ensure species survival; indeed, universal investment in the rearing of large families may lead to species destruction instead. Since sex roles may be determined at least in part by parental training, what will the future bring? It seems certain that it will bring changes in parental behavior and child raising. However, these changes may not be caused only by the movement of women into the labor force, but also by males who feel that their important role in child raising has been short-changed. Recent studies in infant attachment, hoping to dispel notions about the father's limited role in the early personality development of his children, indicate that children form an "active and close relationship with the father during the first 2 years of life [Kotelchuck, 1973, p.9]." Perhaps the best that can be hoped for with the change in parenting is that we will see parents responding to infants and children more on the basis of their behaviors and needs, rather than on the basis of expectations of sex-appropriate behavior. In order for further successful evolution of the human species to occur, recognition of intellectual, social, and emotional needs of all persons of all ages of both sexes seems imperative.

II. The Parental Imperative: The Limits of Explanation

The other issue that needs elaboration is interrelated with the first and concerns the parental imperative as an important focus for explaining adult development and behavior, or, more importantly, attitudes. Gutmann feels that "ideas . . . concerning the keystone role of parenthood in the normal human life cycle have helped . . . to understand and organize certain age and sex regularities and variations that show up in . . . data, across sites [p. 163, this volume]."

The parental imperative may indeed be a major factor in human development for a signficant portion of the life cycle. However, this can be true only for women and men who meet several criteria. First, the persons must be married; second, they must have had one or more children who have survived for a period of time. In addition, what has been depicted in

Gutmann's model is the "traditional" view of marriage and parenthood; meaning that the "wife is bound to the house and is dependent on the husband for material and also for social rewards, and in which the non-working wife has few alternatives to the relationship [Ahammer, 1973]." Ahammer goes on to discuss this view of marriage: "While this model of marriage has guided most research and has unquestioningly been accepted by most investigators . . . the theory of marital role differentiation has received very little empirical support [p. 268]." Other studies indicate that the traditional marriage may represent only one special case in the role distribution in marriage and parenthood (Ahammer, 1973). Certainly this is borne out by the fact that almost 40% of American married women work outside of the home as well as in it (U.S. Department of Commerce, 1973). In addition, the advent of family planning and early childhood education programs has decreased the number of years that either parent spends in full-time nurturance tasks. The role changes associated with parenting, at least for the female, may be much more temporary and/or occur much earlier than previously.

Further, Gutmann's model implies that these are personality and attitude changes in the same persons over time, but, in fact, the majority of the data showing age changes have been cross-sectional, using persons of different ages at the same time, reflecting generational changes and not changes in a particular individual's attitude or personality.

In addition, parenting is not the only important event that occurs in the years from 20 to 50. Occupations are chosen; leisure time activities are planned; property is acquired; stature is gained; persons move in and out of the immediate family situation. Each of these affects the particular family constellation differently. Needless to say, there is a multitude of interactions and interrelationships happening that might have crucial importance to development. In regard to these, other theoretical models might account for the data that spawned the parental imperative in a different fashion by focusing upon different variables. For instance, Erikson (1968) might postulate psychosocial crises involved in the conflict between generativity and stagnation or integrity and despair. Likewise, social learning theory might focus on changing environmental variables and their impact upon the individual. Unfortunately, these views of the development of adulthood are restricted by the same lack of data as the notion of a parental imperative. Until more data are available, the parental imperative serves as a useful explanation, or at least a focal point, for adult development. However, it might be added that the parental imperative may have been more important to the human species in its earlier evolutionary history than it is in modern civilization. The human species, at least in urban society, is now moving away from a recognition of persons based on expectations of sex-appropriate behavior and toward an appreciation of individual differences among persons. This appreciation will be based not only on the distinct sexual nature of a person, but on her or his distinct social, emotional, and intellectual characteristics.

REFERENCES

Ahammer, I. M. Social learning theory as a framework for the study of adult personality development. In P. B. Baltes & K. W. Schaie (Eds.), *Life-span developmental psychology: Personality and socialization.* New York: Academic Press, 1973.

Cooper, R. M. & Zubek, J. P. Effects of enriched and restricted early environments on the learning ability of bright and dull rats. *Canadian Journal of Psychology,* 1958, **12,** 159–164.

Erikson, E. *Identity, youth and crisis,* New York: W. W. Norton, 1968.

Kotelchuck, M. The nature of the infant's tie to his father. Paper presented at the meeting of the Society for Research in Child Development, Philadelphia, Pennsylvania, 1973.

Thoman, E. B., Leiderman, P. H., & Olson, J. P. Neonate-mother interaction during breast-feeding. *Developmental Psychology,* 1972, **6,** 110–118.

U.S. Department of Commerce, 1973. We the American women, Number 4 in a series of reports from the 1970 Census. Washington, D.C.: U.S. Government Printing Office.

Will, J. E., Self, P. A., & Datan, N. Maternal behavior and sex of infant. Paper presented at the meeting of the American Psychological Association, New Orleans, Louisiana, 1974.

CHAPTER 12

Sex Roles and Depression

LEONARD I. PEARLIN

NATIONAL INSTITUTE OF MENTAL HEALTH
BETHESDA, MARYLAND

ABSTRACT

Women are decidedly more susceptible than men to symptoms of depression, and the present paper is concerned with identifying some of the conditions contributing to this important sex difference. Using data from a sample representative of an urban population, the analysis focuses on stress-provoking circumstances to which women are often exposed but from which men are typically shielded. Such circumstances are found especially in the demands and burdens that impinge on homemakers and in the conflicts occurring between the work and family roles of women employed outside the home. The findings indicate that sex differences in depression can be in part accounted for by the problematic experiences of women in these areas.

I. Introduction

There is an accumulation of evidence indicating that women are more likely than men to suffer from mental disorders and psychological impairment. Much of the research bearing on sex differences in mental illness has been assembled by Gove and Tudor (1973) and, while there is not perfect agreement among relevant studies, the overwhelming weight of the materials reviewed by them points up a greater vulnerability of women to functional psychoses and to neurotic disorders. The same sex differences appear in very different types of data, such as sample household surveys of communities, comparisons of first admissions to public and private mental hospitals and to psychiatric units of general hospitals, tabulations from the rolls of people participating in programs of outpatient clinics, and, finally, comparisons of people in psychiatric treatment with private physicians. In each instance women are present in greater numbers than are men.

Side by side with the rather striking accumulation of data pointing up sex differences in psychiatric disturbance is an equally striking absence of empirical studies aimed at learning why these differences exist, how they might come about. The limited research into this question certainly cannot be explained by lack of interest. On the contrary, the general awareness of sex differences that currently prevails has stimulated a particular sensitivity to the potentially negative consequences of inequality between men and women. Nevertheless, a situation exists at the present wherein interest has developed at a much faster pace than has knowledge. Inevitably, this kind of situation leads to a good deal of speculation. Embedded in much of the speculation is the conviction that sex differences in mental disturbance reflect differences in the social experiences of men and women. The data that are reported here are consistent with such a view.

II. Background and Methods

This analysis is drawn from a larger investigation into the social origins of stress. A major purpose of this study is to learn something about the conflicts and frustrations that are built into activities of the normal life cycle. Unlike those studies that focus on crises and ephemeral threats as the major precursors of stress (Rahe, 1968; Myers, Lindenthal, & Pepper, 1971; Dohrenwend, 1973), our research focuses on durable, structured experiences that people have as they engage in their various social roles, such as economic, occupational, family, and parental roles. It is concerned with ordinary people doing rather ordinary things. Essentially it is a study of how people become stressed without really trying.

It is obvious that research into the social origins of stress must eventually take sex into account. Sex, of course, is one of the pivotal ascribed statuses around which a variety of critical and potentially stressful experiences are organized through the entire span of life. Because of the very structure of society itself, many experiences having the potential for arousing stress differentially impinge on men and women. Men and women, first of all, have different roles in society and, even when they are playing the same role, such as in the occupational realm, they are exposed to different constraints and imperatives that shape their behavior. In attempting to account for sex differences in psychological disturbance, it seems a very good bet to pay special attention to those social role areas in which women are exposed to stress-provoking experiences but from which men are relatively insulated. This is precisely what will be done in the present analysis. In so doing, we shall perhaps come to a better understanding both of psychological distress in urban society and of the organization of experience around sex roles.

The data for the study were collected through the use of interview schedules that were developed over a 2-year period. They were administered to a carefully selected cluster sample of 2300 people living in the Chicago Urbanized Area (U. S. Bureau of the Census, 1972), which includes parts of northwestern Indiana as well as the suburbs and outlying towns around Chicago proper. The sex of the person to be interviewed was predesignated in order to come as close as possible to having equal numbers of male and female respondents. However, because women outnumber men in the adult population, and because the households of single people are likely to be headed by women, there are more women than men in the sample (58% women and 42% men). Interviews were also limited to people between the ages of 18 and 65 years of age as a way of ensuring that the sample would have a preponderance of people actively engaged in occupational life. The interviews took an average of about 1 hour and 40 minutes to complete. Despite its length, the subject matter of the interview seemed to maintain the interest of respondents at a fairly high level. One indication of this comes from a question presented at the conclusion of the interview that asked respondents if they would be willing to be reinterviewed in a year or two for a possible follow-up study. Eighty-eight percent indicated their willingness. All in all, then, the survey was a sample representative of a large urban population with an instrument that seemed to engage the involvement and interest of the subjects.

The interview included a large number of questions commonly employed in surveys as indicators of psychological well-being or distress. Five sets of items are used in this inquiry and with each one of them women indicate significantly more disturbance than do men. Thus, women report more ailments that are commonly psychogenic than men do (asthma, colitis, allergies, stomach ulcers, high blood pressure, and rheumatoid arthritis). Second, they more frequently use medications "to give you more energy," "to help you sleep," "to calm your nerves," "to put you in a better mood," and "to relieve you of pain." Measures of cognitive disturbance, anxiety, and depression were also used, each of them adopted from very well-developed symptom measures (Lipman, Rickles, Covi, Derogatis, & Uhlenhuth, 1969; Derogatis, Lipman, Covi, & Rickles, 1971). Women were found to have more cognitive disturbance than men, involving experiences such as trouble in remembering, difficulties in concentrating, problems in making decisions, and having one's mind go blank. They have more anxiety, as judged by psychophysiological signs of trembling hands, racing heart, faintness, shaking inside, trouble catching breath, and so on. Finally, women are more subject to symptoms of depression than are men, the measure of which is described later. It would be somewhat clumsy to deal with each of these aspects of mental health within this paper. I have elected, instead, to focus on depression. This choice is made not because it is of greater theoretical importance than other types of disturbance, or because there is any special set of factors lying behind depression. Indeed, a parallel analysis reveals that the very circumstances that underlie depression also contribute to anxiety. Our findings indicate that depression is more prevalent than other types of mental disturbance, however, and for this reason it is being singled out.

Our measure of depression is a variant of other measures that have been employed in a large number of studies over the past 25 years. It is derived from the frequency (never, once in a while, fairly often, very often) with which people experience each of eleven symptoms: "lack of enthusiasm for doing anything," "poor appetite," "feeling lonely," "feeling bored," "losing sexual interest," "having trouble sleeping," "crying easily," "feeling blue," "feeling low in energy," "feeling hopeless about the future," and "having thoughts of ending your life."

The tone and content of the items defines depression as a condition of malaise, apathy, or weary disaffection. It should be emphasized that such items, when used in a survey of a normal population, are not discriminating a clinical depression. That is, they do not identify psychiatric cases; they do not reveal who needs psychiatric help; they do not indicate functional impairment—whether or not people are able to fulfill in a usual manner their social roles. Scores on these measures have no absolute clinical meaning. They only permit us to establish an order among people based on the relative degree of depression they express. Because these scales are constructed from the presenting symptoms of patients in clinical treatment, it can be mistakenly assumed that a high score thus indicates a need for treatment. But, though depressed people in treatment have high scores, high scores do not necessarily earmark people needing treatment. In field studies using representative samples these scales are not diagnostic tools and scores are not indicative of whether or not people are in need of clinical care.

III. Sex Differences in Depression

I have already indicated that women are appreciably more likely to be depressed than are men. Thus, when scores on our depression scale are divided into five categories of equal size, there are almost 20% more women than men in the highest two categories (chi square $= 115.6$; $p < .001$). One possible explanation of this difference that must be considered at the outset is that the sexes are not *really* different in their susceptibility to depression, but differ only in their responses to questions supposedly asking about depression. It is not likely that response styles play an appreciable part here, however. I say this for several reasons. First, the measures have been developed and validated from clinical symptoms presented by both men and women. Second, the results of our survey are entirely consistent with systematic epidemiological studies of depression (Silverman, 1968) and with the results brought together by Gove and Tudor (1973) from a variety of sources. And, finally, there is direct evidence that the higher depression scores of women do not merely reflect a greater openness on their part in revealing their feelings. This evidence comes from the examination of denial as measured by a nine-item scale constructed for this study.[1] Somewhat surprisingly, men and women do not significantly differ on this scale; but more pertinent, people who are high on denial show a slight (statistically insignificant) tendency toward greater depression, not less. This, then, would discount any explanation arguing that men manifest less depression on the type of measure we are employing simply because they are denying more. Not only do they not deny more, but if they did, they would probably express more depression, not less.

It is safe to conclude, I think, that sex differences in depression are not an artifact of our measuring device, but may reflect, instead, real differences in the conditions of life that are experienced. One of these life conditions concerns the employment of women. It has been suggested (Bernard, 1971, pp. 157–162) that women who have no employment outside the home are in effect barred from an important alternative source of gratification with ultimate dysfunctions for happiness and mental health. By contrast, men who do not find gratification or self-fulfillment in their family roles are presumably able to substitute their occupations as an alternate means for finding whatever it is they might be searching for. Thus, women who find

---

[1] The scale consists of the following statements to which respondents either strongly agreed, agreed somewhat, disagreed somewhat, or strongly disagreed. Scoring was done in Likert fashion, with the scores on the nine items ranging from 9 to 36.

1. It is a sign of weakness for a person to admit that he has problems.
2. I usually try to talk out my problems with other people.
3. When things are going badly, I tend to show it rather than hold it inside.
4. It is difficult for me to talk about myself to other people.
5. I am a person who tries to tell himself that everything is always O.K.
6. For me laughing is a good way to keep from feeling bad.
7. Most of my problems are just a state of mind.
8. As long as I keep smiling, difficulties don't get the best of me.
9. I'm better off when I look only on the positive side of my life.

homemaking unrewarding or frustrating, but who have no outside employment, are more likely to be entrapped in noxious circumstances from which there is no regular relief.

A first step in learning if these arguments are correct—i.e., if differences in employment might help to explain sex differences in depression—is to see if women who work outside the home are less depressed, and therefore more similar to men, than are full-time homemakers. The answer, in brief, is that *there is no difference between employed women and full-time homemakers with regard to depression.* Having an outside job or being a homemaker are by themselves not predictive of depression. But this does not necessarily mean that these roles make no difference to the mental functioning of women. What it does indicate is that in order to understand the relevance of either homemaking or outside employment to depression, we must look at the meanings of these roles for people and at the conditions that are encountered within the roles. We shall first look at homemaking, at some of the experiences of women in this role that seem to have a bearing on their susceptibility to depression. Following this, the same kind of examination will be made of women's work roles.

IV. Disenchantment with Homemaking

The meaning of homemaking, the preparation of women for the role, the priorities they assign to it, and the organization of activities within it vary considerably among individuals and among social groups (Lopata, 1971). Some find it a source of pleasure and pride, seeing it as a most important calling for a woman to follow, an opportunity to put to practice skills they have learned and values to which they have been socialized. Other women may find homemaking an unchallenging and unrewarding trap, something they did not look forward to in the first place and in which little goes on that could make them change their minds. Most of the homemakers we questioned are somewhere in between these extreme views, neither uncritically accepting the role nor unreservedly rejecting it. In our survey six items are used to assess the degree of disenchantment that exists with this important role: "How often are you (1) uninterested or bored with doing household chores; (2) really enjoying the work you do at home; (3) using your talents and abilities in doing your housework; (4) feeling that you should be doing more important things; (5) able to have free time for yourself; (6) not appreciated for your work in the home?" The six items probe the extent to which homemaking succeeds in engaging the interests, skills, and pride of women. Answers to the questions distinguish women who experience the role as a rewarding and involving activity from those viewing it as an onerous chore, lacking the ingredients necessary to stimulate enthusiasm. Although each of the items touches on a somewhat different facet of homemaking, taken together they constitute a suitable indicator of role strain or disenchantment.

Looking now at the relationship of role disenchantment to depression, we find—as could be expected—that the chances of women being depressed increase with the degree of role disenchantment they feel ($r = .34, p < .001$). It would be difficult to argue that this is a one-way relationship, with depression only following from role disenchantment. There may be some reciprocal effect as well, with disenchantment possibly reflecting a preexisting depressive state. Clearly, we need a fuller understanding of the relationship in order to be confident that there is a flow of influence leading from experience in the role to depression. We can achieve this by exploring some of the social conditions that underlie disenchantment. This will help to provide a broader picture of the contexts in which this role strain is likely to arise. At the same time, the more we are able to account for disenchantment by social circumstances, the more able we are to reject any assertion that being turned off on homemaking is merely an expression of depression, rather than the other way around. For the present, then, the analysis will be concerned only with explicating some of the factors resulting in disenchantment with homemaking. Following this, I shall bring the issues back to depression.

A. Aspirations and Disenchantment

I originally thought with some certainty that homemaking would be least liked by and most stressful to women whose aspirations and experience orient them to major roles outside the home, and who would consequently be disposed to experience housework as frustrating or demeaning. Thus, for one thing, I expected that extended formal education—to the extent that it prepares people for rewarding occupational life—would be associated with disaffection. I considered it likely, too, that women with previous occupational experience would be most vulnerable to role strains as homemakers, simply because they have had some taste of the options and alternatives available in the outside world. This, I further predicted, would be especially true among homemakers whose experience had been in jobs of relatively high status; deprivation should be keenest in this group because they have tasted a level of gratification and reward in the past that exceeds that provided by homemaking, a role that supposedly bears little prestige (Gove & Tudor, 1973, pp. 814–815). Finally I anticipated that middle-class housewives would be least likely to find homemaking to be a self-fulfilling and satisfying role, since the values of this class are especially likely to orient its members to career achievement. As it turns out, none of these variables bears any relationship to role disenchantment. It would seem, then, that *women do not particularly dislike homemaking because it stands as a frustrating barrier to the realization of aspirations outside the family domain.* Their acceptance of or aversion to the homemaking role will have to be explained by other conditions.

B. Family Life Cycle and Disenchantment

Some of the conditions that are relevant to disaffection are anchored in the immediate family and in the very mundane problems of mobilizing the time and energy required to run the household. Two closely joined pieces of information are revealing in this regard. One is that role disenchantment tends to increase with the number of children living at home ($r = .26, p < .001$). Second, it increases to an even greater magnitude as the age of the youngest child declines ($r = -.31, p < .001$). Assuming that homemaking tends to be more difficult and more relentlessly burdensome in relatively large families and with relatively young families, it seems evident that role strain—and ultimately depression—are in part determined simply by how tough the job is. It can be said, although possibly with some exaggeration, that being a homemaker would not be such a difficult job for many women if it did not also entail raising a family. When we juxtapose these findings with what we learned earlier about the unimportance of unrealized aspirations as a source of disenchantment, we are led to the conclusion that role strains result not because women prefer employment outside the home but because they experience severe demands in their employment inside the home.

Returning for a moment to the hard work that homemaking occasionally entails, it should be noted that demands on time and energy are especially apt to be experienced as strainful when women have to wrestle with the job by themselves, without the benefit of aid from a husband. An indication of this is seen in the correlations between the number of children and disenchantment among single mothers and, by comparison, among mothers with a spouse in the household. The original correlation between family size and disenchantment, remember, is .26. However, among single mothers this correlation jumps to .33 ($p < .001$), while among married mothers it drops to .12 ($p < .001$). Apparently the hard work of family life, when it must be borne without the aid of a husband, is especially likely to be a strainful experience.

Age is another strategically important variable to consider here, because it embodies life-cycle changes as well as cultural changes that may be under way in the definition and acceptance of the homemaking role in the society.

The relationship between age and role disenchantment is negative: As age increases, the chances of there being disaffection decreases ($r = -.26$, $p < .001$). It is apparent that, contrary to popular view, young motherhood is not a rosy, carefree time of life. Some of the reasons for this may not be so obvious, though. Apparently older women are less turned off by home-making not only because they might have had more time to adapt to the role, or because they operate within a more traditional set of values, but also because age is interlaced with the family age and size factors that have been shown to be related to disenchantment. In families of older women, in other words, there are fewer children living at home, and those that are in residence tend to be older; the family is at a more advanced stage of its life cycle. Consequently, in order to see the relationship of age to disaffection with homemaking in an unobstructed way, it is necessary to control for the age and size of families. When this is done, the correlation is reduced from the initial $-.26$ to a partial of $-.16$ ($p < .001$). Thus, older women are less strained by homemaking both by having been socialized to a different set of values and because the job of homemaking is just plain easier for them. When faced with similar family conditions, there is a smaller difference between older and younger women in their reactions to homemaking. What makes the difference is not age alone, but the location of families in the life cycle as well.

C. Social Relations and Disenchantment

I shall now turn from the composition of the nuclear family to a different type of circumstance having some influence on whether or not homemaking is an unpleasant experience or one that is positive and self-engaging. This concerns the extent to which women are isolated from or involved in a network of social relations. Respondents were asked a number of questions pertinent to this issue: if they have relatives living in the area; if they have friends close by; how long they have lived in their neighborhoods; and if they have membership in voluntary associations. The more separated women are from these kinds of social contacts, the more disposed they are to be disaffected with homemaking. Although the magnitude of the multiple correlation of these factors and disaffection is on the modest side ($R. = .16$, $P < .05$), its implications are nevertheless important and should be spelled out.

There are at least three functions performed by social networks in the lives of homemakers. Such networks are, first, a potential source of information pertaining to the recognition and management of problems arising in homemaking. This information provides standards for defining what to ignore, what to get excited about, and how to deal with crises. Social relations, in other words, help place the events and demands of homemaking in a normative framework, thereby clarifying and stabilizing their meaning. Second, social relations may serve as sources of emotional support and encouragement, something to lean on for help when the going is tough. And, finally, social contacts and affiliations can provide a haven to which one may flee for a bit of relief from ordinary routines. In this manner social relations function as real safety valves and vehicles of escape for the hassled homemaker. Women who are isolated from networks of social relations not only are deprived of these functions, but, in addition, become exclusively locked into marriage and other family roles, and the immediate family simply cannot easily satisfy by itself the full range of emotional and affiliative needs of women.

D. Coping with Role Disenchantment

Let us return now to the original relationship we observed between the disenchantments that women experience as homemakers and depression. There is, of course, a great deal that goes into this relationship that lies outside the scope of this study. As incomplete as our knowledge is, however, it is evident that homemaking is more likely to be stressful because of the hard work and demands it imposes than because of its frustration of dreams and desires for work outside the home. Furthermore, when the duties of homemaking are borne without the presence of a husband or in isolation from people other than immediate family, there is a greater chance that the role will be disliked—possibly because the homemaker under these conditions is deprived of the norms, the support, the emotional outlets, and the alternative gratifications that social contacts ordinarily provide. But whatever the etiology of disenchantment with homemaking may be, when it is present in intensified form there is a good chance that depression will result. The activities embodied by homemaking are too important, involve too much time and energy, to allow strains to be easily shrugged off without their eventually taking a psychological toll.

Yet not everyone who is disenchanted with homemaking ends up depressed. A great deal depends on how women cope with the problems and difficulties they encounter in this role. Part of a coping repertoire, in turn, involves the appraisal of these problems and difficulties. Two types of appraisal are relevant here. The first concerns whether women see the present conditions of homemaking as extending and entrapping them far into the future, or whether they optimistically anticipate that the strains of the role will abate in the foreseeable future. In this regard women were asked if they see their homemaking "getting easier in the next year or two, staying about the same, or becoming more difficult." When they see the role as becoming easier in this time frame, any strains that they experience as homemakers are somewhat less likely to result in depression than when they expect things either to remain the same or grow more difficult ($r = .29, p < .001$ for "easier," $r = .36, p < .001$ for "same" and "more difficult"). Their view of the future, therefore, affects homemakers' appraisals of present objective reality, and an optimistic outlook blunts what might otherwise be depressive consequences of strain.

The second kind of appraisal having some influence on the probability that role strains will contribute to depression involves the comparisons homemakers make with others engaged in the same role. In this connection the following question was presented: "How would you compare your life as a homemaker with other women your age? Is it easier, about the same, or more difficult?" Among women who see themselves as having experiences more difficult than those confronted by other homemakers, the correlation between strain and depression is .54 ($p < .001$). Women under the same strains, but evaluating themselves as similar to or better off than others, are considerably less likely to be depressed; the correlation in this group drops to .27 ($p < .001$). It appears, therefore, that both the temporal and group frames of reference can help shape the evaluation of experience and in this way serve either to increase or decrease vulnerability to depression These appraisal techniques, incidentally, describe only a small part of a coping repertoire. They do demonstrate, however, why it is difficult to predict psychological distress directly from role strains without also taking into account coping responses.

V. Occupational Strains and Depression

I am going to turn now from the homemakers to focus more directly on women who have employment outside the home. It will be remembered that having an occupation does not, by itself, shield women from depression, for there is virtually no difference in this regard between the homemaking and employed groups. In the light of this fact it would seem that the impact of occupation on mental states will depend on the conditions that women encounter in the course of their working and the meaning these conditions have for them. The ways that occupational roles come to be relevant to depression are thus very similar to the processes involved in the relationship between homemaking and depression. It is not simply *having* a role that matters; what is important are the experiences one has while in the role.

A reasonable place to look for occupational experiences having some bearing on depression is directly within the job itself, its activities, rewards, interpersonal relations, and so on. Since employed women are more apt to be depressed than employed men, one would assume that women experience more hardships on the job than do men. The interview deals at some length with problems and strains that people encounter in their work. It asks about unfavorable conditions in the work setting, such as the presence of dust, dirt, and exposure to injury or illness. Other questions inquire more into the demands of the work tasks themselves. asking about repetitiveness, overload, and pressures resulting from technological changes. A third area of questioning concerns the adequacy of various kinds of rewards: income, job security, fringe benefits, and future opportunities for advancement. A final set of questions was designed to identify any occupational strains existing around work relations, the fairness of supervisors, recognition for accomplishments, and experiences of depersonalization. Many of these conditions, when they do exist in occupational experience, are indeed associated with depression. Thus, out of 19 problematic conditions probed by our questions, 9 are appreciably related to depression. However, in every instance where there is such an association between an element of occupational strain and depression, the correlations are greater for men than for women. Furthermore, the problems and frustrations encountered in the job realm are consistently more likely to have depressive consequences for men than for women when they are of the same occupational status. It should be underscored that these results do not indicate that the strains that men experience are more severe than those impinging on female jobholders. What they do indicate is that in the occupational domain men are more vulnerable to depressive consequence of strains than are women; women withstand the strains of work with greater equanimity than do men. The fact that men are more depressed than women by the same job strains indicates that the work place and its events, in our society, more closely regulate the psychological fate of men than of women.

A. Occupational and Family Role Conflict

This being the case, the greater disposition of employed women toward depression cannot be explained by a more problematic daily work life. Though women are less depressed than men by adverse conditions they find on the job, they are more exposed than men to problems and dilemmas attendant upon taking a job in the first place. While the occupational experiences of men certainly have a broad range of consequences for their family roles (Pearlin, 1971), men do not have to grapple with the same problems as women in reconciling outside employment with these roles. Female workers, a group whose decisions and dilemmas have received considerable attention (Myrdal & Klein, 1956; Nye & Hoffman, 1963; Coser & Rokoff,

1971; Epstein, 1971), have a more difficult and conflicting time in accommodating their jobs to their three principal family roles: their housework, their marital roles, and their maternal roles.

Questions were designed to tap the presence and intensity of conflict between having an outside job and each one of these family roles. The first, that involving housework, is ascertained through four items asking about the sheer overload that results from a woman's having major responsibilities both as a wage earner and as a houseworker. They were asked: (1) Is there anyone who regularly helps you with the housework? (2) How often do you just have more to do than you can handle? (3) How often do you have too little time for household jobs? (4) How often do you have no free time for yourself? Marital conflict is represented by disagreements between women and their husbands arising out of employment. To evaluate this type of conflict women were asked several questions about the consequences of their working: whether it was something to which their husbands objected or something they supported; if it interfered with joint leisure time activities; if employment led to disagreements over money; to disagreements over the sharing of household chores; and if it led to any ambiguities over which of the spouses is the main breadwinner and head of the family. Conflict over maternal roles, finally, was measured by asking the employed mother, first, about the adequacy of her arrangements for child care; how often she feels that she may be missing out on maternal pleasures by working; the frequency of concern over children getting into trouble while she is at work; and worry that children may not be receiving proper attention.

The three conflicts were measured in Likert fashion by scoring the frequencies or intensities with which the various issues are experienced. As could be predicted, each conflict is significantly ($p < .001$) related to depression (overload, $r = .16$; marital conflict, $r = .23$; maternal conflict, $r = .20$) and together they have a multiple correlation of $R = .28$. These relationships indicate that whether or not a job has negative consequences for depression depends somewhat on how integrated it is with family roles. The more easily work outside the home is accommodated by these roles, the less depression there is likely to be. On the other hand, the greater the conflict between work and home, the greater are the vulnerabilities to depression. It should be noted that by their very nature these conflicts and their depressive consequences will rise and abate as the woman enters adulthood and passes through the various stages of her (and her family's) life cycle.

B. Social Factors in Role Conflict

Conflicts between work and home do not arise randomly among working women. Their occurrence depends on the interplay of a variety of factors, including the meaning and importance of work to individuals, the nature and composition of the family situation, and certain social characteristics, especially class and age. In trying to specify some of these antecedents it is not possible to treat the three types of conflict as one, for each type has its own somewhat different configuration of circumstances leading up to it. Instead of attempting a detailed and separate accounting, I shall simply focus on maternal conflicts as a way of illustrating a few of the conditions under which conflicts between work and family roles can emerge and be exacerbated.

To begin with, I find that the women's ego involvement in their work increases the risk of being caught up in maternal conflict. One indicator of involvement comes from the answers to an item asking workers how strongly they agree or disagree with this statement: "As soon as I leave work, I put it out of my mind." Women who strongly disavow such a practice, presumably because they are involved in their jobs, more often find themselves in conflict between job and child care than do women who are able to mentally segregate work from other activities ($r = .15, p < .01$). However, the social class standing of women affects this relationship in an important way. In this regard we find that job involvement is more closely associated with maternal conflict among middle-class than working-class women. Thus, the correlation between the answers to this item and depression is .22 ($p < .02$) for middle-class mothers, while for working-class mothers it is .11 (n.s.). It is almost as though the employed middle-class mother who is really into her job may end up feeling she is abandoning her children. The safe course is to hold work at an emotional distance.

The same phenomenon can be traced from another statement, this one distinguishing workers who are primarily interested in the extrinsic rewards of work from those oriented to its intrinsic rewards. It says: "The most important thing about my job is that it provides me the things I need in life." Agreement with this statement is probably indicative of an orientation to intrinsic rewards. Predictably, the more strongly a woman rejects this statement, the more likely she will also be in conflict over child care ($r = .16, p < .01$). And again, the relationship is much stronger among middle-class than working-class women ($r = .26, p < .001$ and $r = .07$, n.s., respectively). Overall, then, it seems that job and maternal roles run the greatest risk of coming into conflict when the mother is absorbed in her work and when it is valued for itself rather than for what it instrumentally provides outside the job. It would appear that under some conditions it is not conflictful to be both a worker and a mother; the conflicts are more likely to arise when the woman is invested in both roles. Bardwick (1971) distinguishes career from job in talking about the cross-pressures that employed women experience, and it would seem that to avoid conflict with maternal roles it is probably easier for a woman to hold a job than to pursue a career. The problem for the career-oriented woman "is not two jobs, but two large ambitions that have trouble living together in a home with young children [Bardwick, 1971, p. 200]."

Our findings are certainly consistent with this view, especially for middle-class women. For working-class women, on the other hand, the main source of conflict lies more in the structure of the family situation than in the meaning of their occupations. The ages of the children of employed working-class women are particularly relevant in this regard. Thus, the lower the age of the youngest child at home, the more conflicted the working-class mother will be over her outside employment ($r = -.25, p < .02$). Interestingly, this same condition does not have any appreciable relevance to middle-class mothers, mainly, I would suppose, because logistical arrangements for child care are easier for these mothers.

Just as it differs from one class to another, conflict between work and maternal roles also does not occur equally among all age groups. As one could guess from material already discussed, the likelihood of intense conflict is somewhat greater among younger women and tends to abate somewhat with age ($r = -.15, p < .02$). But it is not age as such that is responsible for this relationship, rather it is family conditions associated with age. As I noted earlier in discussing homemaking, age is interconnected with the number of children living at home and to the ages of the children. Indeed, these variables are so closely connected to mothers' ages that it is necessary to control for the number and ages of children before assuming that the age of the working mother has an independent part in arousing maternal conflict. When this is done the initial relationship virtually disappears. What this indicates is that when older and younger working women face similar family conditions, they are also likely to face the same dilemmas as they strive to accommodate their jobs to their family roles. Age is related to conflict among working mothers only by virtue of changes in family conditions that occur within the life span.

Keep in mind that while we have been trying to identify some of the conditions associated with role conflict, our ultimate interest is still with depression. A number of conditions have been examined that either directly or indirectly bear on depression, the key antecedent being the dilemmas and strains that may arise between work and family roles. Indirectly contributing to depression through their effect on these conflicts are circumstances such as the meaning of work, family compositon, and social class. There are undoubtedly other circumstances not treated here that are also relevant to the arousal of conflict and to emotional depression. But even this scanning should indicate how insufficient it is to look only at work activities in trying to understand the emotional distress of employed women. The meaning of these activities, their relevance to other activities, and the social characteristics of the employed women must be treated as prominent ingredients in processes leading to depression.

VI. Summary and Conclusions

In summary, it will be recalled that this paper started out by asking what might account for differences between men and women in their disposition to depression. Unfortunately, at the conclusion of the paper the question is still very far from being obsolete. It was possible to show, however, that women are indeed exposed to conditions contributing to depression from which men are shielded. Thus, women alone encounter conflicts in being homemakers, or in juggling both occupational and family roles. To whatever extent such experiences feed depression, the fact that they affect only women would perhaps explain part of the difference between the sexes.

It should be emphasized, though, that this analysis just scratches the surface in revealing how social experience affects well-being and the differences that exist among groups in this regard. What I hope is evident, however, is that a psychological state such as depression is more than just a psychological problem. It is intimately intertwined with the values and aspirations that people acquire; with the nature of the situations in which they are performing major roles, such as in occupation and family; with the location of people in broader social structures, such as age and class; and with the coping devices they use, such as temporal and group comparisons. Clearly, our mental states may have diffuse social origins, resulting from the convergence on individuals of diverse and interacting forces. It is in the identification and explication of the connections between our inner psychological states and properties of our social environments that we can achieve what C. Wright Mills (1959) saw as the proper task of social science: to demonstrate how the psychological problems of individuals may also be public issues.

REFERENCES

Bardwick, J. M. *Psychology of women: A study of bio-cultural conflicts.* New York: Harper, 1971.

Bernard, J. *Women and the public interest.* Chicago: Aldine, 1971.

Coser, R. L., & Rokoff, G. Women in the occupational world: Social disruption and conflict. *Social Problems,* 1971, **18**, 535–553.

Derogatis, L. R., Lipman, R. S., Covi, L., & Rickles, K. Neurotic symptom dimensions. *Archives of General Psychiatry,* 1971, **24**, 454–464.

Dohrenwend, B. S. Life events as stressors: A methodological inquiry. *Journal of Health and Social Behavior,* 1973, **14**, 167–175.

Epstein, C. F. *Women's place: Options and limits in professional careers.* Berkley, California: Univ. of California Press, 1971.

Gove, W., & Tudor, J. Adult sex roles and mental illness. *American Journal of Sociology,* 1973, **78,** 812–835.

Lipman, R. S., Rickles, K., Covi, L., Derogatis, L., & Uhlenhuth, E.H. Factors of symptom distress. *Archives of General Psychiatry,* 1969, **21,** 328–338.

Lopata, H. *Occupation housewife.* New York: Oxford Univ. Press, 1971.

Mills, C. W. *The sociological imagination.* New York: Oxford Univ. Press, 1959.

Myers, J. K., Lindenthal, J. J., & Pepper, M. P. Life events and psychiatric impairment. *Journal of Nervous and Mental Disease,* 1971, **152,** 149–157.

Myrdal, A., & Klein, V. *Women's two roles.* London: Routledge & Kegan Paul, 1956.

Nye, F. I., & Hoffman, L. W. (Eds.) *The employed mother in America.* Chicago: Rand McNally, 1963.

Pearlin, L. I. *Class context and family relations.* Boston, Massachusetts: Little, Brown, 1971.

Rahe, R.H. Life-change measurement as a predictor of illness. *Proceedings of the Royal Society of Medicine,* 1968, **61** (November), 44–46.

Silverman, C. *The epidemiology of depression.* Baltimore, Maryland Johns Hopkins Press, 1968.

U.S. Bureau of the Census. *Census of housing: 1970; block statistics: financial report (HC–3)–68. Chicago, Illinois–Northwestern Indiana Urbanized Area.* Washington, D.C.: U.S. Government Printing Office, 1972.

CHAPTER 13

Situational Stress: A Hopi Example[1]

ALICE SCHLEGEL

UNIVERSITY OF PITTSBURGH
PITTSBURGH, PENNSYLVANIA

ABSTRACT

This paper examines stresses that are built into the normal life cycle, from a cross-cultural perspective. The case of the Hopi female is examined in some detail, showing how the role of the adult Hopi woman and the socialization she undergoes for this role puts her into a position of stress during her adolescence. For most women, this is a mildly troublesome period that is successfully overcome when they marry and have children. For some, however, stress can lead to severe depression; and this depression is culturally recognized as a situationally induced pathology.

This paper introduces a cross-cultural perspective on the issue of situational stress in everyday life and psychopathological reactions to it. Pearlin (Chapter 12, this volume) refers to everyday stresses on American women which lead to depression. My own research on the life cycle of Hopi Indian women also reveals stress at one stage of the life cycle, stress that the Hopi believe can lead to reactions of depression and even death.

[1] The field research on which this paper is based was funded by the National Institute of Mental Health, whose assistance is gratefully acknowledged.

I.   Sex Roles and Depression: Cross-Cultural Findings

Two general findings in Pearlin's study receive support in the anthropological literature. The first is that disaffection with homemaking, shown to be related to depression in women, rises with the number and declining age of children in the home. The interpretation of this finding is that care of children, particularly young children, puts a strain on women. We have evidence that this is true not only for our own society but also for traditional societies, in which presumably children may be more desired and valued than they are in the United States. Minturn and Lambert (1964), in a carefully controlled study of mothering in six cultures, show that "maternal instability," by which they mean moodiness and irritability, increases with the degree of child-care responsibilities the mother has, regardless of the number of other demanding tasks in or out of the home. The authors state: "It may be that few tasks are as harassing as caring for small children." Thus it is not only our society that puts burdens upon young mothers, or in which women react negatively to the demands of sole responsibility for young children.

The second point with cross-cultural support is Pearlin's finding that the lack of a supportive figure in the home, or a supportive social network outside the home, puts stress on mothers. Stack (1974), in an analysis of domestic and kinship organization among poor urban blacks, shows how support from the bilateral kindred complements or replaces support from the husband with relation to children. In fact, where women have to choose between loyalty to the kindred and to the conjugal bond, they may choose to remain unmarried, in the belief that the kindred are more likely to be reliable than the husband. So these women have two kinds of resources open to them, and their strategy is to choose whichever one seems more promising. Therefore, in an urban American population, the absence of a husband may be less stressful for poor blacks, and perhaps other ethnic minority groups, than for women of the middle class, where spatial and social mobility tend to break up the network of the kindred, and which does not have a tradition of the kindred members' taking responsibility for one another.

II.   Hopi Women and Stress

Pearlin (Chapter 12, this volume) has discussed stress in everyday life as illustrated by women in depression. I have collected data applicable to this issue among the Hopi Indians of Arizona. My observations come out of my research among older Hopi women and reflect their early socialization, in the period roughly 1910–1930. Since World War II there have been major changes in Hopi life, particularly in some of the conciously modernizing villages, so that these data do not necessarily characterize all younger women today. More ethnographic details can be found in Schlegel (1973).

The stress period that is built into the life cycle of the Hopi woman is the adolescent stage, roughly between puberty at around age 12 and marriage at around age 18. It is during this stage that intense socialization for her adult sex role is carried on. Up to puberty, the girl has been treated more or less the same as boys of her own age: mixed-sex play groups occur, both sexes go through the same childhood initiation ceremony at the same time, and there are few differences in punishment for the two sexes, although in general girls are treated a bit more gently than boys. The girl, of course, has been learning her sex-specific tasks with her mother, as the boy has been learning his with his father; but both within the home and in the community, boys and girls are relatively undifferentiated.

This changes at puberty. Whereas boys continue in their rather carefree lives until their intensive responsibility training, which comes later, upon marriage, girls are drawn ever more strongly into the house, both literally and figuratively. The Hopi are matrilineal and matrilocal, so that the mother during this time is training her daughter to be her eventual replacement within both the house and the lineage. The ownership of the house, its furnishings, its food supply, and ultimate authority over household property and household activities of its members reside with the women: Men are said to "stand outside the house." In anticipation of this heavy responsibility, the mother begins full-time training for the girl's adult role. She keeps her daughter inside the house working at the laborious task of corn-grinding, and she discourages her from running about the village. Girls get together in small groups to grind, go to the well, or chat, but they are watched, and mixed-sex activities such as picnics are supervised by younger siblings, much to the chagrin of their older sisters.

In order to understand the goals of female adolescent socialization and why adolescence should be a stress period, it is necessary to know the role that women play in the society and in the ideology of the Hopi. I have already indicated that they play a central role in lineage and domestic group organization. They participate in productive and distributive activities as well. While men do most of the work contributing to subsistence— horticulture, hunting, and herding—they work land that has been allocated to them through their wives and which belongs to the wife's clan. Men and women share the tasks of processing raw materials for consumption and trade, the men weaving and the women making baskets and pottery and preparing foodstuffs according to the elaborate Hopi cuisine. Men go on long-distance trading expeditions, but women control much of the trade that takes place within the community, either intravillage small-scale exchange or the trade with nomadic or other Pueblo peoples who bring their goods to the Hopi villages. Economically, then, women are in control of their own property and that belonging to the common household store. The roles they play in the community political and ceremonial systems are necessary but minor, and most of their activities are focused around household and lineage activities. However, the household, as the core unit of the lineage and the clan, assumes an importance that it lacks in many other societies. Village activities are played out within a structure of interclan relationships, so that the households are the building blocks with which the community is constructed.

In many societies that conceptualize their worlds in terms of sexual dualism, the female plays a necessary but secondary or inferior role in the conceptual scheme. This is not true for the Hopi, perhaps because their key value in the total religious system is life. Ideologically, males and females, and the male and female principles, are equal and complementary. The female is associated with the earth and life, as the male is associated with the spirit and death. As mothers and feeders, women are the fountain and maintainers of life, and men provide the physical, emotional, and spiritual protection they need to fulfill their function. Thus, the women stand, so to speak, at the core of the conceptual universe, just as they stand at the core of the lineage and clan in the social world.

Training for a woman's adult role precedes marriage, and women are accorded full adult status upon marriage. This puts a strain on the mother, who must temper her indulgence with disipline and some severity, and the daughter, who must learn to take her place as a central member of her household, at the expense of her erstwhile freedom.

In addition to this intensive socialization, another strain is put upon adolescent girls. The choice of marriage partners is up to the young people involved, with the parents and close lineage members having some veto power; Rosenblatt (1966) lists the Hopi as one of the societies characterized by romantic love. Because the woman is the dominant figure in the home, it is her responsibility to induce the young man of her choice to come into it as her husband. In fact, it is girls who formally propose to boys. There is some tension involved in this, for the young husband holds little honor in his wife's house, where he is under the direct authority of his father-in-law and ultimate authority of his mother-in-law. He will have to prove his worth through long years of hard work as provider. No wonder, then, that he is reluctant to leave the comforts of his mother's house, his "real" home, and take up residence as a stranger and outsider in his wife's house. The delicacy of the situation is given cultural recognition in the formal etiquette governing the rejection of marriage proposals and the treatment of brides.

III. Stress and Depression

We have seen that the adolescent period is one of stress for Hopi women, and it arises out of the radical restrictions on freedom, the intensification of the mother's disciplinary role, and the pressure put upon the girl to find a husband. Let us now look at the girl's reaction to stress.

The normal reaction that women recognize in their own histories and in their daughters is one of moodiness and irritability. Girls become difficult to handle, and tensions arise between them and their mothers. Usually these tensions are reflected in such behavior as tearful outbursts or running away from home to the house of a relative. Other female kin are supportive, and the girl can always find sympathy in the house of a "mother" (mother's sister) or an "aunt" (father's sister); but ultimately she must accept her mother's discipline and learn to control herself.

There is a pathological reaction, however, which the Hopi recognize and dread: a state of depression, a feeling of apathy that robs the victim of her appetite and her will to live. There are numerous stories about people succumbing to depression and dying as a result.

Any Hopi can fall victim to depression, and there are two situations that are seen as particularly conducive to a depressive reaction: the death of a loved person, and the rejection of a woman by her lover. Anyone is vulnerable to depression from bereavement. A newly dead corpse may be scolded "for leaving us," and it is feared that the newly dead may appear in dreams to the living and seduce them into following him into the afterlife. To obviate this, the dead spirit must be chased away from the village. The theme that runs through the relationship between the newly dead and the survivors is one of rejection: rejection by the dead, especially the one dying an untimely death, and rejection of the dead by the living.

The second form of depressive reaction is found only among women. In folktales, when a man or boy is rejected by a girl, he gets a spirit helper either to win the girl's affection or to take revenge upon her. When a woman is rejected by a man, whether she is a wife who is neglected or abused by her husband or a girl who is rejected by a lover or prospective husband, she is considered to be likely to succumb to depression and possibly eventual death.

Whether or not the Hopi are more vulnerable to rejection than are people of other cultures cannot be determined from any evidence we now have. Nor do we know, statistically, whether women actually do become depressed more than men. It is believed that they do. The dynamics of family organization place women in a position of vulnerability vis-á-vis men. While the woman is dominant in the home, it is a fragile dominance: She depends upon the husband for support, yet he is put into a position in which he gets little honor for his work beyond his satisfaction in successfully fulfilling his protective and supportive role. She can order him out at any time, but by the same token he is free to leave and go to another woman or return to the house of his mother or sister, where he always has a right to live. In spite of the strong clan organization, households are quite independent of one another, and help from kin to needy women may be given grudgingly if at all. Women must win and hang onto men, who may not always be willing to cooperate if they can make more satisfactory arrangements elsewhere. The result of this is that men are not always reliable. The girl's appraisal of her situation, and her reaction to it, is due in part to the evidence of male unreliability that she has before her. It may also be that her relationship with her father serves as a model for male unreliability, and that rejection responses are triggered by sensitivities developed during earlier childhood. (This psychodynamic explanation is covered more thoroughly in Schlegel, 1973.)

Whatever the genesis of the depressive reaction, whether in response to immediate stress or as a delayed response to earlier rejection fears, it is clear that this feminine reaction arises within the context of the stressful situation in which the adolescent Hopi girl finds herself. Her relationship with her mother is strained and she is pressured to find a husband. This is a period of normal stress in the Hopi female life cycle. Once the goals of adolescent socialization are achieved—after the girl has married and produced a child, and she has taken her place alongside her mother as the person in charge of the household—the stress is diminished. Unlike the women in Pearlin's Chicago sample, young Hopi mothers are subject to fewer stresses (unless deserted by their husbands and otherwise unsupported). This is a particularly happy period of the woman's life, when she is the center of attention of the household and, to some degree, the clan. Having established herself, she gains much of the freedom she gave up during adolescence, and she has successfully become a Hopi woman with the right to respect and recognition in her household and the village.

IV. Stress and the Life Cycle

It would appear that every society places stress on its members at one or more stages in the life cycle. In urban areas of the United States it seems to be early adolescence, young adulthood, and old age. For the Hopi, it is adolescence for women and young adulthood for men. It is likely that periods of biological transformation—adolescence or the transition into old age—lend themselves to being periods of stress as well, but here we must look at cultural interpretations of stages of the life cycle and the ways in which these stages are handled in order to understand the social and psy-chological stresses put upon individuals as they move through life. The Hopi man or woman passes into old age without much social recognition of the fact and little or no change in status. The Sicilian peasant, on the other hand, goes through a dramatic transformation from a vigorous man in his prime to an "old man" in a matter of weeks after he turns over his land to his sons (Constance Cronin, personal communication).

Such stresses as these are interconnected with a wide range of social arrangements, including such factors as residence patterns, inheritance practices, the transfer of authority from one generation to another, the inevitable breakup of the household or lineage as it grows beyond its re-source base, and the struggle for positions of honor in open, competitive societies. These arrangements put stresses upon people at different stages of the life cycle. We can say in conclusion that normal or situational stress is built into the life-cycle plan, times of stress being determined by culturally determined patterns and the exigencies of social life.

REFERENCES

Minturn, L. & Lambert, W. W. *Mothers of six cultures*. New York: Wiley, 1964.

Schlegel, A., The Adolescent socialization of the Hopi girl *Ethnology* 1973, **4**, 449–462.

Stack, C. B. Sex roles and survival strategies in an urban Black community. In M. Rosaldo & L. Lamphere (Eds.), *Woman, culture and society*. Stanford, California: Stanford Univ. Press, 1974.

Rosenblatt, P. C. A cross-cultural study of child rearing and romantic love. *Journal of Person-ality and Social Psychology,* 1966 **4**, 336–338.

CHAPTER 14

Widowhood: Societal Factors
In Life-Span Disruptions and Alternatives[1]

HELENA ZNANIECKI LOPATA

LOYOLA UNIVERSITY
CHICAGO, ILLINOIS

ABSTRACT

The death of a member of a social unit always disrupts the life-span flow of that unit. The forms, depth, and range of disruptions as well as the process of reorganization can vary considerably. The size of the unit disrupted by death also varies. The importance of the deceased to the functioning of the unit can be determined by the unit's own definition and by the effect upon its life of the presence and the actions of that member and of the interaction of others with him or her. Social units. cognizant of the disruptive possibilities of the death of important members, try to ensure succession without traumatic disorganization. The effectiveness of such succession procedures depends to a great extent on the individualistic quality of the deceased's contribution to the unit; the more charismatic and

[1] These comments are based on two studies of widows in the metropolitan Chicago area. The first, "A Study of Widowhood: Changes in Roles and Role Clusters," was conducted between 1967 and 1968 and was based on interviews with a modified area probability sample of widows aged 50 and over, funded by the Administration on Aging (grant no. AA–4–67–030–01–A1) and facilitated by Roosevelt University. Thanks go to the staff of the National Opinion Research Center at the University of Chicago for interviewing and some of the statistical work. The second study, begun in 1972 and still in progress, consists of interviews with a sample of over 1000 widows of all ages drawn from the Social Security Administration lists and focuses

217

significant his or her contribution, the more difficult is the solution of the succession problem. Social research on the effects of the death of a member of a social unit can be limited to immediate consequences; the effects of the removal of a unit's member can also be studied over time, longitudinally or cross-sectionally, through the direct and successive waves of change this death produces in a small social unit. This second approach will be followed in this analysis of widowhood as a consequence of the death of a member of a marital dyad in direct and repercussive disruptions of the life-span flow of the survivor.

I. Widowhood

The disruptive consequences of the death of a member of a marital dyad, seen as a social unit, upon the survivor depends on several factors.[2] One of these is the dependence of the survivor upon that particular person and upon being a member of a team. This dependence can be analyzed in terms of financial, service, social, and emotional support systems involving both the inflow and the outflow of sentiments, actions, and objects. A second factor influencing the disruptive effects of the death of a member of a marital dyad upon the life of the survivor consists of the ways in which the deceased, the team, and the survivor had been immersed in larger social units, be they a family, a community, a work organization, a couple-companionate circle of friends, a society. A third factor, or composite of variables, consists of the resources and limitations for future action and life styles of the survivor individually and as a member of other social units. A fourth factor is the procedure by which the "gap is closed," the affective,

---

on the "Support Systems Involving Widows in Urbanizing Societies." It is being funded through a contract with the Social Security Administration (#SSA-71-3411) with the cooperation of Loyola University of Chicago. Special thanks go to Dr. Henry P. Brehm, Chief of Research Grants and Contracts, in the Office of Research and Statistics, Social Security Administration; to the staff of the Survey Research Laboratory at the University of Illinois; and to the staff of the Center for the Comparative Study of Social Roles at Loyola. The comparative data were obtained during an early stage of the first study as background and for a chapter on "Role Changes in Widowhood: A World Perspective," in Donald Cowgill's and Lowell Holmes's (Eds.), *Aging and Modernization* (Lopata, 1971b) and through extensive interview planning discussions with Dr. Adam Kurzynowski of the Szkola Glowna Planowania i Statystyki, Warsaw, Poland, and Dr. Nada Smolic-Krkovic of the Institute of Social Work in Zagreb, Yugoslavia.

[2] The concepts of disruption or disorganization do not contain negative value judgments. The point being made here is that widowhood not only requires unexpected and purposeful change, but that this change is a consequence of a disruption of an ongoing life style. This life style may include the late husband as a very ill person, even if he no longer consciously participated in the activity surrounding him. The "normal" period of family life that was disrupted by the death may thus have been one of constant care for an ill patient, rather than one of full family functioning.

behavioral, and integrative steps taken to establish the survivor comfortably in that status role if it is a permanent one, or to convert the survivor into a member of other units or life style if the society does not demand that he or she retain the status of survivor for the rest of the life span.

The death of a spouse disrupts not only this relation but also other relations organized around the marital role, and related social roles sociologically perceived as sets of functionally interdependent social relations (Znaniecki, 1965; Lopata, 1971b). The death of a wife disrupts a man's role of husband, modifying his relations with in-laws, the wife's friends, their mutual couple leisure-time associates, and sometimes even his kin group, since he is now wifeless and particularly if she were the connecting link of interaction. It can also disrupt the many sets of relations involved in his being in other roles: father, church participant, neighbor (Lopata, 1973a). The greater was his dependence upon her as a total human being and as a member of the social circles of the many roles in which he was an active participant, the greater can be the disruptive effect of her death, unless a substitute can be found soon who really replaces the deceased. Some of the secondary effects of these disruptive consequences can make it impossible for the husband to continue functioning in his occupation, or as a "normal" human being in the society. Furthermore, the presence of a widower in a community or any other social unit may have reactive consequences within that unit in that, for example, other husbands may fear for the loyalty of their wives. After all, a widower is not just a survivor of a marriage, but a certain kind of social person, an unattached male, or even a deviant in a social unit composed of married men and women.

II.   Widowhood in the Lives of Women.

Most societies of the world have been, and in varying degrees continue to be, patriarchal, with a history of patrilineal and patrilocal structuring (Murdock, 1949). This means that the authority channels follow the male blood line, adjusted for age gradations, and that women are brought into the extended family units to perform specific functions, obtaining their internal and external status from their relation to established members rather than through independent achievement. Since they are strangers and since they enter alone, no matter how close their own families are in proximity and influence, they are almost invariably not assigned positions of great authority over the existing members. This means that their contributions are seen as supplementary to those of the main family members, the males organized by age and the more established older women. Furthermore, since in most historical and many modern societies the reproductive and mothering functions of women have been the most valued of their contributions, being a wife and legitimized mother forms the main source of identity and interaction, particularly in the absence of alternative roles, or their unavailability to any but the exceptional woman.

Because of the preponderance of patriarchal social structures in most of the world and because we have more data on the disruption in the life-span flow of widows than of widowers, the remaining part of this paper will be devoted to the discussion of widows (Lopata, 1971b). Analyses of comparative data indicate that what happens to widows, directly as a result of the death of the husband, indirectly as other aspects of life become disrupted, in consequence of the very status of "widow" and as a result of the restructuring of their life styles, not only varies considerably from society to society but is highly indicative of the social structure and complexity of the social system at large, as well as of the status of women in it. Each society develops a multiplicity of social roles available to members; however, societies vary in the roles they contain and in the proscriptions prohibiting entrance into a specific role by selected categories of people. The system keeps some members from entering some roles by specifying the qualifications necessary for entrance; these can be inborn traits, such as sex or skin color, or acquired characteristics, such as skill or knowledge, which make entrance impossible without long-range training. Some of the resources of a society, be they roles or services, are ascribed in that appropriate categories of members have them automatically included as part of their support systems; others must be achieved in the process of building individual support systems and life styles. Societies differ in the proportion of the roles and resources that are ascribed and which are achievable. They also differ in the methods by which different categories of members are encouraged and prepared to enter certain roles and prevented from entering others. Two very effective methods of ensuring the matching of the candidate for a role and the role are socialization into appropriate identities and personality tendencies and the control of education by which appropriate knowledge and skills are acquired.

In the nomadic or agricultural past of most societies, the main functions of women were the bearing of children within specified family systems, that is, to specified men, and the maintenance of a domicile with the help of the spouse. According to Paul Bohannan (1963), men have universally acquired certain rights in women upon marriage, although these vary by the strength of the patriarchal system, proximity of residence to the male consanguine family, and the availability of other than family roles to women. These are the rights to share a domicile managed through a division of labor, to the products of work and any other economic goods deemed by the community as rightfully belonging to the husband, of sexual access, and of *in genetri-*

cem filiation of the children born to the wife with the male family line. These rights were sometimes inherited by the husband's male agnates after his death. Some societies demanded that the widow continue performing the functions she was carrying forth prior to hisdeath. If she were still able to bear children for the family, arrangements were made for a levir or widow inheritor to "enter her hut" to "raise the seed" of the deceased; or she was remarried, which meant that her new husband became the legal and social father of her future children, sometimes with the rights of adoption of the children previously conceived with the late husband.[3] If the children were filiated to the male line, the widowed mother was expected either to continue socializing them as members of this unit or to leave the unit by herself so that others could perform the socialization function. Which material goods were considered hers in widowhood and the manner by which she was allowed to handle these goods depended upon the culture and the local community variations.

In highly patriarchal societies not only was the wife and consequently the widow under control of the male family line, but women were often not allowed to become involved in social roles outside of the family institution, particularly during the years in which they were preparing for, or being active in, the role of mother. Agricultural and nomadic groups, of course, had few social roles outside of those connected with the family, it being the main economic, political, and recreational unit, while the functions carried on outside of the homestead were usually designated for men. Even more complex societies of the world which had evolved social roles outside of the family unit could forbid or at least discourage their entrance by women. The final consequence of widowhood in such societies also depended upon how important women were as sexual objects, able to conceive children by the wrong man or disrupt other families by enticing their male members. In all but recent Europe and America, and especially in countries influenced by the Muslim religion, women have been encouraged to remain in or near their homes while societal roles in other spheres of life were located in the male province of activity.

The importance assigned to the function of reproduction and the rights of sexual access to wives in an economically more complex society can be exemplified by the differences of social role assignments and the variations in flexibility given women widowed at different stages of their life spans in traditional India. Until forbidden by law during the English control of India, the idealized solution to widowhood among high-caste Hindus was

---

[3] Bohannon (1963) makes a point of distinguishing between levirate and widow inheritance practices on the one hand and remarriage on the other hand, stating that the former arrangements do not involve total husband and wife roles.

self-immolation upon the funeral pyre of the husband. Suttee was justified religiously, in that the spirit of the husband needed continued service in afterlife from the wife as it awaited rebirth. An equally important, though latent, function of self-immolation was the protection of the spirit of the deceased husband from insult by ensuring that his property, especially such important property as a wife with whom he had enjoyed intimate relations, not be made impure by being touched or sexually "violated" by lesser men. The wives of very powerful and prestigious men were most often expected to volunteer to die in this way. Although the actual number of such deaths was small, the very presence of such an ideal assisted the enforcement of alternative behaviors upon surviving widows.

A basic reason for the imposition of strong controls on widows in India was the proscription against remarriage. Widows were defined as dangerous beings, particularly if they were young, and the most restrictive status role (Lopata, 1964) imposed on such women fell upon the child widow, the child bride who had not had her marriage consummated prior to the death of her husband. Since "impure" women were not desired sexual objects, and virgins were, the whole social system imposed elaborate rituals designed to make the child widow as physically unattractive as possible in spite of her sexual purity. Older widows who were no longer sexually dangerous, and especially those who had grown sons to defend and maintain them, were given relative freedom of action and movement not only in India but elsewhere in patriarchal societies (Goode, 1963; Ward, 1963).

As in agricultural and highly structured societies with a strong division of labor along sexual and age lines, most social groups in the world's history have been influenced in their assignment of social roles to widows, or in the roles they leave open for their acquisition, by their view of women in general and wives in particular.

III.   Social Roles of Women in Modern Societies

Although most European societies and their subgroups are anchored in a highly patriarchal family culture, the life styles of women widowed in them are highly divergent from those described earlier and from each other, dependent to a great extent on the structure and culture of society itself and of the community in which they are located, as well as on their personal resources. Numerous social changes of revolutionary strength have modified these two parts of the world considerably, freeing most women, including widows, from total dependence upon roles within the male family unit, although this freedom varies considerably. These social changes include wars of centralization of political states expanding the complexity of societies, the expansion of the size of organizations carrying out segregated institutionalized sets of procedures for conducting their lives, and scientific and commercial revolutions, technological development associated with rapid industrialization, urbanization, mass education, social mobility, ideological democratization, and concentration upon functional more than status components of social roles, etc. These trends have repeatedly multiplied the complexity of the society, introducing an enormous number of social roles within each institution, particularly the focal one (Herskovits, 1966), which becomes the most developed area of culture and social structure (Winch & Blumberg, 1968). The focal institution of American and much of European life became, in recent centuries, but particularly within the twentieth century, the economic one.

These trends first considerably modified the lives of men, breaking the power of the extended patriarchal family and freeing the young to enter achieved roles and to function independently in the economic and other spheres of life. The young male is no longer dependent upon his family for the training, tools, and work-group assistance in order to maintain himself and his family of procreation. Mate selection shifted from matchmaking bent on finding the appropriate young woman to join the family unit as worker, bearer and carer of children, contributor to the status, and cooperating member to mutual selection by the young man and the young woman. The voluntary selection of a mate has been facilitated by the concept of romantic love between relative equals who meet during the performance of similar social roles in the complex educational or occupational systems. From the time of marriage, or at least parenthood, however, they are supposed to go separate ways, he remaining in societal roles outside of the home, to which he is expected to devote primary attention and identification, she to the traditional world of women within the home. He is then expected to be the only breadwinner, supporting the economically unproductive wife and also the children until they leave home to establish independent existences. If he dies, he is expected to leave sufficient funds for the widow and the nonadult children to maintain themselves without extended family support. In return, his widow is freed from being dependent upon his family and can even remove the children from contact with it.

The changes brought about by industrialization, urbanization, and increasing complexity of society in the lives of women have had two major but mutually exclusive and even conflictfull effects. The first has tied them to the home upon marriage and in spite of extensive prior education into societal knowledge; the second has opened up avenues toward involvement in a multiplicity of roles outside of the home.

The very dissolution of the extended patriarchal family as the basic economic and authority unit has increased rather than decreased the importance of the roles of wife and mother, particularly in the absence of societally developed replacements for the larger unit. Although shortened in time, daily and in the life span, the wifehood and motherhood functions of a woman increased in importance because the man and the children become dependent upon a single human being instead of an extended unit for their care.[4] She is needed, by cultural definition, in the home, not outside of it. Simultaneously, however, industrialization and the other social movements changed the home from being the center of social life into being a restricted place to which members active in economic, political, religious, recreational, and educational roles outside of its walls withdraw to rest and restore their energies (Aries, 1965). What is important in life takes place outside of the home, particularly within economic organizations, and the attention of all members has been focused out. Those people who are not actively participating in the economic institution and not drawing visible economic rewards for this participation have been expected to live vicariously through those who do and to adjust their needs to those of the breadwinning member.

As the home lost its significance as a focus of societal life, and as the economic institution acquired focal significance, the role of housewife, of the woman who maintained this home because she was the wife of the breadwinner, decreased in importance. By the twentieth century the traditional functions of women of bearing and caring for children were also foreshortened in their life spans by the decreasing need for many children and an even larger number of pregnancies and by the expansion of the societal claims on the time and education of children. Women's life span itself expanded dramatically with the advance of medical science, which cut into insignificance death from childbirth and communicable disease in areas of the country where its services are available.

Although the functions of women as members of family units, as main-

---

[4] Extensive research on what Litwak calls the "modified extended family" conducted by Litwak, Sussman, and Shanas, much of which is brought together by Shanas and Streib (1965) documents help patterns across households and generations preventing the "isolated nuclear family" (Parsons, 1943) from being completely isolated. However, the widowhood studies indicate that help patterns carried forth from separate households are seldom a source of complete social engagement unless the families live in "flats" in the same apartment building or within very easy walking distance. Each nuclear family develops its own life style out of the social roles and relations of its members. This does not mean that extended kinship roles are absent, only that they are not likely to form the focus of the unit's social system. In addition, the widowhood studies indicate that the relations a woman has with her siblings and her offspring are not symmetrical, in that each one does not fit into her support system equally, often leaving areas of life in which she must operate in isolation. This is particularly true if all her relatives are integrated into nuclear family units geographically isolated from her household.

tainers of a home, and as bearers and carers of children decreased in the time they took either daily or within their life cycle, modern societies developed no action to solve the economic and social parasitism of women during the remaining parts of their lives. Trained in a manner similar to men in the early years of life, and experienced in social roles away from home, they have still been expected to withdraw from the majority of societal life once they were married or pregnant with their first child, never to return in any but voluntary capacity, although they outlived the presence of children in the home by 30 years and the presence of a husband in the home by 15–16 years (Glick, 1957; Duvall, 1967). The traditional patriarchal family institution retained sufficient hold until very recent years. with the help of the Protestant and Puritanical (Dulles, 1965) ethics, assisted by the Freudian-based *Feminine Mystique* (Friedan, 1963; LaPierre, 1959), to keep women from being seriously committed to roles outside of the home, even in preparation for widowhood or divorce and in spite of the fact that the role of housewife lost so much of its prestige and complexity (Lopata & Norr, 1974).

In spite of these societal trends and the restrictive influence they had upon women in recent centuries, there have been contravening tendencies opening up the doors to complex societal participation. The whole labor structure has been modified by the numerous wars in which Europe and America have been involved. Not so much on this side of the ocean but in Europe, young women, even mothers of young children, have been forced to earn an income by the prolonged absence and even death of their husbands. The wars have also shaken the ideological boundaries and frameworks of political states and societies, with consequent changes in the roles of women. Communism, with its ideological rejection of family controls, and the scarcities produced in economies by wars and political policies have modified the lives of all members dramatically, although vestiges of the prior systems linger on. Few adults in countries such as Poland and Yugoslavia can afford not to work, and women able to gain pay in this manner do so, while others are caring for their children, often in specially designed centers.[5] The numbers of widows are proportionally large and, in spite of a tradition of patriarchal control, the conditions under which many people in Europe and America are living require active participation in the society

[5] Many of the papers given by sociologists in the Communist countries during a seminar on women and work organized by the Family Research Committee of the International Sociological Association in 1972 reported that, although women have to work for pay away from the home in order to help maintain the family, few are assisted in the home by the husband. They carry a double burden of the traditional role of housewife and the new role of worker, complicated by the scarcity of consumer goods requiring long waits in lines in order to purchase the necessities of life.

and relative freedom in the daily lives of many women. There are simply not enough men to take over the responsibilities of caring for and supervising husbandless women. Such changes are occurring even outside these two continents. Israel could not, and cannot, afford to retain half of its population in roles limited to the home. Housing shortages require cooperative pooling of resources in many countries. There are whole villages, even islands in Mediterranian Yugoslavia, which are totally managed by widows and women whose husbands are absent most of the time in seasonal and even more extended work in industrialized countries such as Germany (Smolic-Krkovic, 1970), leading to a feminization of agriculture and increasing control by women of their own lives.

The 1960s in American society witnessed a dramatic reentrance of married women into the labor market after the children were grown to an extent judged as reducing the need for a mother at home 24 hours a day (Lopata, 1971a). This action was often accompanied with increased training or education, necessary in order to obtain a paying job after years of economic inactivity. The behavior was initially justified by economic arguments only, as necessary to maintain a desired style of life above the poverty level by lower class women and utilizing some of the products of a society of abundance by women whose husbands earned more than the minimum. Divorce and widowhood added incentives to reentrance into the labor market and other societal roles.

A major recent trend opening up social roles in complex societies to women at various stages of their life cycles has been the women's liberation movement. Its immediate effect has not as yet been in the direction of decreasing prejudice and discrimination with the help of which many societal roles are closed to women, as much as in changing the world view of increasingly large numbers of women and the ideology by which they have voluntarily held back from acquiring the requirements and entering a variety of roles. It has attempted to break through the traditional socialization system, which retained the patriarchal division of the world into "his" and "hers" and persuaded women not to enter voluntarily and individually into many societal roles. In spite of extensive mass education, this socialization system has prevented women from effective and flexible functioning in the modern, complex, voluntary society throughout their life spans. Many have not learned the skills and personality tendencies needed to analyze societal resources, choose desired ones, plan and carry out steps necessary for social engagement, engage, and then turn to new resources as the definitions of needs are modified by events or changes in the life span. The women's movement is attempting to help women break out of the traditional mold of dependence upon a family and particularly a husband in determining their social role engagement.

IV. Social Roles in the Lives of Widows in Modern Societies

The cultural background of the American society and the changes in the social structure and life patterns touched upon in the preceding section can be expected to have profound effects upon the lives of widows in one of its metropolitan centers. These expectations, framed as basic hypotheses in two studies of widowhood, come from sociological literature dealing with the modern family. One of the assumptions was that the lives of American wives would be highly disorganized through the deaths of their husbands because of the characteristics of marriage and the nuclear family with its division of labor. The next assumption was that the immediate consequences of the death of the husband upon his new widow would be handled through the rituals of mourning and bereavement, which supposedly cover the periods of shock, confusion, disorientation, psychosomatic health attacks, and similar reactions of grief. This expectation ran contrary to the claims of Geoffrey Gorer (1965) that modern Western society has deinstitutionalized these rituals sufficiently to cause serious problems for the bereaved, accentuated by a "pornography of death" which has made it an obscene event to be ignored. Eric Lindemann (1944) stressed the importance of allowing the bereaved to complete the "grief work" by which they can rework their past and cut ties with the deceased sufficiently to be able to build new relations and a new life. Although Gorer (1965) may be right in showing how mourning has become deritualized, it is still sufficiently active to allow for at least some "grief work"; otherwise there would be higher incidences of traumatic problems following the death of a significant other. The psychiatrists and sociologists connected with a major study of grief at the Harvard Medical School, especially Maddison (1968, 1972; Maddison & Walker, 1967), Parkes (1964a,b, 1965; Parkes & Benjamin, 1967), and Weiss (1969, 1974), devoted considerable research to the grief process and to the factors that contribute to various outcomes.[6] Of special sociological concern is the process by which a woman who had been socialized into the role of wife and immersed in that role and other roles in the family institution becomes resocialized into the status of widow and the

---

[6] Dr. Phyllis Silverman organized a project called Widow-to-Widow as a result of this research in the Boston area and has also written extensively on this subject. The Foundation of Thanatology in New York City, at at Columbia–Presbyterian Medical Center, held at least two symposia on related subjects, one on death and bereavement in 1973 and another on acute grief and the funeral in 1974. The papers of the symposia will be published in book form and are undoubtedly available from Dr. Austin H. Kutscher of the Foundation of Thanatology. Dr. Robert Fulton has formed a Center for Death Education and Research at the University of Minnesota, organized several conferences, and brought together a cassette tape program on "Death, Grief, and Bereavement."

roles and life styles she develops as a husbandless woman after the grief period has passed.[7]

Regardless of how well the rituals of mourning and bereavement are functioning in modern American society, problems of adjustment to the withdrawal of the husband through death were anticipated in the research. Current literature on grief provided a timetable to this process, and the first study of older widows investigated the extent to which the "stages of grief" and its timing were known to the respondents. Finally, the long-range consequences to a woman's becoming a widow were seen in terms of the degree to which she is expected to remain a widow, as a person whose major focus of life has been removed, or to which she has to or is allowed to change her life. This change can be forced on her if she is expected to take another husband or enter specially designed roles for widows. Since modern urban life does not really contain the social role of widow, there was little expectation of such involvement. On the other hand, we expected the lives of wives and the lives of former wives to be different. In modern society the woman who has performed the function of wife but no longer needs to do so because the husband is dead, particularly if she has already but no longer needs to perform the role of mother as a total commitment, could be expected to be granted freedom to select nonfamilial roles in the broader society. We can expect the most dramatic change in the life of a woman if she had been committed to the role of wife, if the husband dies suddenly, and if she is unable to reproduce this life after the death of the husband.[8] Such change could be predicted as especially strong if she does not have to remain in the role of widow as a former wife but can voluntarily and individually enter new roles. Such engagement can be expected as prevalant in societies in which the patriarchal controls over women by the husband and his family have diminished considerably in strength and in which there is a multiplicity of social roles outside of the home and the family institution which are at least theoretically available to women who no longer need to continually bear children. In other words, the social structure of modern society leads to the expectation that women who become widowed after their children are no longer small shall move into new levels and complexities of social engagement, particularly if they live in American metropolitan centers.

The studies of widows of all ages in metropolitan Chicago indicate the

[7] The problem of identity reconstruction in widowhood and the part played in the process by grief have been the topics of two papers in secondary analysis of the data because I have been increasingly struck by its importance. (See Lopata, 1973a,b.)

[8] Dr. Parkes concluded that sudden death creates greater problems in grief work of survivors than does prolonged dying, in a speech to the 1973 symposium of the Foundation of Thanatology referred to in footnote 6.

extent to which these expectations are reflective of analyses of broad societal trends rather than the reality of life for women in this historical period of time. The respondents form a very heterogeneous sample, reflecting their own and the society's backgrounds and resources. They vary in the way they were involved in the role of wife and in other social roles prior to the death of the husband; in the form, depth, and range of life-span disruption they experienced immediately after the death and in repercussive waves over time; and in the role clusters in which they are currently engaged. The importance and meaning of the role of wife, as reported in retrospect and apparent from the changes the death of the husband forced on a women, spans a wide range. At one extreme are the women—and these tend to be more educated and more middle class than the others—who were strongly involved in the role of wife when the husband was still active and built many other roles upon his presence as a person, a father, a partner in leisure-time activities, a member of couple companionate groups, a coresident in a household in which they were the housewives, a member of two kin groups, and so forth. Even without considering the emotional quality of their relation, which is difficult to obtain retrospectively because of the "sanctification process" that most widows find necessary, these women report strong life disruption after the death of the husband.[9] At the other extreme of involvement in the role of wife are women who lived in a sex-segregated world, but even they varied in the amount of dependence upon the husband in the filling out of the male-designated functions. Some of these wives were relatively independent of their husbands in sex-segregated marriages, solving their problems without their help or having their role engagements clustered around a role in which he was not an important member. The wife immersed in her family relations, in neighboring, in a job, or in voluntary associations may report that she is lonely for her husband or a man in limited ways, but simultaneously that her identities and life style have not changed much (Lopata, 1973b,c,d). Voluntary mate selection does not automatically lead to multileveled involvement with the husband.

The expectations concerning grief were found to be too simplistic, partly

[9] The fact that some widows tend to sanctify their late husbands, accentuating positive points of the man, their marriage, and life prior to his death through selective memory, was recognized sufficiently early in the study of the support systems of widows of all ages to enable inclusion of a sanctification scale into the final interview. I am very much interested in the factors that contribute to various levels of sanctification and which items are selected by different types of women. The items forming the scale include statements such as "My husband was an unusually good man," "My husband and I felt the same way about almost everthing;" "My husband had no irritating habits" etc. A semantic differential-type personality scale was also included. The results should be available in late 1975.

as a consequence of the dissemination of social science knowledge about the supposed "stages." Many of the respondents were familiar with the supposedly "normal" sequence of stages and became alarmed or depressed when they found themselves unable to "move on to the next stage." In fact, it was not the early period of grieving immediately after the death of the husband that presented the greatest problem to them, but later periods, when the ritualized support system was withdrawn, leaving the widow feeling helpless, inadequate, often unlovable and unacceptable to others, and with "no place to go" in terms of future identities (Lopata, 1973b). These are women who are caught in the squeeze produced by the combination of traditional socialization of women and the changes in social structure and ideologies. They are unable to retain a role of widow, since such a role really does not exist in any but the ethnic enclaves of new immigrants. Some of the older ethnic women wish they could retain such a role, but the communities within which they are living will not support it. Others are too habituated to being wives to convert their identities through individualistic engagement in new social roles. The extended family has dispersed, they no longer have ties with their in-laws, often by mutual consent, they cannot devote themselves fully to the role of mother or grandmother. They prefer to live alone rather than with others because of a host of privacy-protecting and hostile attitudes toward other people if they are not related and the fear of conflict with those to whom they are related.

The long-range consequences of widowhood are reflected in the life styles of the women interviewed in metropolitan Chicago. Few of them are "liberated women," able to lead truly urban and multidimensional lives as individuals with rounded-out identities. Some are able to lead the lives of "merry widows," involved in a round of social activity, dating and utilizing the resources of the city in pleasurable interaction with friends. The few women who fall into this category vary in their activities and companions depending upon age, financial resources, and other social roles, such as mother of small children or worker. The third type of widow, who tends to utilize at least some of the societal resources, is the working woman who is widowed but who operates on the job, to which she is committed, individualistically. This type of woman is likely to have been trained early in life, or after an educational interruption, into skills guaranteeing an interesting job with satisfactory economic returns, increasing self-confidence. A second subtype of the working woman is, however, more typical. Having withdrawn from the labor market upon marriage or the first pregnancy, and being untrained into the utilization of educational or job-finding societal services, these working women haphazardly take any job that happens to be available, with minimal economic rewards. This does not mean that the woman does not like her job, since there are many aspects of the routine of going to work, of interacting with others, and of being "out in the world" and away from an empty house which are reported as sources of satisfaction.

The fourth category of respondent which is sufficiently specific to draw attention is the "widow's widow," who joins the "society of widows" found prevalent in Kansas City by Cumming and Henry (1961); she joins in a round of activity out of an independently run home in which she is the only resident. Although some women deeply resent being relegated to such company at social affairs or by the withdrawal of still married friends, and although others sit home wishing for male companionship, there are women in both of the Chicago samples who enjoy other widows, not just during the grieving period (Silverman, 1973) but because of similarities in life style. They often report feelings of independence and an unwillingness to give it up through remarriage or devotion to grandparenting or other helping roles in family groups.

The traditional widow remains immersed in family roles and relations, devoting herself to her children and grandchildren, sometimes also interacting with a sibling group. She tends to live with one of her children, usually a daughter, and to limit her financial, service, social, and emotional support systems to relatives. No other person or secondary group enters the detailed listing of these support systems and all friends are also relatives. There are other types of women whose life style is sufficiently strong to warrant such generalization, including the "grieving wife" who simply cannot enter new social relations or complete her "grief work" (Lindemann, 1944). Very frequently such women become socially isolated and bitter, as prior associates withdraw from the asymmetry of the supports demanded from them. There are also isolated widows who wish they could develop new life styles but who do not have the personally developed resources even to know how to start the series of steps needed for social reengagement. They do not know how to train for or enter a job, join a club or even a church, move to a new neighborhood and develop satisfactory levels of interaction, or convert a stranger into a friend because they were socialized according to the traditional ideal of passive femininity, which did not interfere with the needs of the patriarchal family. Even when offered a range of alternative life styles in widowhood, many women are constrained by internalized assumptions about what women in general, and they themselves, are capable of doing. They tend to have always been minimally engaged, and a basic difference between their backgrounds and those of the multidimensionally involved women is formal schooling. It is within the formal schooling system that people learn to understand societal complexity, the skills with which to engage in it voluntarily, and the behavioral, attitudinal, and identification tendencies that enable them to mobilize their resources, reach out for new ones, and enter new social relations and social roles. Thus, there are many women who are widows living in metropolitan Chicago who are "urban villagers" (Gans, 1962) or at least incompetent to function in the voluntary and individually engagement-demanding society in which they find themselves. Some of them are lucky in that they are surrounded by a protective social unit, be it a family or a neighborhood in which they can exist in spite of a dearth of personal resources. Others somehow find ways of at least minimal social engagement, but there are many widows who are socially isolated because they have neither socially supplied support systems nor individually achieved ones.

V. Summary and Conclusions

The situation of widows, in comparative and historical perspective, is symbolic of the influence of societal changes upon their members. The nomadic and agricultural social units maintained a closed system of subunits of ascribed membership, in which each participant had specified roles and relations varying by sex and stage in life span. The importance of these social units and of villages and other concentrations of more than one family continued even through increasing societal size and complexity. The social and ideological movements beginning in the seventeenth century in Europe and dramatically expanding the world internally and in contact with other movements and societies changed the very structure of people's roles and life-cycle involvements. The initial change was the freeing of almost all men entering noninherited economic roles from the patriarchal control of their families, and of increasing the freedom of large numbers of men and their nuclear families from social-class limitations. This movement was facilitated by the nature of the extended family breakup itself; by the fact that, under the leadership of men who moved out of the home for their major roles, the extended family broke into small nuclear units. The freeing of the men pushed them out of the home to be tested and to perform against high standards of functionality in the expanding and increasingly complex society. While increasing demands on them, possibly contributing to their death rate from causes other than communicable disease, these trends decreased the demands upon women, and, in the long run, the value assigned to their contribution to the system through home-based, economically only indirectly productive functioning. The need for a homemaker affected not only the socialization of girls and the lives of married women; in the end it made widowhood as a stage of life or as a social role functionally meaningless, unless the role of mother was in full operation.

Thus, while the society expanded social roles and resources, the lives of women became more restricted than in the agricultural past for any but the continually engaged upper classes. Although there are some very recent indications that even married women are changing their levels of commitment to, and involvement in, roles outside of the home, there is a whole complex of social and psychological constraints placed on widows that has put them into a double-bind position. Few widows take advantage of societal resources to lead multidimensional lives. On the other hand, the major spearhead of the next wave of change in human societies may come from the nonmarried women if they are focused out of traditional roles and have the opportunity to reconstruct their identities into new directions. After all, they are freed from the constraints placed on the role of wife which still dominate the family institution of societies that have in the meantime built complexities into the other institutions. What may be happening, although there are not many indications as yet of an overwhelming trend, is that women freed from the controls of the family institution through widowhood may be purposely disrupting the vestiges of their prior role clusters after the "grief work" is done and entering roles and life styles that they never would have considered in girlhood and wifehood, becoming independent functioning units rather than being dependent upon passive acceptance of membership in units dominated by others.

REFERENCES

Aries, P. *Centuries of childhood.* New York: Vintage Books, 1965
Bohannon, P. J. *Social anthropology.* New York: Holt, 1963.
Cowgill, D., & Holmes, L. (Eds.) *Aging and modernization.* New York: Appleton, 1971.
Cummins, E., & Henry W. *Growing old.* New York: Basic, 1961.
Dulles, F. R. *A history of recreation,* New York: Appleton, 1965.
Duvall, E. *Family development,* Philadelphia, Pennsylvania Lippincott, 1967.
Friedan, B. *The feminine mystique.* New York: W. W. Norton, 1963.
Gans, H. *Urban villagers.* New York: Free Press of MacMillan, 1962.
Glick, P. *American families.* New York: Wiley, 1957.
Goffman, E. *The presentation of self in everyday life.* New York: Doubleday, 1959.
Goode, W. *World revolutions and family patterns.* New York: Free Press, 1963.
Gorer, G. *Death, grief and mourning.* New York: Doubleday, 1965.
Herskovits, M. *Cultural anthropology.* New York: Knopf, 1966.
LaPierre, R. *The Freudian ethic.* New York: Duell, Sloan and Pierce, 1959.
Lindemann, E. Symptomatology and management of acute grief, *American Journal of Psychiatry,* 1944, CL, 141–148.
Lopata, H. Z. A restatement of the relation between role and status. *American Sociological Review,* 1964, 25, 385–394:
Lopata, H. Z. *Occupation: Housewife.* New York: Oxford Univ. Press, 1971. (a)
Lopata, H. Z. Role changes in widowhood: A world perspective. In D. Cowgill & L. Holmes (Eds.), *Aging and modernization.* New York: Appleton, 1971. (b)
Lopata, H. Z. Loneliness: Forms and Components. *Social Problems,* 1969, 17, (2), 248–262. [Reprinted in Robert S. Weiss (Ed.) *Loneliness: The experience of emotional and social*

isolation. Cambridge, Massachusetts: M.I.T. Press, 1973; also reprinted in L. Rainwater (Ed.), *Deviance and liberty.* Chicago: Aldine Press, 1974.]

Lopata, H. Z. Self-identity in marriage and widowhood. *Sociological Quarterly,* 1973, **14,** No. 3, (Summer), 407–418. (a)

Lopata, H. Z. Grief work and idenity reconstruction. Paper given at Foundation of Thanatology Symposium on Bereavement, New York, November, 1973. (b)

Lopata, H. Z. *Widowhood in an American city.* Cambridge, Massachusetts: Schenkman, General Learning Press, 1973. (c)

Lopata, H. Z. The effect of schooling on social contacts of urban women, *American Journal of Sociology,* 1973, **79,** (3). (d)

Lopata, H. Z., & Norr, K., Changing commitments to work and family among American women and their future consequences for social security. Proposal for future study, 1974.

Maddison, D., & Walker, W. L. Factors affecting the outcome of conjugal bereavement, *British Journal of Psychiatry,* 1967, **113,** 1057–1067.

Maddison, D. The relevance of conjugal breavement for preventive psychiatry, *British Journal of Psychiatry,* 1968, 1968, **41** 223–233.

Maddison, D. Crises in the family: The family in crisis. *Mental Health in Australia,* 1972, **V** (1), 4–13.

Murdock, G. *Social structure.* New York: MacMillan, 1949.

Parkes, C. M. Grief as an illness. *New Society,* April 1964. (a)

Parkes, C. M., Effects of bereavement on physical and mental health: A study of the medical records of widows. *British Medical Journal,* 1964, **2,** 274–279. (b)

Parkes, C. M. Bereavement and mental illness: A clinical study. *British Journal of Medical Psychology,* 1965, **38,** 1–26.

Parkes, C. M. & Benjamin, B. Bereavement. *British Medical Journal,* 1967, **3,** 232–233.

Parsons, T. The kinship system of the contemporary United States, *American Anthropologist,* 1943, **XLV,** 22–38.

Shanas, E., & Streib, G. F. (Eds) *Social structure and the family.* Englewood Cliffs, New Jersey: Prentice–Hall, 1965.

Silverman, P. R. Another look at the role of the funeral director, paper given at the Foundation of Thanatology symposium on Bereavement, New York, November, 1973.

Smolic–Krkovic, N. Social relations of widows in the villages of Croatia, 1970, Yugoslavia. (Mimeographed.)

Ward, B. Men, women and change: An essay in understanding social roles in South and Southeast Asia. In B. Ward (Ed.), *Women of new Asia.* Paris: UNESCO, 1963. Pp. 25–99.

Weiss, Robert S., The fund of sociability, *Trans–Action,* 1969, **6** 36–43.

Weiss, R. S. *Loneliness: The experience of emotional and social isolation.* Canbridge, Massachusetts: MIT Press, 1974.

Winch, R., & Blumberg, R. Social complexity and family organization. In R. F. Winch & L. W. Goodman (Eds.), *Selected studies in marriage and the family.* New York: Holt, 1968.

Znaniecki, F. *Social relations and social roles.* San Francisco, California: Chandler, 1965.

NORMATIVE LIFE CRISES
AND THE SOCIAL SYSTEM

CHAPTER 15

Adult Socialization: Ambiguity and Adult Life Crises

GARY L. ALBRECHT

NORTHWESTERN UNIVERSITY
EVANSTON, ILLINOIS

HELEN C. GIFT

AMERICAN DENTAL ASSOCIATION
CHICAGO, ILLINOIS

ABSTRACT

Individuals who approach and experience adult life crises are frequently caught in ambiguous situations that lack clear definitions of behavioral expectations. As the person attempts to define the situation and adopt a strategy for dealing with the crisis, he often discovers that he is ill prepared for the changes induced. We suggest that people are not well prepared by prior experience for the life crises they meet in their adult years. The processes through which an individual prepares for and deals with adult life crises and the processes of socialization of noninstitutionalized adults are emphasized throughout the chapter.

I. Adult Socialization

In this discussion, adult socialization is defined as the processes through which an adult learns to perform the roles and behaviors he expects of himself and others expect of him. Socialization is a process through which norms, values, and expectations are transmitted from one generation to the next. Adulthood, in this context, refers to the time during which an individual completes his formal education and enters into a career until his death. Since the transition from student to worker occurs at different times for individuals, adulthood does not begin at the same age for each person.

Adult socialization is a way of looking at life-span development from a social learning viewpoint. The emphasis is upon the active, reciprocal participation of the individual in the life-span developmental process. Socialization is frequently age and sex specific. But the age of a person is not as important in socialization as are his reference groups and the major life events that impinge on his behavior at a given time. The person's age, sex, previous experience, and stage in life exert influence on his adult socialization and life-span development.

In this discussion, adult socialization is studied in relation to adult life crises. The processes of anticipatory socialization, role entrance, role performance, and role exit are looked at in terms of life crises.

These observations are based upon the socialization processes of "normal" adults. The normal are those who are noninstitutionalized and who are not demonstrably deviant.[1]

II. Social Learning Approach to Adult Socialization

The social process approach is an application of social learning theory to adult socialization, placing emphasis upon process, transition, and adaptation. It examines behavior in terms of the rewards that reinforce activity and establish patterns of behavior. The social learning theory approach to socialization takes into account group norms and expectations while also attending to the individual's definition of the situation, his personal expectations, and the reward structure. While the social learning approach has seldom been applied to processes of adult socialization, it seems to hold

---

[1] While some readers may argue that the use of "normal" introduces bias into the discussion, it does have meaning and does imply certain ranges of behavior (Scott, 1968). The study of personal adaptation to adult life crises has more generality if it is based upon the socialization processes exhibited by the large number of adults who are not labeled as deviant or who are not institutionalized.

It should also be noted that demonstration of behavior is differentiated from role competency. Many persons can exemplify behaviors and satisfy minimal requirements, but the levels of competency of role performance might be quite variant. While performance is often measured by basic task completion, personal competence is evaluated in terms of the quality and level of performance. Thus, people are not only expected to learn to behave as adults in specific age, sex, and experience grades, but they are also judged in terms of the quality of their role performance.

considerable promise (Ahammer, 1973; Looft, 1973), as indicated by its application using the exchange model in related areas (Friedrichs, 1974).

Scanzoni (1970, 1971, 1972) has examined behavioral exchange within the family; Kunkel (1970) has used social learning theory to develop a behavioral perspective of social change; and Crosbie (1972) has demonstrated that power-compliance activities in social interaction are affected by basic principles of social exchange. These studies indicate that engagement in, performance of, and disengagement from social roles can be studied as a process, using the cost–reward framework of social exchange.

The social process approach also takes into account the *reciprocal* effects of social learning. Bell's (1968) provocative article on the direction of effects in studies of socialization was followed by numerous empirical studies that demonstrated that socialization is characterized by bidirectional effects. This principle holds within and between age sets, peer groups, cohorts, and occupational groups. Infants and parents (Rheingold, 1969), infants and caretakers (Bell, 1971), students and teachers (Gray, Graubard, & Rosenberg, 1974), prison inmates and guards (Cressey, 1961), and husbands and wives (Scanzoni, 1972) socialize each other. Adults are continually socializing one another through the exercise of social exchange principles. Adult socialization is, then, a reciprocal interactive process.

III. Anticipatory Socialization

The competent performance of a role assumes that an individual clearly perceives and defines role expectations and has the resources and experience necessary to accomplish his tasks. In adult life, an individual may have resources and experiences but lack a clear definition or perception of what is expected of him, if his anticipatory socialization has been inadequate. The result is that the individual is confused about how to mobilize his resources for action. He is not prepared for his problems; he does not know how to define the situation and respond. Ambiguity frequently arises as a result of unclear and/or conflicting expectations surrounding the social situations and events. Situations and events are defined as crises when they are not anticipated. Present problems are crises when they are not easily solved. If the expectations associated with an event are clear and the individual possesses sufficient resources to meet the expectations, there usually is no adult life crisis.

A. Anticipatory Socialization and the Life Cycle

Socialization differs over the life cycle. The child quickly learns and establishes behavioral patterns for which he is rewarded (Gewirtz, 1969); his social learning is specific in response to demands of a particular event but is general when the expected behavior is not immediate. When the adult is active in the social learning process, he brings with him his previous experience, behavioral skills, aspirations, physical and emotional resources, and demonstrated performance abilities.

Since behavior is patterned on the rewards received for activity over time, the adult is likely to have established a wide variety of role-related behavioral repertoires, problem-solving techniques, adaptations to stress, and methods for making role transitions, but these are not necessarily adaptive to current situational demands (McCandless, 1967; Rovee & Rovee, 1969). Thus, there is a continuous need for socialization in adulthood. Learning to respond to new demands does not stop at the end of childhood. It is a continuous process.

Previous successful role performance seems to be a foundation for positive self-conceptions, confidence, and high self-esteem (Gordon, 1971). Positive self-image is in turn related to achievement and performance (Rosenberg, 1965; Rosenthal & Jacobson, 1968). Therefore, rewarding experiences and successful problem solving in a variety of roles during childhood and adolescence tend to facilitate competent adult role performance and achievement. The relationship between successful task performance and positive self-esteem is reciprocal and synergistic.

Much of the social learning of adult roles begins with anticipatory socialization. Children and adolescents are usually expected to perform a limited number of roles with well-determined boundaries. As the individual grows older, the number of roles the person can perform increases while role boundaries and definitions become more obscure. Recent overviews suggest that the social learning of adult roles occurs through modeling, imitation, and/or identification (Parke, 1972). Such role learning can be by trial and error or can occur in a no-trial learning situation where correct behavior responses are acquired through observation (Bandura, 1965). In any case, when anticipatory socialization for adult roles occurs, it does so through preparatory education, planning, observation, and attempting some of the role requirements in situations where competent performance is not critical.

B. Future Orientation

Anticipatory socialization requires a future orientation. In relatively stable and unchanging societies, anticipation of the future was not difficult. However, in industrialized societies with rapid communications, individuals often prepare themselves to perform in one world only to find that within a short time the role expectations have changed. The recent turmoil surrounding sex-role definitions (Bardwick, 1971; Harbeson, 1971; Safilios-Rothschild, 1972), sexual norms (Green, 1973; Reiss, 1971), marital stability

(Scanzoni, 1972), and occupational achievement and its consequences (Dodge & Martin, 1970; Duncan, Featherman, & Duncan, 1972; Scanzoni, 1970) are illustrative of the difficulty in accurately predicting future role expectations so that orderly anticipatory socialization can occur.

Anticipatory socialization occurs within both formal and informal contexts. While much is learned about responsible adult behavior in school, the family, and the church, the testing of behavioral limits and competence frequently occurs in informal peer groups. Adolescents learn how to drink by drinking beer with their friends in cars (Albrecht, 1973). Job skills are learned in part at school, but the full impact of the work world comes when the young person works for pay (McCandless, 1970). The tangible rewards of being paid for each unit of work, the discipline required to perform a regular job, and the responsible allocation of the money earned are an integral part of the anticipatory socialization process that prepares the adolescent for the adult work world.

C. Informal Sources

Other powerful sources of informal anticipatory socialization are found in the media, for example, "Dear Abby," "The Playboy Adviser," *The Whole Earth Catalogue,* and underground newspapers. The range of appropriate behavior is quite diverse, and it is not unlikely that the individual selects his own mass-media reference group according to his own needs and goals.

While many of the roles in adult life are anticipated and met with some degree of participation, others are not. Most Americans expect to live until their 70s, to marry and have children, to possess good health, to work at a rewarding job, to retire, and even to die in due time. However, few anticipate joining the considerable number of adults who never marry, or have sexual problems, or confront divorce and the possible loss of their children, or find themselves unable to control the behavior of their children, or experience disability, or endure physical illnesses, or see a spouse die prematurely, or lose jobs, or undergo the functional limitations of advancing age.

Just as people do not anticipate setbacks and unpleasant experiences, they also are not often prepared for rapid financial and occupational success. From many points of view it is just as difficult to cope with upward mobility as with downward mobility. When the role expectations of unanticipated transitions are not clear, or unanticipated change occurs, the individual finds himself uncertain of the rules of behavior, situational goals, and expectations. These conditions frequently produce poor performance, psychological stress, and feelings of anxiety (Dodge & Martin, 1970; McGrath, 1970).

Both anticipated and unanticipated entrances into roles may be complex and stressful processes with far-reaching social, psychological, and physical consequences. Adaptations into new and sometimes unanticipated roles involve resolutions of the ambiguous role expectations regarding performance, acquiring satisfactory levels of skill and competence, and reduction of the stress that results from the transition into a new role. These role changes are more stressful if the transitions are perceived as crises.

D. Formal Sources

Institutions and formal education do not prepare the individual for a life of continual change. For the most part, individuals are prepared for a static world. Unfortunately, by the time people finish school the world has changed and the knowledge and expectations that they integrated during the educational process may, in large part, be obsolete. There is also an implicit expectation that learning stops at the end of formal schooling, which makes it difficult for many adults to adapt because they do not make use of new learning situations. Individuals who live in the present but anticipate and prepare for the future by being open to change and growth have less trouble in adapting to new facts and conditions.

Just as the individual is not always prepared for his future occupation and community responsibilities, he often is relatively unaware of the more general, personal adjustments that will be demanded of him in his future life. As a consequence, many of the major events and adjustments in life take on crisis proportions when they could have been anticipated and managed.

IV.   Adult Life Crises

Adult life crises are here defined as events and processes that the individual cannot fully understand and control but which threaten to reshape his entire life. These crises have both objective and subjective dimensions. What appears catastrophic to one person might seem manageable to another. While there is consensus that birth, loss of job, marriage, departure of children, divorce, serious illness, moving, and retirement are events across the adult life span that require adjustment (Lowenthal & Chiriboga, 1974), the magnitude of the crisis is determined by the individual's definition of the situation, his preparation for the event and its contingencies, and his skill in successful problem solving.

A. Fear of Failure

While anticipation of major life events helps one prepare for their occurrence, many situations become crises because the individual is not prepared to risk and accept failure. Anticipatory socialization, definition of the situation, and fear of failure exert major influences on individual responses to adult life crises. Most members of American society are socialized to succeed or to achieve, or at least not to fail (Alexander & Campbell, 1964; Crandall, 1964; Turner, 1962). There are many studies that show that when legitimate opportunities to achieve are not available, individuals may use illegitimate means to achieve the goals for which they have been socialized (Cloward & Ohlin, 1960; Merton, 1961; Shelton & Hill, 1969; Short, Rivera, & Tennyson, 1965).

The question arises: If the individual is not prepared for failure and does not anticipate it, how does he define failure and adjust to it when it occurs? If one's values dictate that failure is not acceptable, every effort will be made to avoid defeat. *Failure means being unable to achieve one's goal.*

When failure is met continuously despite repeated, innovative attempts to achieve, futility and a sense of resignation stifle further attempts to attack the problem. However, if the avoidance of failure is impossible, frustration and defeatism are not the only possible outcomes. Failure is defined in terms of the goal expected of the individual by himself and others. When faced with a potential failure, the individual can redefine situations, events, and expectations so that defeat is not viewed as a failure (Aronson, 1969; Festinger, 1957). In this fashion, goals and expectations can be redefined so that failures are avoided.

Atkinson and Litwin (1960) pointed out that the motivation to achieve and the fear of failure are closely related. Yet, although we are continually socialized to achieve, we receive little preparation for resolving defeat. Within this context, failure can be viewed in two ways: According to the Protestant ethic, failure is a result of inadequate striving; alternatively, failure can be viewed as an anticipated consequence of attempting to solve difficult problems and as an *expected* part of adult life. These two perspectives on failure reflect divergent values. One indicates that failure is never acceptable. When setbacks occur, the individual should try harder, work longer hours, and utilize more resources. The other approach suggests that failure to solve problems and accomplish tasks is a reasonable consequence of growing and learning. In this view, setbacks do not reflect poor intentions, lack of ability, laziness, or amorality, but are expected, useful learning experiences.

The view of failure as a learning experience is more typical of youth. The family and educational system frequently instill the attitude that adulthood means maturity or ability to cope with all problems *without* additional learning. While problems are not surprising to anyone who attempts difficult tasks, there is little expectation of failure. Adaptation to major life crises is exceedingly difficult because most adult life crises (divorce, death, or loss of a job) usually entail some sort of perceived failure, which is not expected and for which the individual has not been directly prepared.

The research of McClelland (1958), Atkinson (1957), Atkinson, Bastian, Earl, and Litwin (1960), and Atkinson and Litwin (1960) on achievement motivation and fear of failure suggests that while an individual is motivated by a desire to achieve or by the fear of failure, he is not prepared to deal with failure itself. In fact, numerous studies demonstrate that children and adolescents will take almost any means to avoid failure, and those who do fail do not adapt well to the fact that they have not succeeded (Crandall, 1972; Nijhawan & Cheema, 1971; Smith, Ryan, & Diggins, 1972; Soar, 1973; Stamps, 1973).

Strongly achievement-oriented individuals have a high perception of their own skills (O'Reilly, 1973), but because of the desire for achievement and the fear of failure select tasks of only moderate difficulty (Veroff, 1969). Since these individuals have high motivation, skills, high self-esteem, and choose tasks of only moderate difficulty, they do not have as great a chance of failure. Furthermore, since the selected tasks are moderately difficult, the individuals feel that they have achieved when others perhaps could not.

An irony in the entire socialization process is that although persons are not socialized to anticipate and adapt to failure (Stein & Bailey, 1973), failure and the stress and anxiety that are associated with it are consistent and integral parts of the adult life experience (Selye, 1973). On the basis of the habitual response patterns adopted in childhood, the person continues to redefine and use middle-of-the-road behaviors since he is not prepared for directly coping with failure or stress. It appears that as persons learn to anticipate and deal with failure, they will be better prepared to handle adult life crises.

B. Failure over the Life Span

The child, adolescent, and adult exhibit patterned behaviors and maintain established means of solving problems, adapting to stress, and learning new roles (Brim & Wheeler, 1966; Gewirtz, 1969; McCandless, 1970). The adult is more likely to know his limitations, strengths, and competence in a variety of demanding roles. Because the adult has these assets, more is expected of him. Because of experience, his habitual behavior patterns are more set and adjustment is more difficult. But what of failure? Do we expect people to fail? Are children and adolescents expected to fail more often than adults? Is it more serious to fail at one role or task than at another? What are the consequences of failure?

One way of looking at failure over the life span is to ascertain whether failure is or is not permissible for any given task or at any developmental stage. Adults do not often admit their mistakes and failures, so it is rare for the child or adolescent to be exposed to adult failures. If the young person is extensively informed of apparent successes but not about failures, he may believe that failures are infrequent and unimportant, or that adults hide and distort the truth. In any case, the young person is not well prepared for failure, or thinks it is something he will not face in adulthood. He learns that it is not permissible for him to fail at school, to be unathletic, to be asocial, to be caught by the police for a delinquent act, and to show a lack of ability to earn money through part-time work (Bachman, Green, & Wirtanen, 1971). While these values are social class and culture bound, they hold for the larger American society (Kerckhoff, 1972).

The young child begins to learn which mistakes are permissible (Yarrow, Campbell, & Burton, 1968), and by adolescence has a clear picture of permissible acts. The young person is permitted to drink beer and wine, violate curfew laws, and engage in experimental sexual behavior if he is not caught and no serious consequences follow (Akers, 1973). He is permitted to make mistakes at first jobs and even to have an avoidable auto accident in his first years of driving.

As the person grows older and makes more commitments, moves from situational adjustment to commitment (Becker, 1968), the opportunities for permissible failure begin to narrow. The adult has decreasing freedom for acts that are considered failures by the larger society. The permissibility of failure is closely related to the sanctions attached to that act. Failing in business or marriage is considered worse than failing at golf or gourmet cooking. The physical and social stresses associated with major crises in the life span result from the fact that the crises represent real or potential failures of major proportions.

Although most of the literature on fear of failure is focused on school-age children and adolescents, one may hypothesize that the fear of failure often inhibits adults as well. Most of the activities of adults have serious and far-reaching consequences if failure results. Adults are expected to marry, have children, be parents, develop an occupation, perform a job, and be politically responsible. Failure in these roles can result in marriages that do not work, divorce, maladjusted children, lack of employable skills, lack of a steady income, and a nonresponsive government. Thus, an adult will be less likely to experiment with a new role (such as major job change) if the rewards in his present occupation are at least moderate.

Children and adolescents are usually prepared for the major adult roles not by formal education or instruction, but by observing those around them. Unfortunately, many adults are not open with their children about marriage, politics, sex, and finances. The young person has to observe and infer a great deal. This socialization mode is not the most effective. By the time the individual reaches adulthood and faces crisis events in the performance of major roles, he might be afraid of failure and improperly socialized to meet the demands. The adult engaged in socialization processes is often caught in the uncomfortable circumstance of having to learn through trial and error (when he does not expect to have to learn) in situations where large reward and punishment contingencies are operating.

In situations where the person has much to lose, his common reaction to fear is constriction and withdrawal. The adult who is faced with change, crises, and adult role demands may attempt to continue to focus his life and energies on those roles and activities that he knows that he can do well. This approach to adult life crises breeds conservatism and is not always helpful in dealing with crisis events.

There are numerous ways of avoiding failure. The adult can refuse to become engaged in those adult roles that have both high rewards and risks associated with them. Yet most individuals will take risks to achieve. Since adults are not socialized to fail, how do they cope when they are confronted with a high failure situation or with a major life crisis that could easily result in failure? While individual reactions to failure are influenced by age, race, sex, social class, culture, and marital status, there is a typology of responses to failure that cuts across all adults.[2]

The first reaction to failure is to *give up* completely. For the high school student this means dropping out of school (Bachman *et al.*, 1971). For the rejected person in the nursing home, the prisoner of war, or the terminally ill patient, this might mean giving up on life and dying (Seligman, 1974). In each of these instances, the individual has a sense of helplessness and a loss of control over his life.

The second reaction to failure is to *play the role of the defeated and the vanquished.* The person does not drop out of the system entirely. He maintains membership in the system but does not actively participate. The person is defeated and has no desire to try again and risk further failure. For the widow, this means maintaining the mourning role for 5 or more years, rather than actively making efforts to redefine a life without her spouse.

The third response to failure is one of *conformism.* The person accepts defeat, acquiesces to the consequences of the loss, and adapts by continuing to perform roles. However, this person does not demonstrate any further desire to change roles, the system, or himself. He survives by conforming to the expectations of those around him in a conservative manner. This may

---

[2] This typology is similar to that developed by Merton (1961) and others on adaptive behavior.

be illustrated by the innovator who tries a new approach at work only to be reprimanded and told to follow the rules or get out. Instead of objecting, he stays on the job and makes no further attempts at changing the system.

The fourth reaction to failure involves *minor risk-taking behavior.* Although this individual suffers defeat, he does not give up. He reorganizes his resources and energies. He takes a small or medium risk in setting out again to achieve and perform a role or accomplish a task. This individual at the same time has minimized his future losses by not engaging in high-risk activity.

The fifth reaction to failure involves *taking a high risk with a large potential payoff* in an attempt to regain all losses in one transaction. This adaptive mode has little long-term possibility of being a satisfactory response to failure because it involves a high risk and high likelihood of failure. This response is often found among the multiple losers. It is the mode of the person who is fired from his job for poor performance and who then pursues an even more demanding job that critically tests the same behavioral maladaptations, rather than selecting a less demanding job during a time of readjustment.

The last reaction to failure is denial. This individual does not accept the fact that he has failed. He either redefines the situation so that he has not failed and is not responsible, or he refuses to acknowledge that failure has occurred. The individual does not accurately perceive himself or his environment and is not able to redirect his activity positively. This reaction is well illustrated in many marriages. The person stays married, redefining needs and goals, rather than admitting failure and seeking resolution through counseling or divorce.

From this discussion of responses to failure, it can be concluded that the manner in which an individual responds to failure in life crises can determine the rest of his life course. If the individual gives up completely, he may die. If he refuses to accept the facts, he is in no position to reorganize his resources and activities. If he integrates his experiences and begins anew by taking calculated small and medium risks in his areas of competence, he is likely to succeed.

It is apparent that adaptation to failure is a component of the adult socialization process. Americans are socialized to succeed, yet everyone must also cope with failure. Adults are not well prepared for failure, which is more than an event, it is frequently a process. The cumulative effect of a sequential series of successes or failures seems to have a marked impact on the way the individual reacts to future risk-taking situations (Zimbardo, 1969). People and their careers are drastically affected by the manner in which they deal with failures in their lives.

While there are various individual response patterns to major life crises, a growing number of informal peer and support groups exist to assist the individual in transition. Parents Without Partners is a group designed to bring together widowed or divorced parents who are looking for companionship. Job retraining programs exist for the benefit of those who do not have skills necessary to perform technologically oriented jobs or whose skills need updating. Encounter groups, sensitivity groups, and sex discussion groups are used to help the individual express his feelings and fears and to help him redirect his behavior. These groups sometimes serve to give the individual direct feedback about his attitudes and behavior, help him to deal with himself, to recognize failure, and to adapt. They have become informal institutions for adult socialization, indicating the need for socialization particularly for crisis resolution beyond childhood.

V. Conclusion

The individual approaching an adult life crisis is frequently caught in an ambiguous situation that lacks clear definition, and he is frequently unable to cope. This is often due to a lack of anticipatory socialization, particularly with regard to stress and failure. Much anticipatory socialization is based on fear of failure. The adult faced with a crisis situation is ill prepared to deal with failure without additional socialization. Adult socialization is a process that helps the individual to deal with crises and to make the necessary transitions and readjustments. One way to prepare for adult life crises is to emphasize the useful functions of failure experiences rather than the fear of failure in the socialization process.

REFERENCES

Ahammer, I. M. Social learning theory as a framework for the study of adult personality development. In P. B. Baltes & K. W. Schaie (Eds.), *Life span developmental psychology: Personality and socialization.* New York: Academic Press, 1973. Pp. 253–284

Akers, R. L. *Deviant behavior: A social learning approach.* Belmont, California: Wadsworth, 1973.

Albrecht, G. L. The alcoholism process: A social learning viewpoint. In Peter G. Bourne (Ed.), *Alcoholism: Progress in research and treatment.* New York: Academic Press, 1973. Pp. 11–42.

Alexander, N. C., & Campbell, E. Q. Peer influences on adolescent educational aspirations and attainments. *American Sociological Review.* 1964, **29**, 568–575.

Aronson, E. The theory of cognitive dissonance: A current perspective. In L. Berkowitz (Ed.), *Advances in experimental social Psychology,* 1969, **4**, 1–34.

Atkinson, J. W. Motivational determinants of risk taking behavior. *Psychological Review,* 1957, **64**, 359–372.

Atkinson, J. W., Bastian, J. R., Earl, R. W., & Litwin, G. H., The achievement motive, goal setting, and probability preferences. *Journal of Abnormal and Social Psychology.* 1960, **60**, 27–36.

Atkinson, J. W., & Litwin, G. H. Achievement motive and test anxiety conceived as motive to approach success and motive to avoid failure. *Journal of Abnormal and Social Psychology,* 1960, **60**, 52–63.

Bachman, J. G., Green, S., & Wirtanen, I. D. *Youth in transition, Vol. III: dropping out— problem or symptom?* Ann Arbor, Michigan: Survey Research Center, 1971.

Bandura, A. Vicarious processes: A case of no-trial learning. In L. Berkowitz (Ed.), *Advances in experimental social psychology, Vol. 2.* New York: Academic Press, 1965. Pp. 1–55.

Bardwick, J. M. *Psychology of women.* New York: Harper, 1971.

Becker, H. Personal change in adult life. In B. Neugarten (Ed.), *Middle age and aging.* Chicago: Univ. of Chicago Press, 1968.

Bell, R. Q. A reinterpretation of the direction of effects in studies of socialization. *Psychological Review,* 1968, **75**, 81–95.

Bell, R. Q. Stimulus control of parent or caretaker behavior by offspring. *Developmental Psychology,* 1971, **4**, 63–72.

Brim, O. G., Jr., & Wheeler, S. *Socialization after childhood.* New York: Wiley, 1966.

Cloward, R. A., & Ohlin, L. E. *Delinquency and opportunity.* New York: Free Press, 1960.

Crandall, V. C. Achievement behavior in young children. *Young Children,* 1964, **20**, 77–90.

Crandall, V. C. *Progress report on the achievement development project.* Yellow Springs, Ohio: Fels Research Institute, 1972.

Cressey, D. R. (Ed.) *The Prison.* New York: Holt, 1961.

Crosbie, P. V. Social exchange and power compliance: A test of Homan's propositions. *Sociometry,* 1972, **35**, 203–222.

Dodge, D. L., & Martin, W. T. *Social stress and chronic illness.* Notre Dame, Indiana: Univ. of Notre Dame Press, 1970.

Duncan, O. D., Featherman, D. L., & Duncan, B. *Socioeconomic background and achievement.* New York: Seminar Press, 1972.

Festinger, L. *A theory of cognitive dissonance.* Evanston, Illinois: Row, Peterson, 1957.

Friedrichs, R. W. The potential impact of B. F. Skinner upon American sociology. *American Sociologist,* 1974, **9**, 3–8.

Gewirtz, J. L. Mechanisms of social learning: some roles of stimulation and behavior in early human development. In D. A. Goslin (Ed.), *Handbook of socialization theory and research.* Chicago: Rand McNally, 1969. Pp. 57–212.

Gordon, C. *Looking ahead: Self-conceptions, race and family as determinants of adolescent orientation to achievement.* Washington, D. C.: American Sociological Association, 1971.

Gray, F., Graubard, P. S., & Rosenberg, H. Little brother is changing you. *Psychology Today,* 1974, **7**, 42–46.

Green, R. Twenty-five boys with atypical gender identity: A behavioral summary. In J. Zubin & J. Money (Eds.), *Contemporary sexual behavior: Critical issues in the 1970's.* Baltimore, Maryland: Johns Hopkins Univ. Press, 1973. Pp. 351–358.

Harbeson, G. *Choice and challenge for the American woman.* Cambridge, Massachusetts: Schenkman, 1971.

Kerckhoff, A. C. *Socialization and social class.* Englewood, New Jersey: Prentice Hall, 1972.

Kunkel, J. H. *Society and economic growth: A behavioral perspective of social change.* New York: Oxford Univ. Press, 1970.

Looft, W. R. Socialization in a life span perspective: White elephants, worms and will-o'-the-wisps. *The Gerontologist,* 1973, Winter, 488–497.

Lowenthal, M. F., & Chiriboga, D. Social stress and adaptation: Toward a life course perspective. In M. P. Lawton & C. Eisdorfer (Eds.), *Psychology of aging.* Washington, D. C.: American Psychological Association, 1974.

McCandless, B. R. *Children: Behavior and development.* New York: Holt, 1967.

McCandless, B. R. *Adolescents: Behavior and development.* Hinsdale, Illinois: Dryden Press, 1970.

McClelland, D. C. Risk taking in children with high and low need for achievement. In J. W. Atkinson (Ed.), *Motives in fantasy, action and society.* Princeton, New Jersey: Van Nostrand-Reinhold, 1958.

McGrath, J. (Ed.) *Social and psychological factors in stress.* New York: Holt, 1970.

Merton, R. K. *Social theory and social structure.* New York: Free Press, 1961.

Nijhawan, H. K., & Cheema, P. Maze learning under stress in normal and high test anxious children. *Journal of the Indian Academy of Applied Psychology,* 1971, **8,** 23–29.

O'Reilly, A. P. Perception of abilities as a determinant of performance. *Journal of Applied Psychology,* 1973, **5,** 281–282.

Parke, R. D. *Recent trends in social learning theory.* New York: Academic Press, 1972.

Reiss, I. The double standard in premarital sexual intercourse: A neglected concept. In B. Lieberman (Ed.), *Human sexual behavior.* New York: Wiley, 1971. Pp. 183–190.

Rheingold, H. L. The social and socializing infant. In D. A. Goslin (Ed.), *Handbook of socialization theory and research.* Chicago: Rand McNally, 1969. Pp. 779–790.

Rosenberg, M. *Society and the adolescent self-image.* Princeton, New Jersey: Princeton Univ. Press, 1965.

Rosenthal, R., & Jacobson, L. *Pygmalion in the classroom: Teacher expectation and pupil's intellectual development.* New York: Holt, 1968.

Rovee, C. K., & Rovee, D. T. Conjugate reinforcement of infant exploratory behavior. *Journal of Experimental Child Psychology,* 1969, **8,** 33–39.

Safilios-Rothschild, C. *Toward a sociology of women.* Lexington, Massachusetts: Xerox College Publishing, 1972.

Scanzoni, J. H. *Opportunity and the family.* New York: Free Press, 1970.

Scanzoni, J. H. *The Black family in modern society.* Boston, Massachusetts: Allyn and Bacon, 1971.

Scanzoni, J. H. *Sexual bargaining.* Englewood Cliffs, New Jersey: Prentice-Hall, 1972.

Scott, W. A. Conceptions of normality. In E. F. Borgatta & W. W. Lambert (Eds.), *Handbook of personality theory and research.* Chicago: Rand McNally, 1968. Pp. 974–1006.

Seligman, M. E. P. Submissive death: Giving up on life. *Psychology Today,* 1974, **7,** 80–85.

Selye, H. The evolution of the stress concept. *American Scientist,* 1973, **61,** 692–699.

Shelton, J. & Hill, J. P. The effects on cheating of achievement and anxiety and knowledge of peer performance. *Developmental Psychology,* 1969, **1,** 449–455.

Short, J. F., Jr., Rivera, R., & Tennyson, R. A. Perceived opportunities, gang membership and delinquency. *American Sociological Review,* 1965, **30,** 56–67.

Smith, C. P., Ryan, E. R., & Diggins, D. R. Moral decision making: Cheating on examinations. *Journal of Personality,* 1972, **40,** 640–660.

Soar, R. S. Accountability: assessment problems and possibilities. *Journal of Teacher Education,* 1973, **24,** 205–212.

Stamps, L. W. The effects of intervention techniques on children's fear of failure behavior. *Journal of Genetic Psychology,* 1973, **123,** 85–97.

Stein, A. H., & Bailey, M. M. The socialization of achievement orientation in females. *Psychological Bulletin,* 1973, **80,** 345–366.

Turner, R. H. Some family determinants of ambition. *Sociology and Social Research,* 1962, **46,** 397–411.

Veroff, J. Social comparison and the development of achievement motivation. In C. P. Smith (Ed.), *Achievement-related motives in children.* New York: Russell Sage, 1969.

Yarrow, M. R., Campbell, J. D., & Burton, R. V. *Child rearing.* San Francisco, California: Jossey Bass, 1968.

Zimbardo, P. G. *The cognitive control of motivation.* Glenview, Illinois: Scott, Foresman, 1969.

CHAPTER 16

A Clinical Approach to
the Theoretical Constructs of
Failure and Normality

PATRICIA B. PORTERFIELD

SCHOOL OF MEDICINE, WEST VIRGINIA UNIVERSITY
MORGANTOWN, WEST VIRGINIA

ABSTRACT

A response to Albrecht's model of adult socialization requires the writer to assume at least three separate roles: human being, educator, and clinician. This paper will speak to all three simultaneously with particular emphasis on the clinical aspects.

Albrecht's position might be called process oriented. The entire universe is in the process of becoming, he seems to say. The human animal, being a part of that universe, is, by nature, programmed for change. However, to admit that everything is in the process of becoming and that nothing is ever still but is always changing can be quite frightening to the individual who spends his entire life looking for security.

Predictability in any specific situation can be synonymous with security, for what is expected can be planned for, or guarded against, as the case may be. To be able to predict is to be able to ensure oneself of a feeling of safety. In my opinion, all research on the behavior of the human animal is designed to give a false sense of security by claiming that, if all the variables are as they are described, the end product must necessarily survive as predicted—an impossibility when applied to the human being and his behavior. For the variables are never quite the same and therefore the results cannot be predicted. Thus, any research on the socialization of noninstitutionalized adults from a process perspective cannot yield answers designed to give a feeling of security, but can only raise more questions about the changes that are constantly taking place.

This tendency of the individual to model his behavioral expectations after the descriptions of researchers is often seen by clinicians who deal with many patients who are familiar with the concept of diagnostic categories and much of the literature on mental health. Often a patient will demand a diagnosis so he can search for studies pertaining to that category. He will often proceed from there to analyze his own behavior with the belief that he can safely predict what will happen and protect himself against all possibilities and probabilities. He is overwhelmed with astonishment when his own behavioral patterns refuse to fit neatly into the compartments designed to describe them.

What the patient tries to do is to regiment himself according to concrete guidelines, based on valid research that was not, however, designed for that purpose. This is no fault of the researcher. However, no matter who, if anyone, is at fault, the problem for the clinician may be great. The patient who is adept at playing clinical games around literature can often quote study after study supporting his position and send his therapist into private tirades against anyone who tries to predict human behavior with supportive data that appear so authentic to the reader that they are almost impossible to refute.

For example, a patient may approach his therapist with the request to "do the primal scream" because he has read something that has convinced him that all those with his symptoms are helped by this method. If the therapist tries to take exception, he cites the literature, and the fight is on. Obviously this is not an argument against research, but against its misuse. But I see this as a step in the right direction—for we can accurately predict that change will take place. Any research that throws light on human behavior is useful, but limited in its scope. The patient cannot expect to reprogram his behavior accurately simply because he has before him certain statistics from which he can make fairly accurate assumptions, nor can the therapist extrapolate concrete step-by-step guidelines from generalized research.

Albrecht states that the need for research on representative samples of the general adult population in natural settings is great. While I agree that there is a lack of such research, I do not agree that there is a "need" for it unless we make it obvious that such studies are useful primarily for descriptive and educational purposes. They cannot be used as prescriptions for altering or predicting individual or group behavior with any degree of certainty.

Research on the human animal points out differences. After differences are catalogued, the tendency is to group the individuals into categories labeled "normal" and "abnormal." While these may be useful terms for the researcher, they may be anathema to the clinician. The whole concept of normality and nonnormality is counterproductive for the clinician.

Again, in its search for security, the public is consumed with the myth of normality. What clinician does not get asked many times, "Is this normal behavior?" Such questions are especially common in the area of sex. Just the reassurance "Whatever feels right and good to you is normal" will give the individual the license he may be seeking to justify his or her own sexual behavior. To be considered abnormal is a fate worse than death, for some. To be labeled sick or perverted is to be labeled a failure.

It matters not to me, as a clinician, whether 9 out of 10 individuals exhibit certain types of behavior when placed in a particular situation except as a guide for making generalized, nonspecific predictions. There are patients who imagine themselves having problems where there are none, simply because they have read or heard somewhere that their particular attitudes or behaviors are not "normal." They may be functioning, but because they are not normal they must be bad. Normal, abnormal, good, bad, black, white—all these are judgmental and prejudicial terms that can cause the clinician numerous problems in dealing with patients who are obsessed with their own failures to conform.

The problem for the clinician is to deal not with the patient's normal or abnormal behavior, but with his functional or dysfunctional behavior. The construct of normality is delusional. Claudio Naranjo in his book *The One Quest* (1972) gives the following illustration from Kahlil Gibran's *The Madman:*

Once there ruled in the distant city of Wirani a king who was both mighty and wise. And he was feared for his might and loved for his wisdom.

Now, in the heart of that city was a well, whose water was cool and crystalline, from which all the inhabitants drank, even the king and his courtiers; for there was no other well.

One night when all were asleep, a witch entered the city, and poured seven drops of strange liquid into the well, and said, "From this hour he who drinks this water shall become mad."

Next morning all the inhabitants, save the king and his lord chamberlain, drank from the well and became mad, even as the witch had foretold.

And during that day the people in the narrow streets and in the market places did naught but whisper to one another, "The king is mad. Our king and his lord cham-

berlain have lost their reason. Surely we cannot be ruled by a mad king. We must
dethrone him."

That evening the king ordered a golden goblet to be filled from the well. And when
it was brought to him he drank deeply, and gave it to his lord chamberlain to drink.

And there was great rejoicing in that distant city of Wirani, because its king and its
lord chamberlain had regained their reason.[1]

Now, to relinquish clinical claims to the use of the constructs of normality and abnormality is to give up a powerful weapon that the public has
bequeathed to those in the helping professions. But in my years as a clinician, I have yet to see a normal or average person. Neither have I seen any
abnormal or other than average person. The normality construct exists because man categorizes and classifies and tries to attach appropriate labels.
So normality is a cultural phenomenon resulting from continual repetitive
validation of behavior and the acceptance of that validation. The search for
a normal person would be determined by the cultural variants of a particular society at a particular time. And even then, the determinants would be
open to question because of the varieties of people and opinions involved.

The categorizing and classifying of man in general terms such as normal
may mean that all individuality has been removed. This is of vital importance to the clinician because it logically follows that in order to understand
the individual, the stereotype of normality must of necessity be disregarded
and the person seen only as himself with no data available to classify him
except that which pertains to him. Research, which has added so much
knowledge to the behavioral field, has failed to give clinicians many, if any,
specific guidelines as to how to make the individual more functional. Such
constructs as normality may hinder the helping process because they suggest more areas of concern to the patient. He will concentrate on whether
his behavior can be labeled normal or abnormal rather than on whether it
is working for him in his particular situation.

The clinician sees many individuals who are dysfunctional according to
the dictates of society. Those persons who are dysfunctional and who like
that role can be helped by assuring that they be institutionalized and kept
that way until such time as they choose to become once again functional.
This presents no problem. The problem arises when society sees the individual as dysfunctional but he sees himself as functional. Then the clinician
becomes the mediator or advocate, as the case may be.

Many human beings may be programmed from the beginning for failure.
They are reinforced continually because society needs them. Where would

---

[1] From *The Madman: His Parables and Poems,* by Kahlil Gibran. Copyright 1918 by Kahlil
Gibran and renewed 1946 by Comité National de Gibran. Reprinted by permission of Alfred
A. Knopf, Inc. and William Heinemann, Ltd., Publishers.

clinicians be if it were not for those who see themselves as failures and who come for help in turning failure into success? The constructs of failure and success are also delusional. Failure is arbitrarily defined with reference to arbitrary criteria—it is a subjective sociological term.

Society is enormously successful at programming people to fail. Albrecht points out that the child or adolescent is often expected to fail, and this is considered part of the learning experience, but that adults are expected to display behavioral competence. I submit that many adults are also expected to fail and indeed must do so if social systems are to survive in their present forms. Vast numbers of people are employed solely to help the failures in our midst: for example, social workers, psychologists, psychiatrists, clergymen, and lawyers. Where would these people be if everyone succeeded at being successful? We can only be thankful for those who succeed at being failures.

There are two ways of addressing this issue: (1) program people to cope with failure, or (2) modify the paradigm of failure.

It would seem that Albrecht is attempting the second when he suggests that adults be prepared through education to adapt to change. The recognition that everything is in the process of changing leads to the discarding of any concept such as failure and replacing it with the concept of difference.

To be seen as a failure can be a devastating experience. To be seen as different can be rewarding and growth-producing. I am convinced that if Albrecht pursues the study of adult socialization, he will find differences so numerous that any attempt at integration into similarities would be futile. Too often, behavioral research has succeeded only in the creation of stereotypes, which are then adapted by society and used to define roles along very rigid expectations. Clinicians may sometimes treat such research on behavior as definitive without sufficient awareness of its limitations.

The housewife has recently entered the ranks as a role construct that is considered by society to be a failure. To say that one is a housewife is to admit that one has failed to achieve success in the world. After all, anyone can be a housewife, but it takes a most extraordinary person to have a business career or to do both simultaneously and with equal success. The well-read woman in American society today can no longer trust her own feelings and intuitions. She faces the clinician with such questions as:

1. I have always been satisfied just being a wife and mother. Now, everyone says that means I don't have an identity of my own. Am I normal?
2. I thought that raising a family was quite an achievement. Now, from what I read, that's not considered much of a contribution to society. Suddenly I feel like I've wasted my life. Am I a failure?

Such questions pose enormous problems for the clinician. It is necessary to move quickly away from the normal/abnormal and failure/success constructs to the functional and dysfunctional paradigm. The therapist must help the patient focus on the poetry of human interaction and deemphasize the mystique that surrounds the areas of normality and failure. The emphasis must be placed on what behavior works best for the patient in his or her own unique situation and not on what is considered normal or abnormal. The clinician cannot afford to set himself up as an expert on what is normal or abnormal—he is interested primarily in what is behaviorally acceptable in his patient's life.

Albrecht has suggested that we study adult socialization from a social process perspective. I would agree that this is the only really viable way of approaching such research. We act as if it were true that certain stages of life are static and that rules can be set up which assure easy transition into and out of roles throughout our life span. Nothing is further from the truth. There are no static stages of life and no rules that we can follow to give assurance that we will progress as we plan.

There is too much of the unexpected for us to rely entirely on structure and planning. If educators and clinicians are to help anyone through life with a minimum of difficulty, we must prepare them to meet and to expect change. In addition, we must work toward eradicating all paradigms that lead to failure or to non-normality and concentrate on promulgating the premise that all life consists of change, that there is no security in anything, that there is no failure or success, no normal or abnormal—only differences. And differences are neither good nor bad; they just are.

I had a moment of amused reflection in listening to Albrecht's remarks about the need for study of noninstitutionalized adults. I was reminded of my youngest daughter a few years ago when she hit upon proof that she is a girl. When asked by a neighbor how she knew that she was a girl, Cara, after much intense deliberation and an air of desperation, said triumphantly, "I know! I know! This afternoon when mother had us out to the skating rink the man said, 'All the boys get off the floor and all the girls stay *on* the floor,' and *I* stayed on the floor and he didn't make me get off! So there!" Proof indeed.

Just as Cara knew suddenly that she was a girl because she was allowed to stay on the floor with the other girls, could I perhaps know that I am a normal, average adult if I find myself an uninstitutionalized, nonvoluntary subject of research on the process of adult socialization?

I find myself always excited at the prospect of learning anything new about human behavior; but I am also apprehensive that we will take our newly acquired knowledge and try to set up more stereotypes and make more rules that will turn out to be of little use and perhaps even harmful.

But to study the human animal in the process of change is to see him as he is—a dynamic, moving force in a dynamic and constantly moving universe.

REFERENCES

Naranjo, C. *The one quest.* New York: Ballantine Books, 1972.

CHAPTER 17

The Life Course, Age Grading, and Age–Linked Demands for Decision Making

ROBERT C. ATCHLEY

SCRIPPS FOUNDATION GERONTOLOGY CENTER,
MIAMI UNIVERSITY
OXFORD, OHIO

ABSTRACT

Life-span developmental psychology intersects with sociology at the point where social systems, whether they be small groups or nations, deal with the biological and social maturation and aging of their individual members. The basic premise of this paper is that age is an important variable that cuts across all areas of social life, and that it does so primarily through three social mechanisms: the life course, the system of age grading, and age-linked demands for decision making.

This paper treats the life course, age grading, and age-linked demands for decisions as highly interrelated social forces operating in the development of human beings. The life course is portrayed as a crude road map with quite a few alternative routes for getting through life's various stages. The existence of the life course provides a conception of successive changes in the structure of an individual's life and an expection that these changes will occur. Age grading. is portrayed as a process that combines with sex to control the individual's access to various groups, roles, aspects of culture(including norms, attitudes, values, beliefs, and skills), social situations, and social processes. Decision demands provide the individual, and those who care about him or her, with motivation for imposing structure on what otherwise would be a chaotic system of sometimes contradictory age norms and age-linked opportunities. Decision demands are a prime normative mechanism for providing the movement that translates the static age grading

system into the life course and ultimately into the biography of an individual. Finally,
some social factors that shape the individual's responses to change are discussed.

This paper represents a preliminary excursion into poorly charted territory. It contains
many speculations intended to promote thinking and spark research in new directions. It
is necessarily short on well-documented answers to the issues it raises. At the same time,
it seeks to provide a more complex approach to the sociology of the life span than has been
available to developmental researchers in the past.

I. The Life Course

The life course is a heuristic and conceptual tool through which sociologists attempt to relate social structure and process to the life spans and unique biographies of individuals. Several terms can be used in place of "life course." For example, Cain (1964) lists "life cycle," "life span," and "stages of life" as roughly synonymous. I have chosen "life course" because I feel that it best serves to differentiate between social time, through which society structures the life span of individuals, and biographical time, which deals with the individual's experiencing of his own life span.

The life course is not merely a composite of age-related modalities in individual biographies. It is comprised of largely preprogrammed alternative sequences of age-related norms that give at least a minimum of structure and predictability to the succession of groups, positions, social situations, and subcultures through which individuals pass in living out their lives. Ideas concerning what is *appropriate* for people to be and to do at various ages pervade life. These ideas are organized into rough timetables, each of which represents an alternative path through the maze of prescriptive, proscriptive, and permissive norms concerning age-appropriate positions, roles, groups, social situations, skills, attitudes, ambitions, and a host of other characteristics. It is because of this complexity that the life course must remain a heuristic concept. There is no one life course; there are many.

Just as a cohort of individuals becomes progressively more differentiated throughout its life span, the life course represents an increasingly more complex maze of age-linked alternatives. At the early stages of the life course, there is a great deal of age determinism. Gradually, however, it becomes more and more difficult to predict an individual's place in society mainly from knowledge of age. The life course is rather like a successively bigger equation made up of a series of *contingent* probabilities; that is, the older a person gets, the more tomorrow's alternatives are contingent on yesterday's selections. However, toward the end of the life span, there is a reduction in the number of variant life courses due to the impact of the symptoms of old age.

As Clausen (1972) has pointed out, individuals do not select at random from among contingencies. Personal resources such as intelligence, appearance, strength, health, temperament, and initiative have an important bearing on what come to be defined as realistic alternatives. The guidance, support, and outright help that is available from others are other important variables that influence choices, even within the constraints of the age-grading system. Likewise, whether age-linked opportunities are open or closed is related to such factors as sex, ethnicity, race, social class, and personal contacts (Clausen, 1972, p. 463). This is another reason why there are many alternative versions of the life course.

Yet with all of the latitude represented by the various alternative life courses,there are general, consensual age standards that comprise a sort of master timetable to which detailed alternatives may, and often must, be tied. Neugarten, Moore, and Loew (1965, p. 711) put it well:

> There exists what might be called a prescriptive timetable for the ordering of major life events: a time in the life span when men and women are expected to marry, a time to raise children, a time to retire. This normative pattern is adhered to, more or less consistently, by most persons in the society.

In the sense it is used here, time refers to stages of life. Stages of life are most often identified in terms of major events. But stages of life also exist on several dimensions. Figure 1 portrays several dimensions of the life course with *approximate* relationships of various sequential stages with chronological age. There are wide fluctuations around any given point on any given dimension. Yet the existence of future stages tied to age on given dimensions exerts a pull that results in more consistency than might otherwise be expected (Neugarten & Datan, 1973).

The life course is thus a convenient device for conceptualizing the sequential aspects of social structure through which individuals pass in the process of social maturation and aging. At the same time, it is also clear that a detailed appreciation of the life course requires more than a linear, structural approach. Accordingly, the next two sections of this paper deal with age grading, which provides a detailed view of structure, and age-linked demands for decision making, which provide insight into the dynamic processes that motivate people to tie themselves to age-related aspects of social structure.

II. Age Grading

Age grading is one of the several social mechanisms through which individuals find out what they can expect to be *allowed* to do and to be, as well as what they will be *required* to do and to be. Age grading systematically links the age of individuals to a large and various body of norms in the individual's culture or subculture.

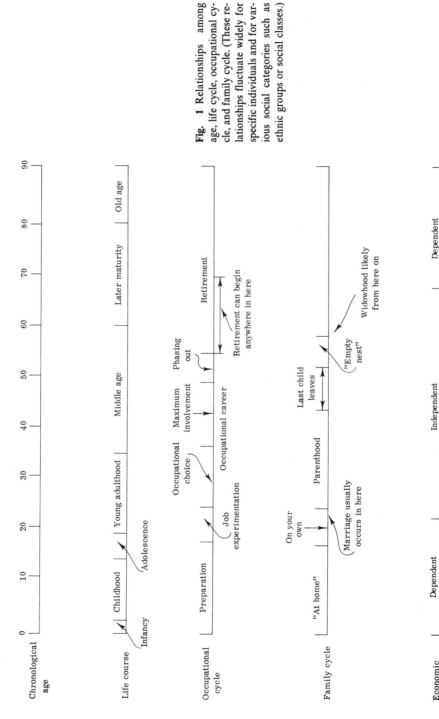

Fig. 1 Relationships among age, life cycle, occupational cycle, and family cycle. (These relationships fluctuate widely for specific individuals and for various social categories such as ethnic groups or social classes.)

SOURCES OF AGE NORMS

Cultural sources for standards

Tradition
Negotiated agreements
Modal behavior

Sources of validity for standards

Natural biological
Natural social
Arbitrary social

Group sources of standards

Primary group
Status group (ethclass- by sex)
Social class
Community
Region
Mass society

ASSIGNMENT CRITERIA FOR
APPLYING AGE NORMS

Chronological age

Tenure

Life stage

Physical appearance

Level of functioning

THE FOCUS OF AGE NORMS

Person

Appearance, dress
Behavorial characteristics

Access to social structure

Role
Group
Social situation
Subculture

Phase of involvement with
social structure

Approach
Entry
Continuity (incumbency)
Exit

Social process

Group
Interpersonal

GOALS OF AGE NORMS

Presciptive

Proscriptive

Permissive

Decision demand

CONDITIONS OF APPLICATION

Types of sanction

Formal-legal
Informal-consensual

Applier

Self
Other

Mode of application

Direct versus indirect
Derministic versus flexible

Age-determined versus
age-linked

Fig. 2. Dimensions of age norms.

The first necessary step in studying age norms is the development of a paradigm that includes both taxonomy and assumptions about the operation of the system. Otherwise researchers have difficulty in establishing or joining dialogue about comparable aspects of age norms. Figure 2 is a preliminary attempt at classifying age norms. It is a synthesis of ideas that have come from a variety of sources (Atchley, 1972; Neugarten & Datan, 1973; Clausen, 1972; Riley, Johnson & Foner, 1972; Cain, 1964, 1974; Neugarten & Moore, 1968; Atchley & George, 1973).

A. Sources of Age Norms

Many age norms are handed down through tradition. However, other norms result from a negotiation process. Cain (1974) has pointed out, for example, that the age of 65 for retirement under social security resulted from negotiations within Congress, and not from a tradition established by Bismarck, as has been widely assumed. Still other norms arise out of the fact that even without tradition or conflict-resolution processes, customs may evolve from modal behavior patterns. Among American working-class young people, for instance, marriage customarily follows soon after graduation from high school. As a result, age at first marriage is less variable for the working class than for the middle class, in which there are several options concerning when job preparation is complete and whether it should be completed before marriage occurs (Neugarten & Moore, 1968).

Regardless of whether age norms grow primarily out of tradition, negotiated agreement, or modal behavior patterns, standing behind these norms is a series of assumptions concerning biological and social development and aging. Many of the age norms that people confront are based on assumptions, often uninformed, concerning what people of a given chronological age are *capable* of doing—not just what they *ought* to do but what they *can* do. For example, Americans seldom try to teach children to play the violin at age 4 because it is assumed that they cannot do it and will only be frustrated by the experience. But the Japanese have had widespread success with the teaching violin to very young children. On the other hand, very few 4 year olds are strong enough to lay cement blocks, and in this case proscriptive age norms seem to make more sense. Thus, what often appear on the surface to be norms based on natural biological limits are often in fact arbitrary social norms based on untested biological or psychological assumptions. Conceptions of social maturation (often called "getting the necessary experience") are also used to justify age norms. It seems justifiable that a child of 3 not be able to vote. But for his 15 year old sibling, the question is not so clear-cut. On both the physical and social dimensions, then, there are natural limits concerning what people can do. Part of the job of setting arbitrary limits is often related to the cost of error, sometimes simply presumed, sometimes discovered through experience.

Age norms thus sometimes rest on actual social and physical limits. But often age norms are only arbitrarily related to relevant aspects of maturation or aging. The greater the disparity between actual functioning and the level of functioning implied by the age norms, the more likely it is that the individual will feel that age norms make invidious, unjust distinctions among people.

At the beginning of the life span, the limits are overwhelmingly natural, biological, and maturational. As soon as children begin to move around, however, they quickly encounter both natural and arbitrary limits centered around social maturation. Throughout childhood there is a mixture of these various types of limits. However, as the individual moves through childhood and into adolescence, there is a sharp reduction of the natural, biological limits and natural, social limits, but the arbitrary social limits diminish more slowly. In early adulthood, all three types of limits are at their lowest point. Of course, individuals are not necessarily free of all types of norms at this stage, they are simply freer of *age* norms. From there, however, aging causes physical limits to begin to reappear. After young adulthood there is also a resurgence of social limits, both natural and arbitrary (Clausen, 1972). Aging brings natural social limits to the extent that with rapid cultural change it is difficult for older cohorts to know enough about the language and culture of younger cohorts to be able to continue to play the role of young adult. More important, however, is the fact that the dictum to act one's age, an arbitrary social limit, will not allow people to play roles too "youthful" for their age. This restriction grows stronger during the latter two-thirds of the life span. It is probably stronger for women than men because standards for women are more closely tied to chronological age (Atchley & George, 1973).

Much of the literature on age norms implies that age norms are uniform throughout society (Cain, 1964; Neugarten *et al.*, 1965; Riley, 1971). However, most sociologists recognize that groups have a way of redefining norms as they attempt to apply them to particular people in concrete social settings (Mott, 1965). Primary groups—intimate pluralities of people with common values or basic standards of behavior, and frequent, direct personal contacts among their members—often serve to reinterpret age norms and apply them with more particularism than would generally be expected in large industrial societies. Likewise, status groups—within social classes, subgroups whose members have frequent contact, share norms, and view one another as social equals—are larger, less intimate groups than primary groups, but they too serve to reinterpret age standards. Status groups are important because they are often homogeneous not only with respect to prestige but in terms of race, ethnicity, and sometimes sex as well. The reinterpreting function of primary and status groups is an important factor influencing the individual's perceptions of age norms. In some cases, these groups may be able to soften the invidious character of age norms, but in other cases they may serve to heighten the individual's outrage at the "unfairness" of age norms.

Social classes are seldom groups except in small communities because they do not experience the interaction among members necessary to form group bonds or apply group sanctions. However, in many medium-sized cities and smaller communities, social classes are small enough to form genuine groups, and when they do, they too can reinterpret age norms in much the same ways that primary groups and status groups do.

Communities are important for age norms because communities represent the smallest social unit with a full array of social institutions—economic, educational, political, family, and religious. And it is through the interaction of social institutions that the system of age norms assumes reality. Thus, many systems of age norms are essentially community-based systems, particulary with regard to nonlegal age norms. When communities exist they have the ability to set their own standards except in those areas covered by state or federal law. We could probably learn a great deal about age norms from comparative community studies, but the work remains to be done.

Regional subcultures also probably differ with respect to age norms, but little systematic study has been made of this subject. For example, in Appalachia, older parents are more often accepted as members of their children's families than is the case in immediately adjacent areas. People generally leave school earlier in the South than in other regions of the United States. These are but two of what may be a great many regional variations in age norms. Of course, the extent to which regional age norms exist is a function of the extent to which there are distinct regional subcultures.

Finally, standards are set by the mass society. Mass societies are large political and social units, such as nations, which rely on mass communications for establishing consensus on norms, age norms included. Mass media messages are especially important for setting standards in areas that lack cohesive community. Advertising messages are a particularly obvious repository of nationwide age-linked stereotypes. Television, magazines, newspapers, and syndicated columns with national circulation all influence community standards.

Age norms, then, are translated into reality at various social levels by particular people in particular situations. Whether the standards applied are local or cosmopolitan differs from locality to locality and from group to group. It is important, therefore, that we keep in mind in research that age norms are problematic, not given. We can be sure they exist, but we have to find out what they are and from which levels of social organization which types of age norms are most likely to emanate.

B. Criteria for Applying Age Norms

How age is defined and applied to persons varies along several dimensions. *Social age* is calculated from several reference points—birth, entry into a given position or situation, or stage in the life course. *Individual age* is assessed in terms of appearance and/or level of functioning. In addition, there are important sex differences in the applicability of these various dimensions of age.

Chronological age is the easiest kind of social time to study. The arbitrary nature of calendar time means that chronological age is easy to compute, and rules associated with specific chronological ages are the most explicit of age norms. Likewise, norms governing tenure—the length of time an individual has held a position(not to be confused with academic tenure)—tend to be tied to calendar time and are therefore easier to observe. Rules based on life stages tend to be more difficult to study, primarily because multiple contingencies are often employed as criteria. For example, it is easy to define the point at which a person becomes ineligible to be a member of the PTA by simply using the exit of his or her children from the school as a criterion. It is more difficult to predict the point at which the individual can form a socially approved marriage, because there are several alternative combinations of life-stage characteristics that can qualify a person for marriage.

With regard to chronological and tenure age norms, sex has less impact on the application of the norms than on whether the person has access to the groups, roles, or situations in which these norms are applied. Sexually segregated groups develop standards that do not apply outside the group. Even when men and women *do* participate in the same groups, their roles within the groups may differ in terms of the application of age norms. Sex differences in certain age norms result from the effects of childbearing and child-rearing on the woman's career. How much this will change in the future we cannot be sure, but there is a tendency toward less sex differentiation in family roles, and this will probably have an effect on the sexual dual standard in age norms.

Physical appearance and level of functioning are important criteria for assigning age norms, but again there is little research on these dimensions. Among children, appearance is an often-used basis for making judgments as to which age standards should be applied. Big, strong-appearing children are allowed more independence than children of the same chronological age who are small and frail in appearance. Gray hair and wrinkled skin cause people to be categorized as "old." To the extent that it exists, the sexual dual standard (Sontag, 1972) makes appearance a more important criterion for women than for men across the entire life span, although people do not necessarily occupy the same position on the scale of attractive physical appearance at the various stages of their lives.

Level of physical functioning is also an important consideration in assigning age norms. Chronologically old people who are gray and wrinkled but still physically spry arouse no particular interest on the tennis court, but a frail older person certainly would. Again there is a fairly well-developed sexual dual standard, particularly during and after adolescence. Men are expected to exhibit a high degree of physical strength and agility and they are expected to exhibit a certain amount of sexual prowess. In these terms, men very often encounter teasing and labeling related to aging in their 30s. Men also often self-assign themselves to an age grade in order to commit themselves to a lower level of physical performance. This is a surprisingly effective social mechanism for "copping out."

Although these various assignment criteria have been presented as analytically separate, they usually occur in various combinations. Furthermore, it should be clear that much research needs to be done before very much will be known about the assignment process.

C. The Focus of Age Norms

Individuals, social structure, social processes, phases of involvement with social structure, and combinations of these are influenced by age norms. This is an issue separate from assigning norms to particular people. It deals with the focus of the norms.

Age norms concerning the person deal mainly with expected appearance and behavioral demeanor (as opposed to specific, instrumental action). That one should dress properly for one's age and behave in a manner appropriate for one's age are examples.

Age norms governing social structure include norms linking age with various groups, roles, social situations, and subcultures. To date, sociologists have been concerned primarily with age-related roles, with little attention to other attributes of social structure (Riley et al., 1972; Cain, 1964). However, roles are usually attached to specific positions within specific groups. For example, one has to be 11 years old and male to join a Boy Scout troop, but within a given troop, roles are allocated on the basis of tenure and performance, and a discussion of a young man's role as a Boy Scout would be incomplete without reference to the rules of the specific group. Age norms for social structure are assigned by all of the various mechanisms. Age norms also apply to unstructured situations. For instance, in a bar with a youth-oriented live rock band, a 40 year old may be exposed to sanctions from younger patrons simply on the basis of his or her appearance. That person is simply not eligible to be in that specific situation. Age norms are also related to access to various subcultures through the effect of age norms on access to age-segregated settings. For example, teenagers develop language that is uniquely theirs and cannot be mastered by non-teenagers simply because of the age-segregated interactional basis of teen-age slang.

People approach, enter, master, and often relinquish their relationships to structural niches in society. Accordingly, age norms related to structure can be differentiated into those that apply to preparation, entry, incumbency, and exit. Most structural elements have age-related entry criteria, but age norms are only sporadically related to the other phases—approach, maturity, aging, or withdrawal—as they apply to particular structural elements. In addition, different assignment criteria are used to allocate people to various age-liked phases, even for a given structural element.

Age norms link people not only to social structure but to interpersonal processes as well. Age is strongly associated with strategies people can and will use in their attempts to pursue their own lives within the group. For example, children and older people are expected to be somewhat deferent and unaggressive in their negotiations with those in between. Middle-aged people are expected to be gentle toward older people. On the other hand, children are allowed to be more physically violent in their relations with each other than they are toward their parents. Thus, age norms have something to do with whether one takes an active or passive stance toward decision making, and aggressive or acquiescent posture in negotiations. The way people deal with change is thus intimately tied to age norms concerning the manner in which people of a given age *ought* to solve their problems.

D. Goals of Age Norms

Age norms can demand that people do or be something or not do or be something. They can also allow people to do certain things, but not require any specific thing. Age norms can also demand that certain choices be made. That is, age norms can prescribe and proscribe specific behavior or relations of the individual to specific structural elements, but they can also delineate a field of permitted behaviors and structural niches. Age norms can also demand that choices be made from this field. More will be said about these factors later.

E. Application of Age Norms

Age norms can be formal or informal in terms of how sanctions are applied. At the one end of the continuum, laws are more or less rigid, universalistic age norms. Age regulations may also be formal and universal-istic, as in the case of mandatory retirement rules. Unwritten laws, or mores, may be informal but they carry a great deal of weight. For example, there is no law against a 40 year old woman's dating a 20-year-old man, but powerful informal sanctions may be brought to bear in such cases. Folkways and mores tend to be consensual, but they may be translated into laws.

Many times age norms are applied to the individual by the individual. This may be simply an accurate view of conformity. But in a changing world, it is also possible for individuals to apply stricter standards to themselves than would be applied by the community at large. Of course, age norms can be and are applied to the individual by others, as in the case of the minimum legal age to vote.

Most of the time age norms are applied directly to the individual, but occasionally age norms are applied to an individual by virtue of the age of someone else to whom the person is tied. For instance, parents are sometimes influenced by certain age norms by virtue of their children's ages rather than their own. Age norms are often deterministic, particularly chronological age norms, but more often a range of age is used. Thus, it is probably more appropriate to say that the application of various norms is *age-linked* rather than age-determined.

F. Age Grading and Human Development Research

It is certainly true that the foregoing discussion is based on a less than adequate research base. However, I have never believed that creativity in science is entirely dependent on a carefully built foundation. It seems to me that the tenuous structure of boxes that monkeys build in order to get bananas may be a more appropriate analogue to the way scientists find important ideas. Thus, I lay the inadequacies of the discussion squarely on my own shoulders. But at the same time, I think it is a more complete paradigm of age grading than we have had up until now, one that can be used as a heuristic tool for developmental research.

There are several ways that research can explore the effect of age norms on human development. It is obvious that, given the extreme complexity of age grading, more attention needs to be paid to interaction among the various demensions of age norms. Legal age norms tend to be arbitrary, direct, externally sanctioned, chronological, and based on community or societal standards. Most other age norms can exhibit a very large array of combinations of dimensions. It is particularly important to see how the various assignment criteria interact with the object of the age norm. For example, which objects—persons, social structure, phase of development, or social processes—are most often associated with chronological age?

Another useful task would be to evaluate the scientific validity of various justifications for age norms which are based on assumptions about human development. It would also be useful to examine the age norms implicit in the work of psychologists such as Piaget, Jung, Erikson, and Buhler. It may well be that their formulations need reconsideration in the light of social change. It is also important to know something about the part group reinforcement plays in the dynamics of age norms as personal standards. It might be particularly interesting to see how age norms affect the presentation of self (Goffman, 1959).

III. Age-Related Demands for Decision Making

Externally, the complex of age norms is tied to the life course by the assignment process, the process through which groups apply age norms to persons. But what about internal processes? How do age norms become translated into significant symbols for the individual? People come to understand what age norms are through socialization, but age norms become salient through interaction and demands for decision making.

Age norms that deal with personal qualities such as appearance or manner of acting become salient when individuals become aware, through interaction with other persons, that particular age norms are being applied to them. Age norms that deal with social structure become salient in a variety of ways. They may be externally imposed, as with formal age norms, or selected by the individual from within a socially defined field of eligibles. This section of the paper deals with age-linked decision-making demands as a normatively dictated mechanism for the internal organization of age norms and the articulation of age norms with the life course.

The division of the life course into a set of "career tracks" was discussed earlier. Each of these tracks represents a prescribed sequence of roles, groups, situations, and subcultures. But these sequentially arranged career tracks are not deterministic. Instead, they represent a series of fields of possibilities along various dimensions. It is almost always necessary to narrow the field further than specified by either the life course or age norms in order to get to the specific structural elements to which individuals are tied. And in complex societies it is impossible for external processes to determine specific assignment completely. The result is a type of age norm—the decision demand—that forces the individual to participate in the assignment process.

Decision demands are norms tied to the life course which set intervals––zones of decision—within which selections must be made from an age-linked field of possible structural niches. For example, following the completion of preparatory education, young adults usually enter a period of job experimentation. The field of possibilities expands dramatically immediately following graduation (certification) and continues to expand while the

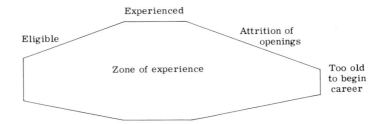

Fig. 3. Dynamics of the zone of decision.

individual gains job experience. But after a time there is an increasing expectation that the individual will find a position of employment into which he will settle, and during this period, the field of jobs for which he is eligible may slowly contract. Contraction also occurs as a result of career choices by others in the cohort. For many jobs, career tracks are difficult to begin after 45. For others, it is difficult to break in after age 35. Clausen (1972) points out that people who make job career decisions relatively late have more orderly careers. This suggests that they simply forgo the job experimentation that usually accompanies entry into a career track. Even within the dimensions of job careers, various occupations and work places differ with respect to the size of the age interval within which career selections must be made.

Figure 3 shows schematically what may happen to opportunities during the zone of decision. Following initial eligibility, opportunities increase with experience until they reach a plateau. Very quickly, however, opportunities begin to decline again as opportunities are selected by others in the age cohort. Finally, the individual may in some cases miss opportunities altogether by delaying a decision too long. For example, postponement of childbearing until the 30s or early 40s may in some cases make pregnancy impossible.

Age-related zones of decision exist with regard to careers in education, the family, employment, residence, retirement, voluntary associations, friendships, leisure pursuits, and in other areas. Although they are often somewhat flexible, the deadlines associated with zones of decision provide motivation for individuals to organize their thoughts and to negotiate an acceptable choice with significant others. Scholars often accept deadlines as a means of pushing themselves into organizing their thoughts and coming to grips with an intellectual issue. Age-related decision deadlines operate in much the same fashion.

The foregoing implies a very active part for the individual in the process of decision making. However, individuals vary a great deal in the extent to which they make their own decisions. Some important dimensions of this include the individual's self-esteem and self-confidence, the support received from others, and age norms themselves. Prior to young adulthood, people are expected to be involved in decisions about their own life courses, but in cases of conflict to defer to those in charge, usually parents. Women are likely to be expected to be deferent longer than men are, and often marriage simply shifts responsibility for decisions about the woman's life from one man (her father) to another (her husband.) This may be changing, but it affected the life courses of those cohorts of women currently in their later years. Likewise, one family may encourage younger members to make their own decisions while others impose fairly specific age-related roles on their members. Older adults are often discouraged by their families from assuming a self-confident attitude about making their own independent decisions. Again, *decisions in response to age-related decision demands remain a variable to be explained in research rather than to be assumed.*

IV.   Turning Points in the Life Course

A turning point is a change in situation that alters the individual's usual strategy for coping with day-to-day life. Turning points often carry along with them immediate demands for action. Turning points represent change beyond the threshold that can be dealt with routinely. They are points at which the individual ceases to be one thing and becomes something else; and many turning points are mandated by age norms.

The disintegration and subsequent reintegration associated with turning points can occur as a result of a long process of erosion or as a sudden shift. In later life, for example, inflation may erode real income to the point where the individual is forced to become financially dependent; or the individual may suddenly lose a spouse.

In the study of human development, the focus has primarily concerned the crises aspects of turning points in the life courses of individuals. I would like to take another perspective and perhaps provide some insights into why turning points often are not crises.

Anticipatory socialization is the process of learning the rights, obligations, resources, and outlook of a position or situation one will occupy in the *future.* Certain aspects of socialization are important in defusing potential crises associated with turning points. To begin with, to the extent that clear-cut cultural definitions exist, future positions do not represent a frightening unknown. To the extent that the context, content, and prerequisites of a future position can be known, it is possible to prepare in advance for change. The individual's capacity to imagine his or her own future is an important aspect of this process. It is quite common to live out, in fantasies, what the future will hold, to identify the potential problems, and to make some decisions in advance.

The success of fantasies in smoothing the process of transition through various turning points depends largely on the resources the individual can command. Concrete cultural prescriptions, such as rites of passage or rituals, make for predictable anticipation, but unfortunately few turning points involve future positions that are so clear-cut. Personal contact with people who are already there can provide models for adjustment to a new position or situation. Of course, the individual must take some initiative in this process, since compared to childhood there are few formal mechanisms for anticipatory socialization in adulthood.

Another factor that serves to help people prepare for subsequent stages in their life courses relates to boredom. Having spent as long as several decades in a given position, people often welcome and even seek the new experiences that turning points bring. The individual's agenda for his or her current phase is also a determinant. For example, people who have achieved most of their job ambitions tend to retire more easily than those who still have "unfinished business" (Atchley, 1972). Finally, by the later stages of adulthood many, if not most, adults have had to cope with several turning points. Skill at coping with turning points probably increases with age.

Another important factor, suggested by the work of Lopata (1973) and Clausen (1972), is the part group support plays in dealing with age-linked turning points. For example, educational decisions, career decisions, mate selection, child rearing, the empty nest, retirement, and widowhood are all age-linked phenomena that most people encounter, not alone, but in the company of age peers who are trying to cope with similar situations. Some of the potential for stress and self-doubt is reduced by the support peers give one another in these contexts.

Seltzer (1975) and Cain (1964) have spoken of people who avoid the preprogrammed sequence implied by various life courses and who end up out of phase. That is, their positions on various career tracks do not match up. To the extent that peer support is necessary to get through a given turning point, being out of phase can heighten the prospect for crisis. For example, in my rese[a]ch I have observed that people who are widowed too early lack a group context and group support for dealing with the new role. This has led Lopata (1973) to conclude that young widows cannot remain widows long. People who begin careers in their 40s often miss the group support among age peers that their younger colleagues may find. Thus, time-disordered relationships offer an excellent lever for studying not only age norms themselves but also the dynamics of group support for coping with turning points.

Thus, society already contains a system of "crisis prevention" through various mechanisms of socialization, and this system deserves more attention in human development research.

V. Conclusion

In this paper I have attempted to show that the life course, age grading, and age-linked decision demands are *problematic* aspects of the sociocultural environment whose effects on human development have yet to be discovered. I have tried to provide some tools for diagnosing and for injecting these factors into human development research. I can only hope that others share with me the sense of excitement concerning the promise this area of sociopsychological research holds for adding to our understanding of human development.

The life course represents a basic, normative ideal to which individual biographies can be related. For example, life graphs (Back & Bourque, 1970) can be used to study both the life course and individual biographies and aspirations. Neugarten *et al.* (1965) have given an example of how age grading can be approached, but more immediate, phenomenological approaches are needed. Finally, age-linked decision demands represent a virtually untapped empirical point at whcih the social impact on human development could be studied. All of these approaches can enrich our understanding of both human development and the social systems that shape it.

REFERENCES

Atchley, R.C. *The social forces in later life.* Belmont, California: Wadsworth, 1972.

Atchley, R.C., & George, L. K. Symptomatic measurement of age. *The Gerontologist,* 1973, **13**, 332–336.

Back, K.W., & Bourque, L.B. Life graphs: Aging and cohort effects. *Journal of Gerontology,* 1970, **25**, 249–255.

Cain, L. D., Jr. Life course and social structure. In R.E.L. Faris (Ed.), *Handbook of modern sociology.* Chicago: Rand McNally, 1964. Pp. 272–309.

Cain, L.D., Jr. The growing importance of legal age in determining the status of the elderly. *The Gerontologist,* 1974, **14**. 167–174.

Clausen, J.A. The life course of individuals. In M.W. Riley, M. Johnson, & A. Foner (Eds.), *Aging and society, volume three; A sociology of age stratification.* New York: Russell Sage Foundation, 1972. Pp. 457–514.

Goffman, E. *The presentation of self in everyday life.* New York: Doubleday, 1959.

Lopata, H.Z. *Widowhood in an American city.* Cambridge, Massachusetts: Schenkman, 1973.

Neugarten, B. L., & Datan, N. Sociological perspectives on the life cycle. In P. B. Baltes & K. W. Schaie (Eds.), *Life-span developmental psychology: Personality and socialization.* New York: Academic Press, 1973. Pp. 53–69.

Neugarten, B. L., & Moore, J. W. The changing age-status system. In B. L. Neugarten (Ed.), *Middle age and aging.* Chicago: Univ. of Chicago Press, 1968.

Neugarten, B. L., Moore, J. W., & Lowe, J. C. Age norms, age constraints, and adult socialization. *American Journal of Sociology,* 1965, **70,** 710–717.

Riley, M. W. Social gerontology and the age stratification of society. *The Gerontologist.* 1971, **11,** 79–87.

Riley, M. W., Johnson, J., & Foner, A. (Eds.), *Aging and society, volume three: A sociology of age stratification.* New York: Russell Sage Foundation, 1972.

Seltzer, M. M. Suggestions for the examination of time disordered relationships. In J. F. Gubrium (Ed.), *Time, roles and self in old age.* New York: Behavorial Publications, 1975 (in press).

Sontag, S. The double standard of aging. *Saturday Review,* 1972, September 23, 29–38.

CHAPTER 18

The Changing Life Cycle of Work

WILLIAM H. MIERNYK

REGIONAL RESEARCH INSTITUTE, WEST VIRGINIA UNIVERSITY
MORGANTOWN, WEST VIRGINIA

ABSTRACT

Life-span development deals with the changes an individual undergoes as he moves from infancy to maturity, which is a dynamic process. This paper discusses the changing life cycle of work during a period of rapid economic growth in the United States, and this turns out to be an exercise in comparative statics. What I have done is to compare the work cycle of an "average" worker in 1870 with that of an "average" worker in 1970. A comparison of this kind involves a considerable amount of abstraction and estimation. Even if there should be substantial error in the numbers I have used, however, my conclusions will not be seriously affected. They do not, in the final analysis, depend upon precision of measurement.

I. Introduction

For a number of years labor economists and some sociologists have been concerned with the "discontent" of blue-collar workers. As early as 1956, Daniel Bell (without specific acknowledgment to Freud) published his well-known collection of notes called *Work and Its Discontents*.[1] The winter 1972

---

[1] This monograph was reissued in 1970 by the League for Industrial Democracy.

issue of *Dissent* concerned itself with "The World of the Blue Collar Worker." Several of the essays in this volume deal with worker boredom, discontent, and alienation. More recently, the Secretary of Health, Education and Welfore appointed a special task force to look into the "blue-collar blues." The authors of the HEW report found job dissatisfaction to be widely pervasive; it is not limited to those who perform dull and repetitive manual tasks (U.S. Dept. of Health, Education and Welfare, 1973; Wool, 1973). Finally, Studs Terkel (1974), the stream-of-consciousness reporter, has recently published his latest set of taped conversations, this time with 135 respondents who were asked how they liked their jobs. Their answer, *in nuce,* is that they did not. While one might question the representativeness of Terkel's sample, since it is unlikely that everyone in the country dislikes his job, these interviews add to the evidence that discontent among workers is widespread.

At a time when most of the disadvantaged peoples of the world are trying to emulate America's economic "success," a substantial segment of the work force in this country appears to have grown weary of the modern world of work (although not necessarily unhappy with the economic benefits they have derived from the system). This has been referred to as the "Lordstown syndrome," in honor of a major strike called by auto workers employed by General Motors at their Lordstown, Ohio, plant. The cause of the strike was worker dissatisfaction brought about by the "depersonalization of work." Many workers complained about the specialized and routine nature of their jobs. Although repetitive tasks and mindless effort are found in many industries, they are epitomized in the minds of many Americans by the auto assembly line. It is important to stress, however, that worker dissatisfaction is not limited to the blue-collar members of the work force. The studies reviewed in the paper by Wool report poor worker morale among many white-collar workers, particularly those in dead-end jobs.

Much is known about the basic characteristics of the world of work today. Numerous government and private agencies gather statistics on hours and earnings, fringe benefits, and production and productivity. Meanwhile, social scientists have expanded their efforts to learn more about the psychological and sociological aspects of the world of work. Unfortunately, we cannot contrast what social scientists have learned about the world of work today with the world of work a century ago. It is possible, however, to make some objective comparisons of hours and earnings, and to draw some inferences from these comparisons. It is also possible to speculate about the probable continuation of past trends.

II.   Hours and Income, 1870 and 1970

The changing life cycle of work can be summarized in a simple diagram (given in Figure 1) which shows the expected lifetime income (expressed in

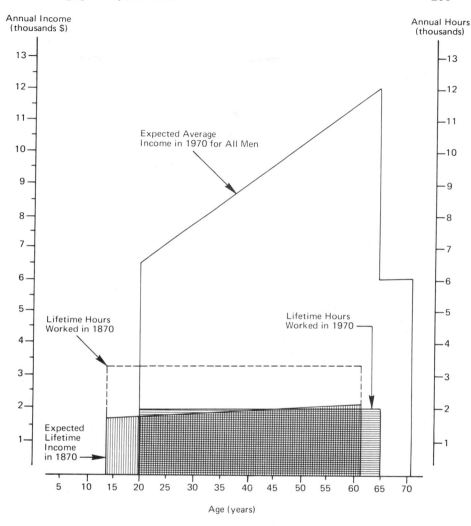

Fig. 1. Income earned and hours worked, 1870 and 1970 (in 1970 dollars). (Source: Calculated from data in: *The Statistical History of the United States from Colonial Times to the Present,* 1965, pp. 25, 91; *Life Insurance Fact Book,* Institute of Life Insurance, 1946, p. 58, 1972, p. 90; *Current Population Reports,* October 30, 1970, p. 13; Lebergott, 1964, p. 524; and *The Economic Report of the President,* 1973, p. 244.)

1970 dollars) of an "average" worker in 1870 and 1970. It also shows the lifetime hours worked by these hypothetical laborers. Expected hours and earnings were calculated from the date of labor-force entry, not from birth.

The 1870 average worker entered the work force at age 14 and left when he died at age 61. He would expect to be on the job an average of 3120 hours per year. Thus, during the 47 years of his working life, he would put in a total of 146,640 hours on the job.

I have assumed that the average employed worker entered the labor force in 1970 at age 20. He would expect to continue to work until age 65. His work career would be terminated by retirement, and he would expect to be employed only 2000 hours per year, or a lifetime average of 90,000 hours. During the century over which the above comparison has been made, therefore, average hours worked per year declined about 36%, and the number of hours spent at work during the typical lifetime work cycle declined by 39%.

The lifetime earnings of the hypothetical 1870 worker expressed in 1970 dollars come to $90,00. His 1970 counterpart would expect to earn, during his lifetime, $360,000. This represents an increase of 300%. The average worker in 1970 would expect to be employed 2 years less than his 1870 counterpart, and he would work only about two-thirds as many hours. In real terms, however, he would expect to have about three times as much income.

The contrast is even greater, as one would expect, if we compare the work cycle and lifetime earnings of a typical college graduate in 1970 with those of the average 1870 worker. The college graduate enters the work force later, between the ages of 22 and 25, and he will work fewer years than the average worker. His earnings also go up substantially, from the expected lifetime earnings of $360,000 to expected earnings that range between $536,500 and $580,000.

The century under review was one of remarkable progress from an economic point of view. The reduction in hours, increase in income, and greater longevity of workers between 1870 and 1970 are the products of technological change. Invention, managerial innovation, and the diffusion of technology have radically altered the structure of the American economy and have affected the life cycle of work dramatically. In 1870, almost 40% of all employed workers were engaged in the primary activities of agriculture, forestry, and fishing. Another 40% were engaged in the secondary pursuits of mining, manufacturing, and construction. Only 20% were employed in "tertiary" activities, by which we mean all of the trades, services, and professions. Today these proportions have been radically altered. Between 5 and 10% of the work force are now employed in farming, fishing, and forestry, and between 30 and 35% are in secondary occupations. The remaining 60% are in the trades, services, and professions. This major change in economic structure is a graphic reflection of technological progress (Mansfield, 1968a,b; Schacter & Dale, 1973, pp. 199–212).

III. The Changing Work Cycle and Worker Dissatisfaction

We now come to the central issue of this paper. How have changes in the cycle of work affected job satisfaction? This is something I can only speculate about, but it is highly likely that 1870 was anything but a Golden Age of Work. A much larger proportion of the labor force was engaged in manual labor in 1870 than in 1970. Four out of five employed workers lived quite literally by the sweat of their brows. Hours were long and work was monotonous, sometimes dirty and often dangerous. There were no paid holidays or other fringe benefits, and workers could not look forward to leisure at the end of a working life. The chances are good, however, that there was less job alienation among workers in 1870 than in 1970. Workers probably had neither the time nor the energy to succumb to the anxieties and neuroses that appear to plague many of today's blue-collar workers. For most workers there was little or no job satisfaction. But because of the instability of employment during the nineteenth century, the thing that workers feared most was "the layoff." The low wages earned by common laborers restricted personal saving, and there was no unemployment compensation for the hapless worker who lost his job. Furthermore, the 1870 worker lived under a much sterner regime of industrial discipline than his 1970 counterpart. Except in a few crafts, there were no trade unions at that time; employers could be as autocratic and capricious as they chose. Workers today enjoy the protection of trade unions; even unorganized workers benefit indirectly from the threat of unionism. But the greater freedom, the democratization of the work place, and the clear-cut economic benefits of economic growth and technological progress clearly have not generated a corresponding amount of that elusive thing called worker satisfaction.

It is also worth pointing out parenthetically that the pathological results of economic progress—that is, the growth of worker anxiety and discontent—have created a demand for the services of psychologists and psychiatrists. We devote a steadily increasing part of our economic growth dividend to medical expenditures, and I assume that this includes expenditures for mental as well as physical cures and treatment.

IV. Some Speculation about the Future

What of the future? Can we expect a further quantum jump in economic growth comparable to that which occurred between 1870 and 1970? Will there be further dramatic changes in the life cycle of work? I think the answer to these questions is an unequivocal negative. There will be further economic growth, but we have reached or are very close to a point of inflection on the growth curve. Future growth in real income will be at a declining rate. Why should this be so? Are there limits to technological progress? Clearly not. We have no reason to believe that there are limits to man's technical ingenuity, or that there are ultimate froniters to the growth of knowledge. But there are other constraints; namely, resources and energy.

In 1870, energy per capita, expressed in terms of the total horsepower embodied in all prime movers, amounted to .42; that is, less than half of one horsepower per person.[2] By 1970, the energy available in the United States amounted to approximately 100 horsepower per capita. *This is more than a two-hundredfold increase!* A somewhat more reliable figure shows an equally dramatic increase in a more restricted form of energy available to each person in the United States over a shorter period. In 1902, the first year for which we have data, the United States produced 75.4 kilowatts of electric energy per person. Seventy years later, this nation produced 7989 kilowatts of electric energy per person, an increase of more than 10,000%.[3]

The past century has been one of unprecedented expansion in the use of energy in all forms. One of the characteristics of historical technological progress has been that each major new developmennt has been more energy-intensive than the one before. Events of the past few months have indicated clearly, however, that in this country we can no longer take abundant and cheap energy for granted (Landsberg, 1974). Because there will be changes in relative prices—and energy will be increasingly more expensive than it has been in the past—it would be unrealistic to assume further quantum jumps in real earnings comparable to those of the past century. We are now entering an era when it will require all of our scientific ingenuity to maintain even modest rates of growth in real output and earnings (Georgescu-Roegen, 1971). The structure of the economy will continue to change, but more slowly than it has in the past. And there is no reason to expect any fundamental alteration in the present life cycle of work. Future changes will be much less dramatic than those of the past. The average man of the future will enter the work force sometime between the ages of 16 and 25, and will retire sometime between 62 and 65. His real income will continue to go up, but much more slowly than in the past.

One economic trend that is almost certain to continue is that of increasing interdependence of the world economy. And if this is so, it seems highly unlikely that the residents of this country, comprising less than 6% of the world's people, can continue to consume two-thirds of the world's energy and roughly the same proportion of its goods and services. I do not pretend to know how or when the basic institutional changes that will provide for a more equal distribution of the world's goods and services will occur. But a shift toward a more equitable distribution is bound to happen (Landsberg, 1974, p. 248; Ford Foundation, 1973, p. 3).

---

[2] The prime movers involved included automotives, work animals, factories (excluding electric motors), mines, railroads, powered merchant ships, sailing vessels, farms (excluding horses and other animals), windmills, aircraft, and central electric stations.

[3] The energy estimates were calculated from data in *The Statistical History of the United States from Colonial Times to Present*, Series A1–3, p. 7, and Series S1–14, p. 506; and *Statistical Abstract of the United States*, 1973, no. 2, p. 5; no. 829, p. 507; and no. 834, p. 510.

I also expect a revival of old-fashioned economics. Our basic concerns will shift away from the problems engendered by affluence and toward problems dealing with the allocation of *scarce* resources. Along with this, I expect to see growing concern about a more equitable domestic distribution of what we produce. Whether or not these changes will have an effect on worker satisfaction is something that is not now clearly predictable. My guess, however, is that a century from now our successors in the social sciences will be less concerned with the pathological consequences of affluence than with a number of more elemental economic and social problems. If alienation, or anomie, is a negative result of a highly productive and competitive economic system, it should be less significant when growing scarcities of energy and resources force men to behave more cooperatively than they have in the past in order to lengthen the time horizon of mankind's survival.

ACKNOWLEDGMENTS

It is a pleasure to acknowledge the research assistance of Luther Thompson.

REFERENCES

Council of Economic Advisers. *Economic report of the president,* Washington, D.C.: U.S. Government Printing Office. 1973.

Ford Foundation Energy Policy Project. *Exploring energy choices.* New York: Ford Foundation Energy Policy Project, 1973.

Georgescu-Roegen, N. *The entropy law and the economic process.* Cambridge, Massachusetts: Harvard Univ. Press, 1971.

Institute of Life Insurance. *Life insurance fact book,* 1946, 1972.

Landsberg, H.H. Low-cost abundant energy: Paradise lost? *Science,* 1974, **184**, 247–253.

Lebergott, S. *Manpower in economic growth.* New York: McGraw-Hill, 1964.

Mansfield, E. *The economics of technological change.* New York: W.W. Norton, 1968. (a)

Mansfield, E. *Industrial research and technological innovation: An econometric analysis.* New York: W.W. Norton, 1968. (b)

Schacter, G., & Dale, E.L., Jr. *The economist looks at society.* Lexington, Massachusetts: Xerox College Publishing, 1973.

Terkel, S. *Work: Working people talk about what they do all day and how they feel about what they do.* New York: Random House, 1974.

United States Bureau of the Census. *Statistical abstract of the United States.* Washington, D.C.: U.S. Government Printing Office, 1973.

United States Bureau of the Census. *Statistical history of the United States from colonial times to the present.* Stamford, Connecticut: Fairfield Publishers, 1965.

United States Bureau of the Census. *Current population reports,* October 30, 1970.

United States Department of Health, Education and Welfare. *Work in America: Report of the special task force to the Secretary of Health, Education and Welfare.* Upjohn Institute for Employment Research, Cambridge, Massachusetts: MIT Press, 1973.

Wool, H. What's wrong with work in America?—a review essay. *Monthly Labor Review,* March 1973, 38–44.

CHAPTER 19

Accommodating Old People in Society: Examples from Appalachia and New Orleans

JOHN LOZIER

WEST VIRGINIA UNIVERSITY
MORGANTOWN, WEST VIRGINIA

ABSTRACT

Successful aging, like successful living in general, requires an accommodating environment, regardless of an individual's capacity to cope, adapt, or adjust. More than research on how old people cope with society, we need research on how societies cope with old people. More than programs for belated socialization, therapy, or counseling aimed at changing old people, we need programs to change society in such a way as to assure old people of society's protection. Case studies provided here are intended to support this argument, and also to recommend an ethnographic approach in gerontology that is conceptually intermediate between the individual developmental approach of psychology and the comparative approach of sociology and ethnology.

Morton Lieberman (Chapter 8 this volume) observes that an aggressive, irritating, narcissistic, and demanding old person is more likely to survive the crisis of institutional transfer than the more gracious and likable old person. This observation seems to fit perfectly with the idea that ours is a gerontophobic culture; after all, anyone who lives to very old age must be a crotchety old buzzard. People are not really supposed to live that long, and thus by his very survival, an individual becomes a violator of the norms—troublesome, uncooperative, unaccommodating. So if it should be found that the crotchety old buzzards live longer than those who are more cooperative and sensitive, it may be because the latter are responding to social cues and behaving appropriately by dying in a timely fashion.

It was suggested that this paper deal with aging and "adaptation" in a rural context. Having studied the old physical anthropology, I knew I could not adapt to that usage, since I am merely an organism and not a species. Since "adaptation" is conceptually inseparable from "survival," the concept is inappropriate to refer to the kind of accommodation achieved by old people who cannot, in the end, survive. Since death is inevitable, and even the most advanced technologies offer only delay, I think we are going to have to stop thinking of death as an "adaptive failure," or a consequence of "inability to cope," by implication an "abnormal behavior." It makes sense to think of death as one possible way of coping, sometimes (or eventually) the socially appropriate way, and surely sometimes the expedient way, as when a secret agent, trapped by counterspies bent on extracting information, bites down on a cyanide capsule.

If we assume that "successful aging" requires "continued survival," then we may as well forget any hope of avoiding failure. On the other hand, success in late life can be seen in terms of meeting social expectations, displaying appropriate behavior (independence without stubbornness, gracious dependency without clinging, emotional warmth without anxiety, authority without tyranny, etc.), and finally, participating as the central figure in a death event, well staged and well attended. I would like to suggest that success in this sense is quite possible, quite common (but not necessarily predominant in America), and probably quite well understood by most old people themselves. Perhaps in modern, urban society we are forgetting how it is done.

I. The Societal Perspective

Althouse and I (Lozier & Althouse, 1974, 1975) have studied old people and the society about them in southern West Virginia. Following the suggestion of Clark Tibbitts, we have attempted to provide a *societal* analysis of aging, concerned with "how . . . society organizes and behaves with reference to its older people [Tibbitts, 1960, p. 11]." This perspective implies that we are not really talking about old people, but rather about *society* as it *accommodates* old people. For us, a societal theory of aging would be a theory of society applied to old people, and not an autonomous theory of the aging process.

The societal perspective, to the extent that it can be found in existing literature, is more implicit that explicit. In 1960 Tibbitts was perceptive enough to notice that this was indeed a distinctive approach, but he could cite few examples. Clearly the most relevant is the work of anthropologist Leo Simmons (1945, 1960a). Simmons provides an excellent nutshell statement of the position I am taking: "Successful aging rests upon the capacity and opportunity for individuals to fit into the social framework of their own societies in a way that will insure security and influence [Simmons, 1960b, p. 74]."

Simmons is acknowledged by two other sources (Maxwell & Silverman, 1970; Cowgill & Holmes, 1972a) as the pioneer in this approach. Maxwell and Silverman apply a model of reciprocal exchange between old and young, showing a relationship between esteem for elders and control of information by elders, using a cross-cultural approach. The work of Cowgill and Holmes (Cowgill, 1972; Cowgill & Holmes, 1972b) is directed at the development of a "meaningful sociological theory of aging," and draws on the ethnographic contributions of a number of authors in this edited volume.

However, the goal of sociological theory of aging continues to be elusive, because too much is expected of the comparative method. This approach, though legitimate, cannot be fully effective until more extensive work has been done in the ethnographic study of aging in individual societies and communities. My own work with Ronald Althouse is intended as a contribution to this relatively neglected area—the ethnography of aging— which lies conceptually between the individual– developmental theory of psychology and the universal sociological theory sought by comparative sociology and ethnology.

We have described (Lozier & Althouse, 1974) a series of individual case histories of careers to old age in "Laurel Creek." Our aim has been to show that younger people (juniors) are required to display attention to the legitimate claims of older people (elders) because a junior's performance with respect to his obligations is publicly judged and sanctioned. Since this can happen only in a social system where people pay attention to what their neighbors do and require, it would seem that this process of *social enforcement* would be most effective in small, stable, and perhaps rural kinds of communities, and least effective in the anonymous context of urban life.

The process of social enforcement or control should guarantee that a person gets what he can rightfully claim, and gives what he properly owes. This obviously means that different persons, with different histories of behavior or performance, will meet with different consequences. This is what is commonly meant by *justice;* for good or ill, you ought to get what is coming to you. Consider two cranky, sick old men, each abandoned by kin and neglected by neighbors. The one has lived a model life, worked hard, helped his children and neighbors to get ahead; the other has been perennially suspect, taking more than he gives, demanding more of children and neighbors than he can legitimately expect. The compassionate observer sees human suffering in both cases, but the honest reporter of social phenomena sees injustice in the one case and justice in the other.

One may view the allocation of a share of collective resources to a particular old person as a consequence of the collective effort of a society to deliver justice (as culturally defined) to the individual.

II.   Retirement to the Porch

We have also attempted to provide a description (1975) of the social process we call "retirement to the porch." Although we have attempted to maintain a societal perspective, avoiding what we consider to be the trap of locating the "aging process" in the individual organism, it is clear that we have here a point of correspondence with the concerns of life-span developmental psychology.

"Retirement to the porch" is not a peculiar characteristic of Appalachian culture, but a local manifestation of a process that can be observed in many rural, small-town, and even urban neighborhoods. In Laurel Creek, it is men, not women, who most typically make extensive use of the front porch in their elder years. This discussion therefore omits consideration of the accommodation of old women.

A major obligation of a male throughout his lifetime in Laurel Creek[1] is to secure and maintain steady employment, but economic conditions make this exceedingly difficult for most. Faced with a period of unemployment, the best a mature man can do is to display his energy, skill, and readiness to work; this can be done by job-seeking activity, and by working about the house and yard. It is dangerous for him to appear too frequently in an attitude of repose on the porch, as this is taken as evidence that he is no longer actively interested in working steadily. But at some time in later maturity, usually well before age 65, it is apparent to him as well as to others that he will not find steady work again. He may then drop some of the appearances of industry and retire to the porch.

In this early period of retirement, a man typically looks for opportunities to join in activities on an occasional basis—helping out a neighbor with a repair job, taking occasional work for pay, and otherwise seeking ways to make himself useful and maintain his exchange relationships with others. Later on, he is gradually released from the obligation to perform useful

[1] "Laurel Creek" is a pseudonym. All data from Laurel Creek were collected by Althouse from 1968 to 1973.

service, and begins to claim privileges that are granted him in recognition for his record of service. He may still help out on occasion, but it is up to him to decide when, where, and how.

As he becomes more incapacitated, he is further relieved of obligations, and others may begin to take responsibility for helping him maintain his house and yard. He ceases to accumulate social credit, and must now draw on that which he has accumulated. This means that he must be careful not to demand in excess of what others consider to be his legitimate due. He may ask children in the neighborhood to run errands for him, and he may report on the child's performance to the parents. If his social credit is good and his demands are reasonable, the child's parents can be counted upon to encourage respectful compliance.

Periodic illness may occur, and the old man may fail to appear on the porch for extended periods. His absence is noted, and information about his condition passes by word of mouth, relayed by close kin. When he reappears, he enjoys a flurry of special attention celebrating his recovery, and then, if his health is stable, he maintains his pattern of appearances for a further indefinite period. But it is likely that during some illness he fails to recover sufficiently to resume routine appearances, and the conversational networks relay the information that his prognosis is negative. This is the situation that all have expected as inevitable but have hoped to delay, for it marks the onset of a *socially terminal* condition. Ideally, death should follow without undue delay, because it is assumed that the dying have a claim to greatly increased commitment of resources that cannot be sustained indefinitely without unbearable cost to others. It is for this reason that the old person feels, and is felt to be, under obligation to maintain his customary routines and to avoid entering the terminal condition until he is very near death.[2] He continues to make regular appearances, perhaps in spite of pain and waning interest, in order to reassure others and to avoid calling on them for intensive care. The longer he can maintain this preterminal performance, the better he preserves his social credit for the inevitable terminal phase.

If things go as they should, when it is known that he will not recover, family and friends will present him for a final appearance on the porch, where he will receive visits from all who have known him. This event signals the onset of the terminal state. He is then withdrawn into the house, where close kin and friends sustain him until death.[3]

---

[2] Stated otherwise, once in a terminal condition the old person may feel under obligation to die, and therefore continuing survival may be a source of dismay even to the old person himself.

[3] Commitment to an institution may follow if death is delayed. In the ordinary course of

The process of retirement to the porch provides what may seem a comforting ideal, and when it is achieved we may consider it to illustrate one form of "successful aging." Unfortunately, success is difficult, and often unachievable, for it requires not only the cooperation of the elder and the rest of society, but also an adequate level of resources in a social system so that the elder may be sustained without undue cost to others. It requires that an individual, throughout his active lifetime, be provided with sufficient opportunity to earn social credit, and it requires that the social system provide some kind of bank where social credit can be safely stored for withdrawal when needed. The collective knowledge of an individual's life history accomplishes this in a traditional community where personnel are not transient.[4]

Before giving illustrations from Laurel Creek, it should be noted that this ideal model is only approximated in reality, and is not intended to support a romantic fiction that finds the circumstances of the rural aged to be generally benign and comfortable. However, the model does help to understand what goes wrong when it does go wrong, which is all too frequently.

A. Fred Chaplin: An Example of Success

Fred Chaplin and his wife live some distance up the left fork of Laurel Creek, where normal traffic consists mainly of a few local residents. But passers-by rarely fail to pass the time of day with him when he is out on his porch, and as he remains relatively fit, he often catches a ride to town to conduct some minor business. He maintains a supply of minor errands—a bill to pay, purchases to make—so that he can justify a request any time he wishes. The request is never an imposition, as the passer-by is never asked to go out of his way.

Fred has about 5 acres of garden land just across the road from his porch. He is now too old to work it, but in the spring he hitches up his mule and plows a couple of furrows along one edge, then leaves the plow standing in plain sight from the porch. The evidence of work in progress cannot fail to provoke comment from passers-by, and before long he negotiates for

---

events, then, the old person is already "socially terminal" before being institutionalized. In many cases, especially in urban life, it may be actual commitment to a nursing facility that constitutes the symbol of terminality. This may help to explain why an old person seeks to maintain a customary routine, and also to delay entry to a nursing home; a failure in either case means that the old person must accept the terminal definition, which implies that his continuing survival is a liability to others and therefore places him under obligation to die.

[4] Legal and financial institutions for retirement have developed in part to compensate for the disruption of traditional institutions that cannot easily survive the effects of extensive migration and urban-scale society, but unfortunately money cannot always purchase the resources that old people require and desire.

others to use the land for gardens, and in exchange it is understood that he will receive a steady supply of produce as it matures.

When Fred purchased a new bathtub and commode, he had them delivered and placed right up front on the porch. After about 3 weeks, during which time talk focused on his remodeling plans, three men from up the hollow came in to help him install them.

Since Fred spends a great deal of time on his front porch, it is assumed that he has no direct access to information about what goes on in the community. Therefore, passers-by are under obligation to provide him with information; and since everyone talks to him, in fact he knows more about what is going on than most others about him. This gives him another resource—information—which he can provide to whomever he may favor. A fieldworker cannot fail to recognize how valuable the confidence of such a person may be.

B. *Wallace Meadows: An Example of Failure*

In contrast, Wallace Meadows has made a failure of porch retirement, in spite of the fact that his lifetime career was very successful by local standards. His children migrated from the community, in part because of attractions outside, but also very much influenced by the fact that Wallace taxed them with excessive demands.[5] He is also troublesome to neighbors. When he asks for a ride to town, he may want to take the driver out of his way or otherwise delay him. He demands small errands from children, and is quick to criticize their performance; but the parents cannot be counted upon to encourage compliance, because they too have come to regard him as troublesome. More and more, Wallace is avoided by both children and adults. The cycle of interactions lead to further deterioration of his position; he is bitter, and others describe him as a "contentious old son-of-a-bitch."

III.   Accommodation of the Old in Urban Settings

The front porch, as we conceive it, is merely one resource available to old people. It is a limited resource in that it cannot be used to create claims, but rather simply provides a setting for maintaining a semipublic presence and asserting existing claims that can be publicly justified. In some urban neighborhoods, porches may be used in the same way. Where front porches are not used as stages for old people to display themselves and assert their claims, other settings may be found—the lobby of a high-rise building, the

[5] Had the possibility of migration not existed, Wallace's situation might be very different.

park bench or bandstand, the dime-store lunch counter, the church, the senior center, fire hall, chess club, or race track. But generally, the opportunities available to old people in urban settings seem to be fewer, and the certainty of success diminished.

The old person in an urban setting may have accumulated through his active life a substantial set of publicly justifiable claims, but it may be very much more difficult for him to find an audience to hear and recognize the justification, and a social institution that can sanction the required performances. A long-time resident of an urban neighborhood may have performed impressive services for his neighbors, but if the neighbors move away, the record of service is lost, and those who come to occupy the neighborhood do not recognize his service or his claims. Local public sentiment is not an effective sanction on obligated juniors who are physically removed. Any help that he may obtain then becomes charity, and he is robbed of the dignity that is due him. If we assume that it is recognition for his accomplishments, as much as any material support, that provides the successful old person with a sense of well-being, then it may be very dismaying for him to receive service as charity.

Althouse contributed an illustration of an old woman in an urban neighborhood who made it a point to minister to the needs of other, more frail old people, and who often called on younger neighbors to help out on their behalf. We suggested that she is attempting to create claims for herself, by helping out in socially approved ways, with the hope that this will provide the basis for claiming reciprocity as she becomes more incapacitated. She seems plainly fearful, however, that the reciprocity may not be forthcoming—that her own claims may not be enforceable.

The social process may be quite different in urban settings, as illustrated by the case of an octogenarian bookie whom I shall call Ben Hobbs. This case is not typical, but it can be understood in terms of the same basic concepts.

I met Ben Hobbs as I ate breakfast at a dime-store lunch counter in New Orleans. From the way he greeted other patrons and counter workers, it was evident that he appeared there regularly. He initiated the conversation by showing me a wad of betting tickets, advising, "Don't ever bet the horses because you'll lose in the long run." I learned that he has no close kin, no children, no wife (she left him a half a century ago because he played the horses). He rooms with an "old crippled woman," and "helps her pay the rent." He shows obvious concern for the problems of the old. Indicating the sausage and eggs being consumed by another patron, he observed that this was more protein than lots of old people get in a week's time. He displayed his own frugality by wiping his plate clean with his bread.

Each day, he revealed, he visits a number of old people residing in the urban neighborhood, and collects from them small amounts of money which he bets for them at the race track in the afternoon. He wanted me to know that he discourages a person from betting more than he can afford to lose. He claims not to profit from the betting operation (he receives a railroad pension), and says he does it because he enjoys visiting people and going to the track.

I do not know for certain what Hobbs would do if he should find one of the isolated old people who place bets with him sick, or hungry, or in need of help to change a light bulb, but I would be very much surprised if he did not administer numerous minor services and arrange major services as he makes his rounds. If this is the way he operates, then we may glimpse a fascinating example of mutual accommodation among old people in an urban setting. A small bettor receives the assurance of regular visits, occasional help, and a monitoring service that may be crucial in an emergency. The bettor who wins is provided with cash that can finance reciprocal favors to Ben, and presumably there are always some winners.

Much must be left to speculation, as I had only a half-hour talk with Hobbs at the lunch counter. But I envision a network of regular bettors who inevitably must collectively lose more money than they win. And yet, in the process, they may be creating enough mutual interaction and enough reciprocity that in terms of social credit, they are all gaining an advantage.

The fact that an enterprising oldster may make a success of old age in an urban setting, in spite of the absence of kin and close lifelong associations, does not provide grounds for complacency; but it forces us to abandon any simple model of what is required in terms of social organization. This should have been obvious already, since we can see that many powerful figures (mayors, businessmen, etc.) are themselves old. With the interests of the old becoming more and more a political issue, we should not be surprised to see increasing efforts to organize the voting behavior of old people. Individuals such as Ben Hobbs could be important in such a process, and it would not be surprising to find that with his keen mind and garrulous nature he is already operating to some extent as a politician.

IV.   Accommodating Old People in Society

From the discussion and illustrations presented earlier, I hope it may be seen that the social process that I call "the accommodation of old people" involves more than simply the coping behavior of the old (or "adaptation," if my objections are considered baseless); it also involves the behavior of others who must cope with the presence of an old person in the social environment. The term "accommodation" is particularly useful because it implies a mutuality; the old person may (or may not) accommodate others, just as they may (or may not) accommodate him. Accommodation may be achieved with adjustment on either side, and one may be *accommodated* only if he is also *accommodating*[6]

This leads me back to Lieberman's thesis. It should be obvious that I am in full agreement with his suggestion that the work of gerontology must "take into account the characteristics and qualities of the social supports around the person. . . ." This position seems generally accepted. Yet we have many examples of efforts to understand how old people cope with their environments (other people), and very little empirical work focused on the people who *compose* the social environments of old people.

There seems to be a rich possibility for psychology along these lines. Could "gerontophobia" (and perhaps "gerontophilia") be studied as personality characteristics in research modeled along the lines of studies of such traits as authoritarianism, racism, and ethnocentrism? Recall that blacks, when they began to comment on the directions for research, recommended the study of "white racism." Such a strategy may be incomplete, but any other strategy is also incomplete without this component.

In part, these observations constitute a criticism of psychology for what seems to be an implicit (and untenable) assumption that the problems of old people can best be understood by studying old people. This assumption tends to support the conclusion that solutions can be found by *changing old people*—through counseling, therapy, behavior modification, and so forth.

My perspective leads me to pay more attention to the problems of old people that arise from the fact that they are *neglected*; these particular kinds of problems do not arise when old people are *accommodated*. Solutions to problems of neglect cannot be found by changing old people, but require *changes in society*.

If we are seriously interested in learning how to solve these kinds of problems, we must study the social environments of the old, which is to say, society as a whole. There is plenty of room here for work by psychologists and social scientists, but joint effort is also needed from such fields as social work, economics, and law.

But even when we know how to solve these problems—when we know what changes in society would be required—there is no assurance that we will collectively decide, in the end, to actually solve them. We will probably find that old people are neglected because it is considered costly to accommodate them; to decide to solve these problems, then, will be to decide *against* the perceived interests of the non-old. Perhaps this is the situation

---

[6] Neglect—the conceptual opposite of accommodation—need not be mutual; either party can neglect.

we have now; and perhaps this is a good definition of "gerontophobia." But there is a great unifying potential, as Grey Panther Margaret Kuhn points out, in the fact that everyone is getting older, and ultimately becomes old if he lives long enough. Thus gerontophobia threatens us all, in the end, and everyone can benefit from eradicating it from our culture.

REFERENCES

Cowgill, D. O. A theory of aging in cross-cultural perspective. In D. O. Cowgill & L. D. Holmes (Eds.), *Aging and modernization.* New York: Appleton, 1972. Pp. 1–14.

Cowgill, D. O. & Holmes, L. D., Preface. In D. O. Cowgill & L. D. Holmes (Eds.), *Aging and modernization.* New York: Appleton, 1972. Pp. vii–viii.(a)

Cowgill, D. O. & Holmes, L. D., Summary and conclusions: The theory in review. In D. O. Cowgill & L. D. Holmes (Eds.), *Aging and modernization.* New York: Appleton, 1972. Pp. 305–323.(b)

Lozier, J. & Althouse, R., Social enforcement of behavior toward elders in an Appalachian mountain settlement. *The Gerontologist,* 1974, **14,** 69–80.

Lozier, J., & Althouse, R., Retirement to the porch in rural Appalachia. *Aging and Human Development,* 1975, **6,** 7–15.

Maxwell, R. & Silverman, P., Information and esteem: Cultural considerations in the treatment of the aged. *Aging and Human Development,* 1970, **1,** 361–392.

Simmons, L. W. *The role of the aged in primitive society.* New Haven, Connecticut: Yale Univ. Press, 1945.

Simmons, L. W. Aging in pre-industrial societies. In C. Tibbitts (Ed.), *Handbook of social gerontology.* Chicago: Univ. of Chicago Press, 1960(a)

Simmons, L. W. Aging in pre-industrial cultures. In C. Tibbitts & W. Donahue (Eds.), *Aging in today's society.* Englewood Cliffs, New Jersey: Prentice-Hall, 1960(b)

Tibbitts, C. Origin, scope and fields of social gerontology. In C. Tibbitts (Ed.), *Handbook of social gerontology.* Chicago: Univ. of Chicago Press, 1960. Pp. 3–26.

CHAPTER 20

Death and Public Policy:
A Research Inquiry

DWIGHT HARSHBARGER

WEST VIRGINIA UNIVERSITY
MORGANTOWN, WEST VIRGINIA

ABSTRACT

Death has been historically regarded as an event that happens to individuals. From a research perspective, death has been conceptualized and analyzed at an individual level. Most exceptions to this level of analysis have been made in the investigation and control of infectious diseases. Over the past 25 years a growing body of data has suggested that our increasingly man-made, carcinogen-containing environment may itself be a major factor in elevated rates of death in selected population groups, particularly among workers in certain industries, e.g., coal mining and asbestos. Further, these industries and other living environments are subject to certain degrees of environmental control through the development and exercise of public policy. This paper presents some considerations for public policy aimed at reducing death rates; policy that would be developed from a data-oriented research base.

An elderly lady, upon visiting a funeral home and viewing the deceased lying in a classic state of repose complete with a lily placed in her clasped hands, remarked to a friend, "When I die, don't treat me like that. Please don't let them put a lily in my hands. Give me a piece of chocolate. Make it Schrafft's. I'm particular."

299

The life situation of the lady differed substantially from that of the 45-year-old business executive who was stricken with a devastating heart attack and died 2 weeks later. For the executive, his family, and his network of associates, death was a far more problematic event than it was for the elderly lady. For him it was unexpected and an interruption of normal developmental events; for her death was anticipated, a natural occurrence in the cycle of developmental events.

The respective life situations of these two people point to the fact that death may or may not be a particulary difficult problem for any given individual; an observation made by Kastenbaum (Chapter 3, this volume). To the extent that we define death as a *life* problem, something to be avoided or postponed, we are likely to commit often considerable personal and public resources to the maintenance of life. To the extent that we do not view death as a problem, we are likely to commit lower levels of resources, both privately and publicly, to the maintenance of life. Even then, those resources are likely to be aimed at minimizing discomfort, rather than more actively attempting to intervene in the preservation of life.

Although defining death as a life problem ultimately rests with the individual and social systems most directly affected by the death, demographic data can be examined for indicators suggesting patterns of death which are likely to be problematic, and for which life-maintaining intervention programs would seem appropriate. For example, in the earlier parts of the twentieth century, Public Health Service research led to intervention programs that virtually ended the deaths of children and young adults from such diseases as smallpox and diphtheria. Along with other programs aimed at ending deaths from infectious diseases, public health research and intervention programs have played major roles in extending the average life expectancy in the United States.

I. Background of the Problem

Other, as yet relatively infrequent, kinds of population research are beginning to report the incidence of death as a function of other, more complex and subtle physical and social problems in the environment. Researchers have recently examined such occupational problems as pneumoconeosis (black lung) among coal miners, asbestosis among workers in the asbestos industry, and types of cancer that appear to be strongly associated with workers' exposure to vinyl chloride in the plastics industry. Further, such problems as death due to alcohol- or drug-related behavior can be associated with particular demographic and occupational variables.

The impact of changes in the social environment on health and mortality has been examined by an increasing number of researchers. For example, recent studies by Cassel (1972), Holmes and Masuda (1970), and Rahe and Paasikivi (1971) have examined the consequences of life changes on health, and the relationship of these changes to such problems as myocardial infarction and other conditions. Parkes, Benjamin, and Fitzgerald (1969) have investigated increased mortality among widowers, and Lieberman (Chapter 8, this volume) has described the sometimes lethal impact of environmental changes on elderly nursing home residents. Overall, these studies have strongly suggested that environmental changes have important and specifiable consequences on the health and mortality of people who are at different points in the life span. As yet there have been few inquiries into the preventive potential of intervention programs based on these kinds of research.

Research in more controlled living environments, such as public mental hospitals in the United States (Babigian & Odoroff, 1969), Norway (Odegard, 1967), and Scotland (Innes & Millar, 1970), have suggested that mortality rates in these institutions are from two to seven times greater for their inmates than for their respective noninstitutionalized counterparts in the population. In addition, a recent and as yet unpublished study of death rates in one mental hospital has suggested that over a 6-year period significant increases in the frequency of death occurred following summer heat waves and winter cold waves (Roth, 1974).

An intriguing and as yet little explored problem in the occurrence of death in large populations is that of the timing of death. Case histories of individual deaths (e.g., Sigmund Freud, Thomas Jefferson, John Adams) have suggested that people may exercise some control over the times when their natural deaths occur. In an investigation of death in Jewish populations in Budapest, Hungary, and New York City, Phillips (1970) found significant increases in death rates among elderly Jews following Yom Kippur, the Jewish Day of Atonement. Similar research among an Appalachian, Christian population indicated significant increases in the frequency of death following Christmas (Marriott & Harshbarger, 1973). However, the deaths did not seem to be related to length of illness or age, as was found in the Phillips study. Further, a major identifying variable of those who died after Christmas was that they lived alone, and thus may have lacked proximal family ties. While one might hypothesize stress as a consequence of being alone at Christmas, more definitive conclusions await further research.

Overall what seems to emerge in the preceding research review is concern with two important kinds of variables. The first is the identification of factors present in or associated with work and living environments that are deleterious to health, ultimately resulting in premature death in certain population groups. The second is an examination of the importance and consequences of stresses generated by the relative presence or absence of supportive social systems and changes in those systems.

It seems clear that patterns of health and death can be discerned through population-oriented research. Further it seems clear that many of these research findings have considerable and perhaps far-reaching implications for community health intervention programs. However, given the present state of the organization of research, and the very limited extent to which practitioner-intervention concerns have been part of research designs, these implications are unlikely to lead to new programs of intervention.

II. Public Policy and Death: Needs of Future Research

A. An Organizing Strategy

The application of research to programs of intervention is difficult. In instances in which it has been successfully accomplished, researchers have worked closely with research consumers in the design and organization of the research (for a full discussion of this problem, see Glaser & Taylor, 1973). More often, research findings have gone unapplied, in part because researchers and practitioners live in different environments and have different concerns, and in part because some research findings, owing to design problems (e.g., sampling), are difficult to apply to population intervention programs.

A first step toward reducing this problem might be to generate an organizing strategy for existing research. An overview might be developed, one within which available research on death could be examined for trends. One effect of such an overview could be to enable researchers and practitioners, particularly the latter, to see the larger, more general issues. That is, individual studies, some of them no doubt conflicting, could be seen in the context of larger bodies of research. Thus an individual study that suggested an intervention strategy, but remained suspect because it was standing alone, could be seen in the context of related findings. While such an organizing strategy may be common to most researchers, and may therefore seem unnecessary, it could be of inordinate benefit to many practitioners.

Based on the general themes of the preceding health–death research review, the conceptual model shown in Figure 1 is suggested as a means of organizing research findings. The model, like the earlier discussion, is aimed at population, rather than individual, research and intervention programs.

Organized around the concept of life-span development, and derived from an earlier life-span model for ecological intervention (Harshbarger, 1973), the model calls for an organization of research across age groupings, relating type of death to living environment. The model attempts to interrelate the person, his long-term environmental experiences, and death. Thus

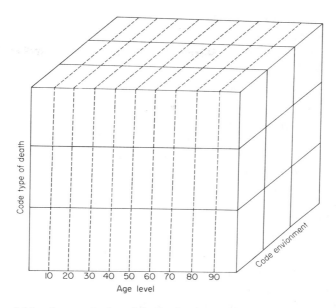

Fig. 1. A model for the organization of death-related research across the life span.

workers between the ages of 40 and 45, who have worked in the plastics industry in an environment containing elevated levels of vinyl chloride, and who have recently died, would be placed in one cell of the figure. Continuing with the frequency of death, or a death rate statistic as the dependent variable, an entry could be made for children who have grown up in public institutions, old people who live in public institutions, and occupational groupings. Carrying out the number of entries necessary to complete the figure for a particular region or community catchment area would be expensive and time-consuming, and no doubt would require the aid of computer technology in order to store, organize, and retrieve the large amount of information. However, the research can be done, much of the information already exists, and the computer technology is available. The motivation to complete the task remains.

B. Public Policy and Death Research

The general unwillingness of most researchers to get involved in matters of public policy, however well motivated and socially and academically appropriate, has too often resulted in research designed with little or no concern for its public policy implications. This has further complicated the already difficult problem of applying research to intervention programs and public policy.

If the organizing strategy suggested by the preceding schemate were carried out, it might be possible more easily to give attention to the kinds of research questions that, if answered, could shed light on significant issues involved in the incidence of death and the shape of public policy. Briefly, they are as follows:

1. Congruence between Death and Developmental Principles

As Kastenbaum noted, there is a certain "fairness" involved in individual's perception of death. Younger people are not supposed to die before older people. Yet they do. These events may be closely related to the frequency and intensity of changes in life events for people. These in turn may be systematically related to the preceding demographic variables. The incongruence of patterns of dying with developmental principles could be ascertained, through the use of the model suggested in Figure 1, and public policy could be designed as a way of attempting to restore congruence to these patterns of death.

2. Parity of Resources in Community Environments

Wealth, by definition, brings with it a certain inequity of resources, creating noticeable differences in the life styles of those who are and are not wealthy. By and large we accept this condition as a matter of fact in Western society. However, if these inequities lead to differential rates of death, rates that are considerably higher among those who earn less income and have fewer resources[1] then we might want to consider ways of reducing these inequities. National health insurance, making health resources available to those now unable to afford adequate health care, would be a step in this direction. In general, a program of health and death-related research at the community or regional level could indicate both the extent to which there is a lack of parity in health resources and some of the health consequences of this condition (e.g., see Harshbarger, Smith, Miller, & Zeller, 1974).

3. The Effects of Life-Span Intervention Programs

To the extent that these exist, the effects of various intervention programs, operating at different points in the life-span and in respective living environments, might be assessed through the use of a model similar to that suggested in Figure 1. A life-span model of program evaluation might be developed in which intergenerational and cohort similarities and differences with respect to health problems and the incidence of death could be noted. Such a program evaluative model should give close attention to the cohort–generational research model developed by Schaie (1966).

---

[1] Here I am not speaking of welfare recipients, but rather of middle- and lower-middle-income wage earners; people who have difficulty in generating the resources necessary for adequate health care.

4. Legislation and Regulations for Controlled Environments

To the extent that research might suggest problematic controlled environments, such as public institutions, new laws and regulations might be developed which would have the potential for reducing health problems and the incidence of death in certain age-cohort groups. Researchers who know the effects of these environments would seem to be in excellent positions to offer proposals for changing them. To the extent that researchers are in close contact with those who would shape public policy, the positive potential for a synergistic relationship is likely to be maximized.

5. The Interdependencies of Social Systems and Death Systems

The GNP or Gross Necrotic Product (Kastenbaum, this volume) is a little understood and rarely investigated set of events. With the exception of a few writers such as Jessica Mitford (1963) and Ruth Harmer (1963), there has been little inquiry into the interdependencies of death and economic life. What public expenditures would be required if the death rates in public institutions were only the same as those of the general population? What if the death rates due to black lung, asbestosis, or even cancer were to be sharply curtailed?

For the first time in history we are beginning to experience the difficulties of a society whose population includes an abundance of elderly people. Not only must careful economic projections be made as the size of this group increases; we should also consider the consequences of sharp rises, beyond normal projections, in this population owing to unanticipated medical advances. Our historical assumptions regarding economic and biologic life with a limited population of elderly persons are less and less true with each passing day.

And what of the social consequences of these changes? Other than in tragedy, death has never been a popular theme in literature. With the possible exceptions of Westerns and detective novels, death has rarely been taken lightly enough to be explored as a major theme in community life. As a consequence, we have little in the way of ideas or conceptual models to guide our thinking and anticipatory problem solving. The 1930s film *Death Takes a Holiday,* starring Lionel Barrymore and Sir Cedric Hardwicke, was one attempt to explore the meaning of death in community life. In the film, the Angel of Death, played by Hardwicke, is in the process of paying the final visit to ar old man (Barrymore) and his grandson, who has taken a bad fall, both of whom are dying. Death is frightened by the family dog and gains safety by climbing a tree. With Death removed from community life, no one dies. The film explores some of the individual, family, and community consequences of this condition. Finally, sadly but gratefully, the characters in the drama allow Death to climb down from the tree and go about his appointed rounds.

As a society we seem to be alternately and capriciously bringing Sir Cedric out of the tree, through wars, industrial hazards, and increased environmental pollution, and sending him back up the tree, through medical and sociotechnical developments in community life. The present consequences of these relationships need to be fully explored and carefully projected into the future. This is particularly critical as we move toward the development of large-scale strategies of intervention, such as national health insurance.

One researcher, Jay Forrester of M.I.T., has suggested that very often, in attempts to make community environments better places, we in fact make them worse (1971). Our well-intended programs of intervention very often do not have the effects we predicted, although our predictions have been based on available historical information and apparently rational predictive models. Forrester suggests that social systems often behave in apparently counterintuitive ways, not because they *are* in fact counterintuitive in their modes of operation, but because the intuitions of humans, and in particular policy planners, are based on an inadequate understanding of the systems involved.

Death is a major component of community life. If we are to take steps that would in important ways alter patterns of death, we would do well to explore fully the potential consequences of our intervention strategies. The problem is too important to treat lightly or to avoid exploring because of cultural taboos or the personal anxieties of researchers. While our values and good intentions will continue to guide much of our behavior with respect to death and public policy, they are not enough. Data are essential.

REFERENCES

Babigian, H. M., & Odoroff, C. L. The mortality experience of a population with a psychiatric illness. *American Journal of Psychiatry,* 1969 **126** 470–480.

Cassel, J. The relation of the urban environment to health: Toward a conceptual frame and research strategy. Report to the Bureau of Community Environmental Management, Department of Health, Education and Welfare, 1972.

Forrester, J. W. Counterintuitive behavior of social systems. *Technology Review,* 1971, **73** (3).

Glaser, E. M., & Taylor, S. H. Factors influencing the success of applied research. *American Psychologist,* 1973, **28** (2), 140–146.

Harmer, R. M. *The high cost of dying.* New York: Collier Books, 1963.

Harshbarger, D. Some ecological implications for the organization of human intervention throughout the lifespan. In P. B. Baltes & K. W. Schaie (Eds.), *Life-span developmental psychology: Personality and socialization.* New York: Academic Press, 1973.

Harshbarger, D., Smith, W. J., Miller, R. W., & Zeller, F. A. *A survey and analysis of human ecosystems and human service systems in Appalachia.* Morgantown, West Virginia: Appalachian Center, West Virginia Univ., 1973.

Holmes, T. H. & Masuda, M. Life change and illness susceptibility. Paper presented at symposium on seperation and depression: Clinical and research aspects. Annul meeting of the American Association for the Advancement of Science, Chicago, Illinois, December, 1970.

Innes, G., & Millar, W. M. Mortality among psychiatric patients. *Scottish Medical Journal,* **15,** 1970, 143–148.

Mariott, C., & Harshbarger, D. The hollow holiday: Christmas, a time of death in Appalachia. *Omega,* Winter, 1973, **4** (4), 259–266.

Mitford, J. *The American way of death.* New York: Simon & Schuster, 1963.

Odegard, O. Mortality in Norwegian psychiatric hospitals 1950–1962. *Acta Genet, Basel, 1967,* **17,** 137–153.

Parkes, C. M., Benjamin, B., & Fitzgerald, R. G. Broken heart: A statistical study of increased mortality among widowers. *British Medical Journal,* March, 1969, **1,** 740–743.

Phillips, D. P. Dying as a form of social behavior. Unpublished doctoral dessertation, Princeton Univ., 1970.

Rane, R. H., & Paasikivi, J. Psychosocial factors in myocardial infraction. II. An outpatient study in Sweden. *Journal of Psychosomatic Research,* 1971, **15,** 33–39.

Roth, S. Seasonal variations in death rates at a state mental hospital. Unpublished master's thesis, West Virginia Univ. 1974.

Schaie, K. W. A general model for the study of developmental problems. *Psychological Bulletin,* 1965, **64,** 92–107.

Subject Index

309